COAST-TO-COAST RAVES FOR TOM AND NITA HORN'S *THE AHRIMAN GATE*

"My reaction is that the world is right on schedule, winding down. Our redemption is ever closer as the world does what it can always be counted on to do apart from God"
- Cal Thomas, LA Times Syndicate, on the GM and Transgenic Research of the Ahriman Gate

"Thomas Horn... has got his answers, and I've got to tell you, they'll put chills down your spine!"
- Barbara Simpson, The Babe in the Bunker, On Art Bell's Coast-to-Coast

"The Ahriman Gate brings the reader face to face with the return of the Nephilim... and that might be a little too close for some folks!"
- Dr. Lynn Marzulli, best selling author of "Nephilim"

"Dr. and Mrs. Horn are obviously conversant with ancient Biblical sources, and make good use of it in their novel."
- Dr. I.D.E. Thomas, BBC Correspondent and best selling author of "The Omega Conspiracy"

"Romance! Intrigue! Thrilling cat & mouse scenes!"
- Raiders News Update

"Instantly on the 'A' list of thrilling Christian fiction! Makes the Antichrist of those 'other' End Times books about as scary as the Tooth Fairy!"
- Christian News Service

THE AHRIMAN GATE

Thomas & Nita Horn

VMI
Publishers

Published by

Inspirational Fiction

a division of VMI Publishers
Sisters, Oregon
www.vmipublishers.com

ISBN 0-933204-00-1
Library of Congress Control Number: 2005926295

Author Contact:
www.ahrimangate.com

Printed and bound in the United States of America

APPRECIATION

Words can never express the deep gratitude we feel toward the many members of our family and friends that helped with this project. Besides these gifts from God, we wish to acknowledge the following technical advisors without whose inspiration and research this project would have suffered.

Ufology, Demonology: Dr. I. D. E. Thomas
Ancient Languages, Ufology: Dr. Michael S. Heiser
Catholic Theology: Father Dick Rossman
Evangelical Theology: Dr. Donald C. Jones, Reverend Kenneth Vanderhoff
Premise: Dr. Lynn A. Marzulli
Mars Mythology: Cryptoarcheologist David E. Flynn
Genetics, Medical Science: Dr. Bob Hakala
Military: William Gallaher

NOTE TO THE READER

While the story you are about to read is fictional, the technology and prophetic speculations presented in this book describe factual advancing sciences and future possibilities as foretold in the Bible for the Last Days.

PROLOGUE

Darkness enveloped the treetops as the dreadful scent of the predator closed in on the herd of elk. The approaching creature was unidentifiable and menacing, a strange presence unlike the animals had sensed before. A blood rush moved through the bull elk's limbs as it froze to survey the murky shadows descending through the trees. Its alert brown eyes gradually settled on the pathway where the pursuer's steps, heavy and temblorous, bent the brush along the edge of the clearing.

As the stalker drew near, it hissed deeply and stepped from around the back side of a large Douglas fir, its eyes smoldering red, its arms grotesque and contorted, its open jaws stretching torturously around its black and oily fangs. The bull, nearly incapacitated by instinct and by the foul scent of the colossal creature filling the woods on every side, snorted and lowered its head at the entity.

The nefarious hunter flared its apelike snout and relished the air, as if amused by the eight hundred-pound bull's defensive posture, the sound of its heartbeat slamming uncontrollably in its chest.

Then, with a throaty, muffled roar, it attacked.

1-ESCAPE

"Human skulls with horns have been found in a burial mound at Sayre, Bradford County, Pennsylvania.... Except for the horny projections two inches above the eyebrows, the men to whom the skeletons belonged were anatomically normal, though seven feet tall..."

Pursuit, 6:69–70, July 1973

July 7

On this damp early evening in July, Joe's heart was pounding like a hammer. He was not sure he could make it through the overgrown flora, tearing his arms on berry vines, trying not to curse as he jumped fallen trees and dangerously random hollows, running for his life.

For a moment, a vague malaise told him it couldn't get any worse, then a new ambush concealed beneath the vines tripped him, and he fell headlong into a dump. Round, black objects, wet from an early rain, glistened in the starlight beneath the leafy growth: Michelins, Firestones, entombed inside the prickly Oregon blackberry.

The smell of rotting flesh was heavy around the tires. The source of the odor stared at him forebodingly from on top the rubber heap. A bull elk's decapitated head, putrefied and bloated, appealing for him to hurry. *Get up!* the dead

1

beast's eyes screamed. Keep running! *Brutal creatures roam these woods!*

He measured his breathing and glared over the animal carcass, behind him through the drapes of forested earth, where weak scalpels of twilight and a reflective reddish moon softly illuminated the angry men and their excited dogs uphill. Sliding quietly on his belly against the foul-smelling garbage, he found a good location and looked deeper into the grove. A security truck's spotlight pierced the foggy shelf like a single strand of aurora borealis, while a cool breeze, chilled by nearby water, carried the unguarded voices and muffled barking down the slope toward him. The light cast eerie illuminations on the bloodhound pack as they continued their relentless pursuit. The canines sniffed the ground, pulling against the guard's ropes as they struggled down the hill. Nearby, he thought he saw something else, lumbering off to one side, tall and indefinable.

Joe lowered his head and wondered how it had come to this.

He was only twenty-six, chestnut brown hair to his shoulders, hazel green eyes, and, thanks to his Lieutenant Colonel father, in excellent physical condition, not that poor dexterity was ever an option in the Ryback household.

Enrolled in the Yuma Young marines at only nine years of age, he had stayed in the program through high school. Later, at the behest of his father, he attended Parris Island where he concluded his marine training at the top of his recruit battalion. After eighteen months in Fox Company's Second Platoon, Third Marine Regiment, Hawaii and six months at Twentynine Palms in California, he received an honorable discharge when his esteemed father, Clarence Ryback, was mysteriously and famously murdered. This was the trigger that brought him back to Yuma, to his own nightmare and to that of his mother alone.

Ten months later, when he felt he could, he'd moved to Portland, Oregon, to work on the docks with Garth, his old high school buddy. He'd told himself that the Northwest was calling him to watch over his adopted younger sister, but he knew better. It was a ploy to get away from home. There were simply too many ghosts in Yuma...although looking back, they didn't seem as threatening as the ones in this grove.

Now something warm oozed along his midsection through his ragged blue jeans. He pushed into a crouch. At once the stench of rotting flesh blossomed even stronger. A maggot cluster, like squirming rice, clung to his belly. He scraped the wiggling larvae off with the palm of his hand and quietly shook it clean.

Inching forward to ease out of the rot, he cracked a branch beneath his foot.

He froze.

The snap of the twig had been so loud it seemed to be amplified over a speaker.

Somebody shouted, "Point the light over there, and release the beast!"

Had he heard that right? A beast?

He clutched the fanny pack containing the graven image, the one his dad had hidden a few years back, and charged over the rubbish into a small opening in the trees, black and cavernous, possibly a deer trail leading deeper into the woods.

Moving as fast as he could beneath the desultory light, he ducked and jumped like a crazed gazelle over decaying trees that had fallen years before.

Though the unfamiliar course was dangerous and

challenging, marine training enhanced his natural athleticism. His breathing synchronized perfectly with the liquid motions of his feet. He slipped, slid, palmed mossy limbs, avoided stone projections, and prayed for protection against a broken arm or leg.

Except for the howling of the dogs behind him, the woods were ghostly quiet, making stealth nearly impossible at the speed he was travelling. He kept the pace anyway, sensing the trail would continue due north toward the Columbia River, and when he finally arrived at an area where low-hanging limbs encased the crooked pathway, the vague light faded beneath them.

Thirty feet further the thicket boxed him in.

He considered turning back, decided against it, and dropped beneath the brambles onto his belly. Crawling forward, he struggled to find space until soon he came into what felt like an oversized briar hole. Now his shoulders became guides, probing both sides of the burrow's claustrophobic walls, testing the area for concealed branches and thorny vines. He explored the darkness with his hands to block the hidden dangers. No matter how he wanted to hurry, he couldn't afford a jagged branch in the eye.

He slid around a rough curve in the passage and smelled what he thought to be an animal nest. He studied the musky void as far as he could reach, feeling with his fingers, searching the swarthy space where he thought he needed to go, inspecting it for hazards.

That's when something inspected *him*.

Wet fur brushed against his hand, bit him, and scrambled onto his arm.

He shouted, shook the bristly creature into the briars, and clambered desperately forward, telling himself not to panic. He would be okay if he only remained calm.

Well, you finally got what you wanted, his alter ego complained as he shuffled along the ground. *You just couldn't leave well enough alone, could you?*

An equal part of him silently argued: Oh yes I could have, if that big shot hadn't pushed me.

Uh-huh. Ever since Dad's death you've been looking for a fight, and you know it.

Bull. I was trying to return the item.

And to kick butt, he rebutted himself as he pushed feverishly ahead.

But I ran, didn't I?

Not until you analyzed the situation and determined you were outnumbered, only then.

What was I supposed to do, stick around to see what would happen? They knew about Dad's death, for Pete's sake. Something was wrong.

Drudging forward...fussing with himself...controlling his breathing...searching for an escape, he thought, *Even so, you should have given them the image. You need to back off and let it go!*

You heard what the man said.

What? That enough people had died already? So what. Whatever this thing is...it isn't worth getting killed over.

Dad must have thought it was. So did those who tortured and murdered him.

If you die, it won't bring him back, you know. Let it go.

It's too late for that. First blood has been drawn.

Suddenly what sounded like the trickling of a stream caught his attention. He knew from the area that the water would be moving toward the Columbia River. He spotted the moon peering through an opening in the brush, headed for it, and heard something else. Uncertain at first, he recognized the baying sound of the well-trained hounds.

Montero's thugs were closing.

For a split second it grew quiet, as if the dogs were afraid of something, then a loud crunch echoed behind him. He propelled himself toward the opening with frantic abandonment, no longer concerned with protecting his face.

Reaching the end of the lair and dragging himself outside, he heard the frenzied sound of the canines closing on the stretch where he'd first entered the crawl space. Something was with them, bigger, much bigger.

He stood and gazed ahead. The area looked odd, dark blue, expansive. When he realized what it was, it was too late. The ground gave way, plummeting him on his heels, arms flailing wildly, until finally he caught a tree limb and jerked to a painful stop.

He was sixty feet above the Columbia, standing on a steep and slippery embankment. A few feet ahead of him was a sheer canyon wall.

It wasn't the trickling of a stream he'd heard, but the weak echo of the river far below.

Of all the luck.

Now a huge presence was plowing through the thicket toward him, the thud of heavy footsteps on dry leaf mold and the hard crack of breaking branches snapping terrifyingly loud. He remembered the top-secret project his father told him about. Biometric chips implanted in soldiers...secret military experiments on unconsenting guinea pigs..."Rambo Chips" he called them.... Somehow the technology increased adrenaline flow and made experimental soldiers temporarily stronger.

With split-second reasoning, he decided to jump into the river. Looping the fanny pack tightly behind his belt, he whispered a quick prayer, drew his breath in, and thrust his body toward the rim.

Just then a creature bolted from the brush, low to the soil, unnerving and rabid, growling as his feet left the ground, its hot breath snapping ferociously for his legs.

And then it was gone.

If the animal had been some kind of dog, it seemed much bigger and unlike any he had seen before. *And that smell!*

His stomach was in his throat now, his eyes bulging widely, plunging down, down, until a tree limb protruding from the crag came out of the mist and smacked him across the brow, twisting him violently into a reverse somersault.

He hit the deafening river like a solid block wall, crushing his tongue and filling his mouth with blood. The bitter substance gagged him as the Columbia's swirls clutched his arms and legs. His forehead was on fire. His thoughts were spinning too, yet he had the presence of mind to listen for the splash of the huge creature.

Nothing.

Whatever it was hadn't followed him over the ledge.

Dazed and descending into the water's ominous throat, his last breath had been shallow; it wouldn't sustain him long.

He knew the augmented muscular movements would likewise diminish as he vanished beneath the waves.

He, like other marines, had been trained in escape and evasion, jungle survival, water aircraft ditching, and sea survival techniques. Although he didn't have an EPIRB emergency radio beacon and he wasn't wearing an immersion suit, he did have the initiative and determination to survive. He focused his energy and fought the would-be grave, scissor-kicking the liquid enemy down in powerful desperate strokes.

With his heart pounding like a hammer for several fear-inspiring moments, his head finally bolted from the water, coughing and sucking in a lungful of the river's misty air. His ribcage felt like a mule had kicked him, his vision was blurred, and he was spitting out drool and blood. The icy current would be impossible to withstand very long; he knew that. He only had minutes until hypothermia overcame him. Delirium and death would quickly follow. This was no ordinary river. It was frigid, powerful, and carrying him out to sea.

"Y-y-you...can...b-beat...this..." he chattered in the freezing water, "and...Montero's...d-devils..."

With the feeble attempt at self-encouragement in play, he noted the soft expanse of the heavens—God's eternal night-light—illuminating random blotches of glittery waterscape in each direction. As the swells lifted him, he pushed up and peered at the images passing by. A canyon was thirty yards south and fading. The water was churning there anyway; it might have pulled him under. The faint silhouette of what looked like a beach flashed to the right. He could try for that. Then something closer caught his attention. It bobbed on the current, matching his drift. What was it? A large log, or was the growing numbness in his arms and neck causing delirium?

He was fainting away, wasn't he...getting dizzy...losing consciousness...hallucinating...dying.

The commanding voice of Gunnery Sergeant Hubert Franklin screamed from out of the past.

"A MARINE DOES NOT KNOW THE MEANING OF THE WORD QUIT, DOES HE, MAGGOT!?"

Joe heard himself, slightly younger, reply, *"NO, SIR!"*

"A MARINE DOES NOT KNOW THE MEANING OF THE WORD FEAR, DOES HE, MAGGOT!?"

"NO, SIR!"

"A MARINE WOULD NOT STOP UNTIL HE CONQUERED THIS OBSTACLE, WOULD HE, MAGGOT!?"

"NO, GUNNERY SERGEANT, SIR!"

"THEN OFF YOUR SISSY BUTT, BOY, AND SHOW ME WHAT YOU'RE MADE OF!"

"YES, SIR, GUNNERY SERGEANT, SIR!"

He shook his head and snapped from the memory, focusing on the log. He started toward it, swimming as strong and as fast as he could, fighting back the blackness that clawed at his vision. The pain was in his chest now, worsening, constricting his upper body strength. He could feel his legs slowing too, and his arms, like a mouse that consumes poison and gradually dies away.

Drawing on inner strength, he thought of his father.

Others might die the death of a dirty rat, Dad, but not me, not today.

Fighting desperately, his heart pounding like a hammer, his chest heaving forcefully for another needed breath, he reached the mammoth log and with some effort pulled himself onto its crumbling bark. He rolled onto his back, feeling the movement of the tree as it lilted to and fro, while from above, the moonlit sky became a swirling, churning fog, quickly filling the vortex of his unconsciousness.

* * * * * *

"There he is!" a voice on the ridge shouted.

"Where, sir?"

"There! In the water! Somebody put a light on him!"

"Is he dead, sir?"

"How should I know!? Do you see the item!?"

The marksman stared through the night vision scope.

"It's tied to his waist!"

"Good. Secure the body. Have river patrol pick him up and take him back to the lab. And private, be sure I get that package!"

As the dogs broke free of the brush overhead, blue flame flashed twice from the tip of the soldier's rifle.

Behind the canines, a large, menacing shadow drew back into the trees.

Sixty feet below, the undaunted Columbia seemed to come alive, its ancient waters ascending like Kraken from the sea, gluttonous, slavering, lapping hungrily for the blood.

2—BUCK AND TATER

"Humanity's monopoly as the only advanced sentient life-form on the planet will soon come to an end, supplemented by a number of posthuman incarnations. Moreover, how we re-engineer ourselves could...raise crucial questions about our identities and moral status as human beings."
"Inside the Movement for Posthuman Rights,"
Village Voice, 7-30-03

July 9

Sheri drummed her fingers nervously on the heavy wooden table. Her knees were rigid, her heels arched upward inside her stylish leather shoes. For the third time in the past five minutes, her pale blue eyes searched the windows hoping to see Joe's familiar gait shadowing up the walk. She had been here nearly an hour already and was just finishing a second bowl of chips, "the best in town," or so the crooked sign on the restaurant's wall said, especially when dipped in "the salsa that's so addicting it should require a prescription."

But a person could only eat so many before etiquette demanded a real order, one from the menu, one that actually cost money.

She snapped the last chip in half and stirred the remaining salsa, then dropped both pieces haphazardly into the bowl.

She looked at her watch again.

Checked her pager.

Still no messages.

She flipped the switch to sound and put the pager back in her purse. She nestled her chin meditatively against the tops of her hands, thinking this was so unlike Joe. He was never late for anything, especially their midweek lunches at Charlie's.

"More while you wait?"

It was Janet, her favorite waitress. She was holding a fresh bowl of chips and salsa.

"Ugh...I couldn't," she said, twisting her pudgy fingers through her sassy short red hair. If Sheri had a nervous tick, it was twirling the curls near the nape of her neck.

"I'll turn into a chip if I eat another."

"Joe'll want 'em I bet."

Sheri knew that was true. In fact, Joe would say he needed them, just like everything else these get-togethers had come to represent. In her own way, she did too. Joe was not the only one affected by Dad's death. Images of her father's tortured body dumped by the roadside haunted her even now. Terrible, gruesome details that startled her awake at night, scorching away the sacred moments she preferred to remember, softer times when laughter had framed the family's warmth.

"So do I leave 'em or not," Janet pressed, swirling the bowl in the air and smiling. She looked like she could tell Sheri was troubled. The brother and sister duo had met religiously at the restaurant for the past six months, and neither of them were ever this late.

"Sure, if you don't mind. But I feel like I'll have to pay rent on this space pretty soon."

"Let me see...a four-foot booth in the corner by a window. That'll be a thousand dollars a month!"

Sheri smiled at the glib humor.

Placing the chips on the table, Janet sat down across from her. "You know what I think?" she said.

"I have a feeling you're about to tell me, whether I want you to or not."

"Of course."

"And?"

"I think the spell has been broken. He's met a girl, and they've run off to Mexico."

The spell, as Janet called it, referred to Joe's fear of attachment. It was second only to his anger issues—both vexations of Dad's untimely death he couldn't seem to overcome.

"Wouldn't that be a hoot," Sheri chuckled. "I'm just hoping his car broke down and he forgot to bring his cell phone."

"I'm serious about the girl thing, ya know. Your brother's a hottie."

"Janet!" Sheri said, slapping her on the hand. "That's my brother!"

"Well! That gorgeous hair and body!"

"Well nothing! You've got a fiancé!"

"I know...but Joe's a hottie," she repeated, blushing.

Sheri wagged a shameful finger at her while siphoning a small drink through her straw. She could hardly blame Janet. Joe's ruggedly handsome features belonged on a fashion magazine. Plus the way he carried himself, so confident, as if he didn't want nor need anybody. It made him all the more appealing to the ladies. Not that it mattered. His disposition had recently become as hard as his marine sense of duty. Somebody was going to pay for Dad's death. Until they did, his life was on hold, no time for long-term relationships and certainly no room for deep love. He was as chained to his self-imposed prison, guarding her, his younger sister, and waiting to toe-tag the culprit of his father's murder, as was the Greek hero Prometheus, who, having been bound to a rock by Jupiter, became the symbol of resistance against unmerited suffering and the champion of magnanimous endurance.

A beeping sound went off, and Sheri looked across the table. She snatched her purse from the space Joe usually occupied and located the noisy device. The return number wasn't the one she was hoping for. Her heart sank to her stomach. It was "Paul the jerk," another in a long line of losers she'd dated recently. Or, as Joe liked to say, "la-hu, za-her."

"Joe?" Janet asked.

"No. Paul. Probably wants another go at me."

"Not dating him anymore?"

"Na-na-na-no thanks!" Sheri quipped.

"Why?"

"He puts the *man* in man if you know what I mean."

"As in, 'what a man'?"

"No, as in, 'Ah, man! Pa-lease stop calling me!'"

Sheri grinned and burst into laughter. Janet joined her until both of them were forced to hold their mouths to keep from annoying the other customers.

"The funny thing is," Janet whispered, leaning forward, "Joe tried to warn you. He said Paul was a joke."

Sheri hunched her shoulders and sat back against the booth, subconsciously twirling the hair at the nape of her neck again. "Well...that don't make him a seer. All my dates are jokes to him. He never thinks anybody is good enough."

"So far, he's been right," Janet teased.

"Okay, but as Grandpa Tony used to say, you'll never get a ringer if you don't throw a shoe," Sheri added, taking a dig at Joe's lack of dating, the usual argument between the two siblings. No man would ever be good enough for Sheri as long as Joe was around. He watched over her like an angry guardian angel, thoroughly intimidating most of her boyfriends, while he rarely dated at all. Their father's murder had affected him so profoundly that he feared love itself, while she on the other hand went through men like a bag of jelly beans. The irony hadn't escaped Sheri. Their mutual psychosis formed the core of their bond. They needed each other—to heal, to figure things out, to find closure, to move on. So they met each week to agree and argue, to laugh and cry, and above all else to nurture this contest about dating. As silly as it seemed, it appeared to be working, at least for her.

"You know he's only that way because he loves you," Janet said after a moment.

"Sure. I know. He's thinks he's filling in for Dad, but sometimes it's smothering."

"Yet he doesn't seem to be that way with Allie or Donna?"

Joe's older sisters, Donna, who lived on the East Coast, and Allie, who lived near Sheri in Portland, had met Janet during Christmas vacation the year before.

"That's because they're married and I'm not. They've got husbands to protect them. Plus, I was adopted, remember? So poor little me, I'm really all alone."

Janet puckered her lips and batted her eyes. "Ohh, boo-hoo, I think I'm gonna cry. No, wait, it was just some salsa in my eyes," she said with a jab. She slid from the booth, stood, and opened her writing pad. "Work is calling. You gonna order?"

Sheri checked her watch again. Joe was ninety minutes late.

"Guess not. What do I owe you for the chips?"

"Don't worry about it."

"Right," Sheri said, digging in her purse and dropping three dollars on the table. "If he shows up, will you have him call me?"

"Only if you can get him to call *me*."

"Knock it off, or I'm telling."

* * * * * *

Am I dreaming or did someone say something to me?

A rhythm of pain beat at the base of his skull as the cloudy mixture of smells and sounds slowly interrupted his oblivion. Trapped momentarily in that surreal place that exists only in waking meditation, Joe struggled against the nightmarish images occupying his thoughts. A distant gunshot, a shadowy creature, a tree limb, something damp and warm bobbing along his cheek, and a soft, metronome-like object tapping systematically against his right leg.

He listened again, trying to determine whether he was awake or asleep. The sound repeated, a little clearer this time. "Tater, leave that boy alone," an elderly voice warned.

Joe raised his brow and stretched his face to force his eyelids open. A whining sound from Tater acknowledged the dog's excitement at the recovery of his patient. A fresh round of saliva poured forth from what seemed an endless tongue.

Lap, lap, lap.

"Wh...uhh...stop, please stop," Joe moaned, raising his

hands defensively.

"Tater!" the grainy voice snapped. "I'm fixin' to kick you in the head, dog! Leave that boy alone!"

Joe could barely discern the lanky silhouette crossing the room toward him. In response to the approaching master, Tater's tail slapped harder and faster against his leg.

He heard the aging voice say something about "fingers."

"Wh...aad?"

The old man repeated, this time with deliberate repose, almost spelling his words. "How...many...fingers...yeh...SEE, hmm?"

"Uh...mmm." Joe licked his lips and drew in a deep breath. "Uhm, I...d-d-don't care...two...two, maybe?"

"Jumpin' Jehoshaphat, give that boy a pig!" the old man howled laughingly. "Yer posalutely right, son!" Then he dropped his voice to a whisper, as if he had a secret to share. "And it's a good thing too, boy—I figur'd yeh was dead fer sure."

The stranger looked like something out of the past—a preindustrialized souvenir, tall and crooked with age, face covered with three month's scrub and skin as wrinkled and as sunburned as leftover orange peels on the summer ground. He wore a red flannel shirt, probably as old as he was, and gnarled suspenders supporting crusty denim jeans. His boots were western, worn at the heel, bent up at the toe. A billed cap featuring a fish leaping out of the water sat sideways on his head. His gray hair shot randomly from beneath it.

Realizing it was not a dream, Joe gestured with his hand for the old man to wait while he used the couch cushion near his right side to push himself up. Clutching the pillow and lifting with both arms, he felt pain erupt through his rib cage like the plunging of a knife blade, and dropped back to the sofa with a groan. His stomach muscles felt like a sledgehammer had beaten them apart. His reaction sent Tater sideways with a *woof* that rocketed through his throbbing head like a white-hot sear. "Ohhh..."

"Yep," the old man said, "I'm gonna kick that dog...outside that is!" he added with a snicker as he hobbled on obviously a bad leg toward the door. "C'mere, Tater, yeh dummy."

Next to the old man, a rustic picture of a B-52 Bomber hung off center above an old woodstove. The frame around it was of rough-sawn cedar, blackened from its proximity to the fire. A tin-colored coffeepot sat below it on the stove, steam rising from its spout. The radiant heat felt good against Joe's bandaged arms and side, especially where he had been damaged at his waist. *Through it?*

He watched the dog get ousted, then asked weakly, "W-where am I?"

"Hey, he speaks." The old man wisped, turning from the doorway and dismissing the question altogether. "What's yer name, boy?"

Joe focused on the man's aged eyes. Like the worn sound of his voice, they beamed with kindness. Every instinct he had said there was no danger here...wherever here was.

"Uhh...Joe...call me Joe, sir."

"Sir? Sir? Why, I ain't been called that since the War."

Moving to the couch, the codger asked, "Yeh want a cup a' hobo-jo, boy?"

Joe knew he meant coffee. His grandpa used to call it that, as did lots of old-timers who made it in the foxholes of World War II.

"N-no...no thanks. Y-you in the second world war, sir?"

"Korean, medic's assistint, but I ain't talkin' 'bout it, and don't call me 'sir.'"

Joe hesitated. "Okay...then...w-what *should* I call you?"

Lowering himself onto a seasoned recliner, the bony man leaned forward and dropped his spittle into a coffee can between his feet. He didn't answer.

The reaction seemed odd to Joe. Why wouldn't the stranger want him to know his name? He took a second suspicious inventory of his surroundings. Several pieces of dusty furniture filled what appeared to be the cottage's front room, including the couch he was lying on and the shabby recliner the old man was using. A woodstove, several burl tables, one with a toolbox or maybe a tackle box on it. That would make sense; it went along with the fishing poles leaned up by what he assumed was the front door. Hardwood floors, dull but clean. A blanket by the woodstove was undoubtedly for the dog. A small kitchen with an antique stove, the kind that didn't require electricity, behind a plywood partition. An opening in the wall on the opposite side of the room housing a standard issue army cot, the old man's quarters, he guessed. Several pictures of a woman, probably his wife, sat neatly aligned on a burl facing the bed. A candle was flickering in front of them.

Hesitating, he said slowly, "L-look, I just need to know where I am. If you don't want to give me your name, that's okay. I'll get out of here and forget about this place and you too, if that's what you want."

The old man winked and spat again. "Tha'd be good, son, and I'll tell yeh somethin' else. Those men who were terrin' up the river a couple nights ago lookin' fer yeh...well, them are strange men. Yeh'd better forget anything yeh know 'bout them too, yesiree."

"Men...looking for me?"

"Uh-huh, it was a real show, boy...yep. And it's a good

thing the fishin' was slow...er else Tater 'n me might a' left yeh there crumbled up on that log."

A faint image formed in his mind...a wet black dog paddling through the river...toward him...catching his arm...holding him until a cloudy figure came alongside in a boat...

Up the mountain...a group of men...no, soldiers...in pursuit of him...it was coming back now.

"Montero. Right?...Montero...," he mumbled.

"What's that yeh say, boy?"

"Just...just...thinking."

Perhaps the elderly gentleman could be trusted after all. He might owe him his life. "Y-you were fishing? On the Columbia at night?" he said, feigning interest out of respect.

"Oh yeah, boy. Some of the best sturgeon fishin' in the world is in that river. Me and Tater love sturgeon fishin'. We go at night so's we can be alone. Otherwise, too many weekend warriors, yeh know."

A smile blanketed the old man's face. Perhaps he was remembering a happy fishing experience with his slobberfest pal. The firelight emanating through the woodstove's open door painted his skin with a brassy, comfortable tone. Joe couldn't help notice how much the entire scene looked like a Norman Rockwell painting.

The old-timer placed both hands on his knobby knees and stood up again. "I'm just glad we was in the cove, uh-huh. I'm just glad we got to yeh b'fore they did. It was Tater what fetched yeh from the log, yeh know."

Shuffling to a window by the front door, the old-timer pushed a burlap curtain blackened by years of soot out of the way. He pointed to a stark canyon on the Oregon side of the Columbia. "That's a long way to fall, boy. The Good Man upstairs musta been watchin' out fer yeh, uh-huh."

Joe tried to focus through the dingy glass, but something about the windowpane's shadows triggered a more important matter in his mind.

The image.

He felt for his belt line. The fanny pack was missing. Carefully, he glanced at the stranger. "Uhhmm...you didn't happen to find a fanny pack...did you?"

Relaxing his right leg and leaning against the wall, the old man pointed across the room and said, "Is that what yer lookin' fer, boy?"

Beneath the splintered top of a homemade table in the corner of the cottage was the belt purse.

"Do you know if it still has...my stuff in it?"

The elderly fellow cocked his head and stared out the window. Joe could see Tater eagerly raise his ears from his position on the porch, as if to say, "Do you want me?"

"Don't know nothin' 'bout that," the old man sighed heavily. Suddenly he looked worn with worry. "But whatever yeh got there, boy, if them Trainers want it, be smart t' give it to 'em, uh-huh."

He glanced suspiciously through the window, then grimly back at Joe. "I'll not hide it from yeh, boy. I gotta bad feelin' 'bout 'em. They don't seem right to me, and Tater don't like 'em either."

"Your dog, Tater...he don't like...who? *Trainers?*"

"Nope. He don't like 'em a bit. And Tater's a good judge of character fer a dog. One time we hear'd roarin' over there, so Tater 'n me sneaked across in the boat to get a listen. The noises we heard, boy, they weren't natural. Unearthly and spooky like. Made Tater 'n me's hair both stand on end!" he said with a nervous grin. "If yeh got somethin' belongin' to the Trainers, I'd give it back to 'em.'"

"But...what do you mean, the Trainers? Who are they?"

"That's what I'm a tellin' yeh," he said, raising his voice as he turned toward him again. "Me and Tater call 'em Trainers 'cause we don't know their real name! They control the apes, we think. They train 'em, uh-huh..."

Joe didn't mean to say as bluntly as he did, "Apes!? They train apes!?" His imagination was suddenly enthralled. Was this old guy nuts? What was he talking about? Apes?

Yet he wondered. Had he seen something running with the dogs above the Columbia? A glimpse of something large, apelike, silhouetting through the forest?

Nausea boiled in his belly.

Run, his instinct shuddered unexpectedly.

"Yeh, apes! Bigfeet, yeh know," the old man continued. "I see 'em up there sometimes, doin' a hoop-de-loop or fetchin' sticks or some dang thang. Could prove it too, if I had to, uh-huh."

Joe steadied himself. The old fellow was eccentric, maybe even a bit crazy, but probably sincere. "I'm sure you could," he said, pausing. "So...as for me...I need to get home...contact my family...make sure they're okay...let them know I'm alive."

Slowly reaching forward, he placed his hands on top of the cushions and pushed up again. Severe pain racked him like before, and he grabbed his side and fell backward against the sofa. *"Oomph!"*

Blood seeped through his waist bandage onto his hand.

The old man, hobbling over, scowled, "Hold on there, boy! Yeh can't do that! Yeh gotta stay still if yer gonna heal up."

"B-but...I've got to check on my family. It's important, sir." He grimaced.

"Well, I ain't got no phone, and yew ain't got no energy, so yer jest gonna take it easy fer a spell whether ya like it 'er not."

Adjusting Joe against the pillows, he pulled the blanket over his legs. "And like I done said, don't call me sir. If yeh jest haft-ta have a name, it's Buck, uh-huh."

3—THE MAN IN BLACK

"A 405-page report sponsored by the US National Science Foundation calls for a broad-based research program to improve human performance leading to telepathy, machine-to-human communication, and enhanced intellectual capacity."
"US Report Foretells of Brave New World,"
The Sydney Morning Herald, 07-20-02

July 23

A light drizzle peppered the windshield of the '68 Ford pickup as it rolled nonchalantly into the parking lot of Shop Right's Grocery in Springdale.

As the truck crept slowly over the asphalt, the old man wrestled the transmission into first gear and manuevered the vehice forward to a gentle rest against the railroad-tie bumper. Nobody seemed to notice as Joe slid from the truck bed and made his way through the parked vehicles, to the east wall of the country store and a canopy of unkept hedges. Joe was familiar with the hideout. He'd seen local kids playing inside and around the bushes before.

It had been two weeks since he first met Buck and Tater. During that time he had grown to respect the old man, and, though he hated to admit it, attached to the guardian fur ball too. Together, they decided he would conceal himself beside the country store until Buck's bimonthly shopping event was concluded. If the gossipy clerk who stood behind the counter repeating every rumor he ever heard asked no probing questions, Joe would assume Buck and Tater were in the clear and that he could move on, that he had not endangered them.

A half hour passed before the little bell hanging from a wire above the entry jingled. A voice inside the building hollered through the door, "See ya next time, Buck!"

"Uh-huh," the old man said, pushing the neatly stacked cart toward the rusty pickup.

A few minutes later, as if on cue, Tater barked, the signal that all was okay. Joe heard the truck start, then sputter off down the highway.

* * * * * *

What Joe didn't hear was the interdimensional breach simultaneously unlocking across the road. Invisible beings stepped through the space-time portal: angels, tall and magnificent, eyes burning like lamps of fire. The golden-skinned figures made their way across the road, toward the grocery, automobiles driving behind, in front of, and through them as they went.

"There's Garth now," the taller of the two angels said, raising his finger in a flash toward a young man exiting the store. The hearty twenty-five-year-old he was pointing at would play a small but important role today.

"Okay, Justice, I see him," Swift replied. "I'll start the sequence as soon as he's off the deck."

* * * * * *

Garth Pumphrey, six feet tall and usually sure-handed, was surprised when he dropped the Mountain Dew. It was as if somebody knocked the twenty-ounce bottle from his hand. Now he stood in his designer jeans and watched the plastic container roll toward the end of the building, picking up steam as it coasted along the slanted parkway, finally bumping into what appeared to be a boot jutting out from the brush.

Was somebody hiding in the hedgerow?

Garth stepped toward the beverage.

"Hello-oooh," he said in a singsong voice. "Somebody there?"

The leather boot withdrew into the shrubbery like a moray eel into its refuge.

Whoever was in the bushes wasn't interested in company, and that was okay with Garth.

"Ah...listen...no sudden moves now...I'm gonna reach over and get my soda..."

No reaction.

"I don't want any trouble...so don't try anything...'cause I know karate..."

Garth's "I know karate" threat must have sounded familiar to the mystery person.

"Garth? Is that you?" a voice within the brush said.

Scrutinizing the poorly maintained plants, Garth tilted his head and looked into the hollow.

He was flabbergasted at what he saw.

After two weeks unaccounted for, beaten and bruised, his lifelong friend Joe Ryback had returned.

* * * * * *

In Arizona, Nettie Ryback sat at the breakfast nook and stared from her self-appointed watchtower by the window as clouds slowly darkened the midsummer sky. It wasn't the monsoon season yet, just a freak storm and another day alone.

On the radio, B. B. King was singing "The Thrill Is Gone."

Striking a match, she touched it to a candle's wick near the windowpane. The soft glow of the flickering firelight cast faint wavering shadows against a pastel yellow ribbon tied to the candelabra, a reminder from her husband of his promise to return, a promise she knew he could never keep.

She recalled the night he placed the bow on the candleholder. It was pouring down rain like today. She believed it when he said he'd be back. Just a short run to the base to meet another officer was all. He'd be gone one hour, tops.

That was five years ago. Eighteen hundred and twenty-five days ago. At least fifty million tears ago.

Wincing, she stroked the moisture from below her doe eyes and leaned back against the chair, sipping slowly from a slender glass of Cabernet, savoring the crisp taste of the fermented grapes with slow delight. Her dependency on the vine had evolved to outright friendship over the last few years—a frequent invitation to chemical obscurity that alleviated her pain, if only for a while.

Yet not her tears. Never her tears. She was such a melancholy baby when she remembered Clarence—his kind, hazel green eyes and thinning black hair; his clean-shaved face framing a broad, honest smile; his strong masculinity complemented beneath his off-duty black

Stetson. Even at middle age he had been disirable to her. Everything about him was as intoxicating as this wine. Her need of him now was as strong as the day they fell in love, stronger perhaps than her passion for life without him.

She rubbed her finger along the edge of the glass and dabbed a bit of the alcohol behind her ears.

Nice perfume, she thought. *Deadly perfume.*

Having thus begun this day's episodic ritual of numbing her wounded soul, her thoughts strayed now—like they had recently—from Clarence to her missing son, Joe.

For more than a week she had told herself he would reappear at any moment. It wasn't the first time he'd vanished only to pop up in some obscure locale later on. Yet after two weeks, her hopes for his safe return were starting to feel as puny as the promises she'd clung to during the terrible days leading up to her husband's discovered corpse—promises as empty as this bottle would soon become.

Leisurely, she tipped the delicately shaped chalice toward her face and smelled the welcome aroma.

A drink was what she needed to alleviate the fear, followed by another one.

Yet before the Cabernet could reach her open mouth, a shadow moved over the trees near the walkway and a *creak* spread through the deck outside.

Her head started to spin.

She knew it wasn't the liquor. The day was early yet.

Sitting forward, she felt primal fear roll over her, black and mindless.

Her intuition screamed. Something dreadful was coming her way. She had the uncanny feeling she was being watched.

Another thump, and something knocked on the front

door.

She froze, glancing at the entry. The lock was set and the safety chain was fastened. The windows were secure, too. Yet it would be easy enough for a determined man to kick his way past the deadbolt.

If only she had installed that bar thing across the door Joe wanted.

If only.

After all, she was alone in the house most of the time. No precaution was unreasonable. Someone had murdered her husband, someone never identified, his reasons never known.

He could be out there, studying her, plotting.

Do not start that again. *Do not.*

Another knock, louder this time.

Gooseflesh crawled on her arms.

Against her better judgment, she rose to her feet and tiptoed to the door. She looked through the peephole. Two men were on the deck: a young, clean-cut marine security guard, and a middle-aged man in a black suit.

And something else.

Strange, unnatural silence.

No neighborhood dogs barking; no birds chirping; not even a cricket sound.

Leaving the chain hooked, her pulse pounding, she surprised herself by seizing the knob and cracking the door a little.

She peeked at the solid young man on the deck.

"Y-yes?"

"Good morning, ma'am. Sorry to disturb you. Would you happen to be Mrs. Annette Ryback?" the officer asked.

His voice was familiar, looks too, probably one of the base kids Joe grew up with. She calmed a little.

"I am," she said, not mentioning that some people knew her as Nettie, her nickname.

"Joe Ryback's mother?"

Her pulse quickened again. "Yes. What's this about?"

"May we come in for a moment?"

She checked the uniform for authenticity. It looked real, though she knew such things could be purchased at a military surplus store.

"Of course, gentlemen," she said after a second.

Unhooking the chain and swinging the door aside, she invited the officer in.

"Thank you, ma'am," he said politely. "My name is Skip Stevens and this is Special Agent Apol Leon. Mr. Leon is looking for your son, Joe."

"My son?"

"Yes, ma'am. Do you happen to know where we can find him?"

Though relieved they weren't harboring bad news about Joe, something felt wrong, antagonistic. Reciting the awful truth, she simply said, "No."

Not only had Joe been missing since visiting her two weeks before, but at the time he had claimed that he was onto something, a lead involving high-ranking officers and cover-ups that might connect to his father's murder. She had warned him to be careful, to leave things to trained investigators. Putting himself at risk wouldn't change the facts anyway, "Except maybe to get you hurt, too," she had argued. Nevertheless he had carried on about the whole mess, as though it was his duty to solve the mysterious crime. Now, sure enough, uniformed men were looking for him.

"No idea, huh," the soldier pressed.

Before she could repeat the answer, the man in black

entered the doorway and gazed at her suspiciously. Though she couldn't see his eyes due to the sunglasses he was wearing, a cynical expression clearly insinuated that he thought she was lying.

"None whatsoever," she said flatly.

For reasons she didn't entirely understand, her eyes darted across the living room to an exquisitely handcrafted eighteenth-century hardwood table. On top of it sat an evenly worn Douay version of the Bible. It called to her as if it were alive, pleading for her to resume the study of it, to reclaim its authority. Why had she felt this now?

As if sensing evasiveness, Apol raised his right hand and repositioned the expensive Armani glasses on the bridge of his nose. In a deep, snakelike hiss that took Nettie by surprise, he said, "Mrs. Ryback, you are aware, are you not, that concealing a fugitive is a federal offenssse?"

Instantly regretful she had gone against her instincts by allowing the men inside, she made a slow examination of the skeptical agent in the doorway: approximately six feet tall, raven black hair combed hard to one side reminiscent of Adolf Hitler, he had pockmarks on his face and arms and a small scar or mark on his forehead that looked like numbers.

"I...I am," she responded, warning herself to be careful what she said. Anybody as unabashed and as lacking in common manners as this man was probably dangerous. Her husband once told her that unchallenged authority ruined some men, causing them to take particular thrills from controlling people. To discover what made such people tick—to define their truest and deepest character—give them power, he had said, and watch what happens. The outcome was typically megalomania.

"And you'd never challenge such authorities by hiding

your ssson, would you?"

"Excuse me?"

"It's a sssimple question, really. Your son. You wouldn't be keeping him from authorities, aiding and abetting him would you?"

"What authorities? You?"

Apol's cheek twitched, as if he was unaccustomed to being questioned, especially by a woman.

"I can assure you, Mrs. Ryback, it would be a mistake to doubt my authority in this matter," he said dryly. "My need of your ssson has to do with an above-top-secret undertaking for the United States Government. As a former Lieutenant Colonel's wife, you understand the term 'classified,' don't you, Mrs. Ryback?"

Of course she did. Who was this man anyway, arriving here without an appointment and talking to her like she was a child?

"It has come to our attention that Joe may be in possession of stolen government property. Specifically, a confidential item related to...the project I'm overseeing."

Nettie amazed herself by blurting, "Don't be ridiculous. Joe's not a thief. He wouldn't steal anything from anybody." She could feel herself shaking even as she said it.

"Yet he's chosen for sssome reason to violate the law by refusing to surrender the classified material to proper authorities," Apol shot back.

The dark man, powerful or not, was quickly wearing out his welcome. Nettie crossed her arms and glowered. "Just what evidence do you have that my son is involved with this...situation?"

"Eyewitnesses for one, video for another."

"Eyewitnesses? Video? Antiquated junk that's easily faked."

Apol tilted his head and ambled toward her, his face grim now, seething, his temples pulsating on both sides, a peculiar sneer cutting on his lips. Even his walk was inexplicable. The way he swayed was unlike anything Nettie had seen before, every stride reflecting indisputable authority, at least in his mind.

She felt like a cornered rabbit too afraid to run.

Noticing a photo of her late husband strategically positioned on the fireplace mantle, he abruptly stopped, tapped the frame of it with the tip of his finger, and looked at her again.

"Ahh, Lieutenant Colonel Ryback, a fine officer indeed. Served his country well, didn't he. It was a terrible day for all of us when he was assassinated, yesss?"

Placing his hand over his heart, he puckered his lips. "Personally, I was deeply moved when he was killed..."

Although she could hardly believe it, the man in black sounded callous, as though he was mocking her husband's death right here in her home.

"...and the mystery surrounding his unfortunate ssslaughter..."

Did he actually lick his lips!? Was he *salivating*!?

"It's never been sssolved...has it?"

The terribly insensitive remark enraged Nettie. Somehow—she wasn't sure just how—she controlled herself. Her eyes narrowed to angry slits as she glared at the stranger, determined to hide her fear.

Her anxiety seemed like honey to him. He continued toward her, slithered actually, his face noxious now, as if feeding on her pain.

"Did you know there are those who believe your ssson could be in similar danger?"

She placed a hand over her mouth. The threat was veiled,

but she understood it. "W-what are you saying?"

"I'm saying your ssson is in over his head. If I can find him, I can protect him, but I may need your help. You don't want to see him come to any harm, do you, Mrs. Ryback? You wouldn't resist me, would you?"

The dark agent's head jerked, and something unseen drifted through the room.

A sharp, intrusive vibration was in her inner ears.

Buzzing, swarming, stirring, like angry particles of static electricity.

Now her thoughts were spinning.

Her mind was...was...being *searched!?*

She stumbled backwards, tripping, falling, her shoulder catching a lamp on the way down, knocking it with a hard whack to the corridor that ran along the stairs, shattering the bulb into a thousand powdery shards.

Who, or what, was this man!?

Officer Stevens rushed to help her.

"What's the matter, Nettie," the man in black said menacingly from behind them, his lips stretching eerily, grinchlike. "Sssomething wrong?"

He knew her nickname! Had she given it to him!?

Blinking in confusion, half mad with fear, hands quaking as if swatting at invisible flies sent by Baalzebub to bore into her brain through the channels in her ears, Nettie stuttered, "I-I-I think it's time you men leave! I don't know anything about this m-matter. I can c-call...can call...if I hear anything..."

"Uh-huh...you do that," Apol hissed as she stood and backed away. "Here's my card. The number's on the bottom. Anytime, day or night, call me...and the sssooner the better."

Turning a hundred and eighty-degree arch, Apol placed the contact information on the fireplace's mantle and quickly walked outside.

Officer Stevens was visibly shaken, obviously unsure what had occurred. He picked the larger pieces of the broken lamp glass up and handed them carefully to Nettie.

Faltering apologetically, he said, "Don't...don't worry, Mrs. Ryback. I'm sure everything will work out."

He turned and pursued Apol outside, closing the door behind them.

Nettie heard a verbal confrontation on the sidewalk to the street before a vehicle started and drove away.

Slumping to the floor, bursting into tears, her eyes drifted uneasily to the top of the fireplace mantle. Photos of her family sat there, neatly tucked inside the antique metal frames she enjoyed collecting. In the middle of them was the one Apol had desecrated with his touch—a black-and-white photo of her and the kids standing with Clarence. Decked out in full military uniform, on her husband's face was the rigid look of marine devotion. His large hand rested gently above her hip. She could almost feel it now, pulling her close, promising to protect her.

She clung to that image as it dawned on her. Something dark and beyond her control was closing in.

4—THE GRAY HIDEAWAY

"We have dozens of photographs of things...on Mars that are unquestionably associated in our minds with intelligence."
Dr. Thomas D. Flowers, renowned astronomer,
World Net Daily interview, 09-24-00

Having instructed Garth to find his sisters Allie and Sheri and to assemble them for his arrival, Joe pretended to be biting his nails as he shielded his face from public view. He inserted several coins into Shop Right's pay phone, then dialed his home number and listened to the machine's familiar recording.

"You've reached the home of Joe Ryback. You know what to do, so do it."

After waiting for the ensuing beep, he punched the two-digit code that allowed remote playback.

"You have twenty-three new messages," the digital voice said.

There were calls from his mom and sisters: frantic, heartfelt inquiries concerning his whereabouts; a contact from a credit card company wanting to know why his bill hadn't been paid; and a different kind of message, one that sounded synthetic. A salivic *hiss* dominated each slowly enunciated syllable as the unusual voice in the recording said, "Mr. Ryback. My name is Apol Leon. I work for the United States Government. I need to meet with you, to discussss the item in your possession. We are willing to pay a substantial finder's fee, and I can guarantee your safety. Please return my call as soon as pos-s-s-ible...."

As the man named Apol recited his callback number, Joe slammed the receiver down and looked around.

The hairs on the back of his neck stood up.

Something in that voice had sounded...dead.

He zipped up the coat Buck had loaned him and crossed the road from the country store in a brisk jog. As he moved through the woods toward Portland, he was overcome by an inexplicable urge to whisper repeatedly: *"The blood of Jesus is against you."*

Two hours later, wet from running through the tall wild grass, he emerged at the base of Mt. Tabor. Though Garth would be waiting for him with the girls by now, he knew that he couldn't hurry. To avoid being seen by authorities, he took the long route, following familiar alleyways, running past commercial Dumpsters and delivery vehicles on his way to one of Portland's oldest neighborhoods, Montavilla.

At Ninetieth street, he paused by a chain-link fence near his destination. Across the road was the rear entrance to the Gray Hideaway—a.k.a. Maxamillion Video—a movie, memorabilia, and arcade store. The proprietor of the deteriorating facility was a friend of his, a colorful personality whose business—a youth dive—was called the Gray Hideaway due to its fading color and mortar façade. What the juveniles and wannabes that hung out there didn't know was that Maxamillion Video also served as an illegal base for hacking government computers. Joe became aware of the felonious habit after meeting Dave Pitzer, the fifty-year-old owner, at a benefit dinner for veterans. The two struck up a conversation and eventually discovered a mutual distrust of certain U.S. agencies. As subsequent months passed and their friendship strengthened, Dave let Joe in on the high-tech breaking and entering. Joe disapproved, but remained silent. Who knew if the quasi operative's expertise might come in handy someday?

He studied the busy parking lot to make sure nobody was watching, then crossed the street and knocked on the paint-chipped rear door. The back hall provided the only means of entering "the computer room." He hesitated, knocked twice more, then repeated the same pattern until finally a crotchety voice blurted over a speaker, "You the pizza delivery man?"

Joe thought the code talk was corny. Although likable, Dave was a slouchy-dressing, Dan Akroyd-type, ill-tempered eccentric, two parts grouch and one part petulant showman who insisted on having things done his way.

"Yeah, I'm from Pizza the Hut, and I've got your Grand Master pizza," he answered appropriately.

CLANK!

As the heavy lever on the right side of the door squealed and turned automatically upward, Joe slipped past the steel panel and waited for the contraption to change motion and close. A moment later, as usual, an electric motor gyrated and the dead bolt reversed through the heavy framing into the concrete wall.

Standing quietly in the dimly lit, musty-smelling chamber, he was aware that nothing much had changed. To his left was a staircase that led upstairs to a vacant office used for storage. On his right was an antique furnace that no longer worked and directly ahead of that, the item he was interested in—an outdated public pay phone once used to promote the television series *Get Smart*. Years earlier, the unique carnival relic had served as the entrance to the state fair's most popular funhouse—"Get Smart's Laboratory!" Dave found it at an auction somewhere and bought it, later installing it as his outlandish computer room door.

Joe flipped the switch beside the rotating gizmo on and stepped into the cubicle. He pulled the door shut and dialed 87-99, the respective numbers of the fictional spies from the television show. As the theme music to the classic program crackled over a fractured speaker, the compartment began slowly turning counterclockwise. Someday, somebody would get stuck in the contraption, Joe thought. That's when Dave, the eccentric, melodramatic "circus performer" would be in a mess.

For now it appeared to be working. The gadget clanked and the familiar whirling-down of the well-worn motors brought the cab to a stop. He grabbed the handle and slid the accordion door aside. That's when he saw them, and they saw him, from inside the secret chamber.

* * * * * *

Near the bank of the Columbia River, in the only bedroom of his tiny cabin, Buck sat on his cot, rubbing his palms together and studying the fading picture. Ruby was still beautiful to him. She had gone to be with Jesus nearly twenty years ago, and yet he missed her, especially on days like today, their wedding anniversary. He leaned forward and clutched the antique photo. If she were here now, she'd know what to do. She always seemed to know.

"Oh, Ruby...yer still th' only mortal I can go to," he said, staring into her soft, understanding eyes. "If yeh could-a seen that boy, all cut up and bruised like a road-killed possum...yeh would've insisted I help 'em. But I'm a-feared I brought a dark cloud down on us. Them Trainers are sure t' come lookin fer that boy. If I go to th' law, they'll be against me too...I jest know it...they'll say I sheltered a criminal...then they'll lock ol' Buck up, and God ferbid it, take Tater t' th' pound...."

He laid the photo on the cot and rocked gently back and forth, nervously praying, "Sweet Heaven...save poor ol' Buck 'n Tater...."

* * * * * *

Momentarily startled by the outlines moving toward him, Joe relaxed when he heard the familiar voice and saw Sheri pushing past the others. She was screaming, "Omigosh! Omigosh! Joe!" He leaped from the cubicle, caught her with both arms, and nearly fell forward with her onto the floor. As she squeezed him with all of her might, Allie, his older sister, wiggled her skinny body through the small group and said, "Joe, thank God you're safe...we were all so worried."

Despite the severe reasons that brought him here, and having undergone a renewed sense of purpose, Joe was thrilled to see some of his family. He closed his eyes and embraced the moment. The smell of his sisters—their skin, hair, perfume—it radiated a powerful, kindred balm to his soul. He was surprised at how much their presence meant to him, their close proximity, their aura, as if an energy field existed between him and them that intensified his interest in life. At one time Dad had been the source of that strength—an indestructible, decorated war hero and larger-than-life father whose reputation as a no-nonsense

Lieutenant Colonel assured he would always be there. But then he was murdered, and Joe wanted to ask God some questions about the lack of justice, the good dying young and the useless living longer. Yet as time passed he realized no argument would bring his dad back anyway, so he resigned to punish those guilty for his death, contemplating that somewhere, someday, he'd kill the miserable freak that took him away. Until then, he'd watch over Mom and the girls, especially Sheri, the adopted one. It gave him cause to live as well as to hate.

Opening his eyes, he finally whispered, "I'm glad to see the two of you again."

In the background, his brother-in-law Carl was saying something to Dave Pitzer. Joe didn't care what it was about, not even when Dave aimed his tough-guy voice at him and demanded to know where he had been. He simply reached around the girls and, even though it hurt his still-tender midsection, pulled them closer, squeezing them so hard that Allie groaned beneath his well-toned biceps and pulled loose. She patted him on the arm and said, "I know...I know...I've missed you too." Probably what she really wanted was an answer to Dave's question: Where have you been? She knew better than to push.

For Sheri's part, her runny mascara said it all. She didn't care about speeches. There would be time for explanations later. She wanted to grab hold and know that God answers prayers. Her brother was home again. He was safe. Physical contact was important to Sheri, and though Joe struggled with expressions of affection, he'd hug Sheri for as long as she needed him to.

"Last chance hotel, buddy boy," Dave pressed, stepping forward. "Where've you been?"

Joe opened his eyes and glared over Sheri's shoulder.

Dave was about as sensitive as a bulldozer, even though it was just an act.

"Well?" Dave pressed.

Joe visually inventoried the others—Garth, Allie, her husband Carl—each was curious all right. It was understandable. He would have been too, if the shoe were on the other foot. He scuffed Sheri's curly red hair and said, "It's okay. I'm here," then ruffled her locks until finally she looked at him with those pale blue eyes and growled, "Qqquuit!"

He smiled. It was good to hear her grumble again.

"So...where *have* you been?" she pouted, studying the bruised area over his eyebrows. He probably looked to her as if he had been in a street fight. "I waited for you at Charlie's for an hour and a half."

"It's a long, long story, Sheri."

Kicking an office chair and sending it rolling across the room toward him, Dave said, "Of course it is! It always is! But let's start at the beginning anyway, hmm? You're not in a hurry, are you?"

As usual, Dave missed the point by a mile in Joe's opinion. Telling his family and friends what had happened might not be smart. He could endanger them. What if they were questioned? Would they be charged with aiding a fugitive? According to marine training protocol, he shouldn't tell them a thing. Plausible deniability could be their best ally. They weren't on a "need-to-know." But then, these weren't soldiers. They were family, and what they might need most of all was a reason to run away. He had one for them.

"What's this nonsense Garth's been blabbin' about you hiding in the bushes, huh? You got somebody after you? Bad guys? You know what we do around here with bad guys, don't you...?"

Here it came, the compulsory carnival barker. If Joe were going to control this situation, he would have to interrupt Dave, probably more than once. "Listen, Dave," he said. "The guys I'm talking about might be too tough...even for you. I'm deep in something I don't fully understand. I may need to disappear long enough to sort it all out."

Dave's pretentiously wise expression widened. "Whaddaya talking about? Too tough for me? Look at this place! Do I look like the kind of guy who don't know his way around?"

Joe glanced through the room. It was the real deal all right. He had marveled at it before. The computer towers, the monitors, the files and maps stacked here and there. These were the tools of Raiders News Update, the website Dave used for broadcasting information "raided" from government resources. All of it reminded Joe of the serious differences he and his sisters had with this man. Hacking computers was a major offense. Someday, he'd burn for it, not to mention the trouble his conspiratorial ideas about prophecy and the New World Order could lead to. Of course, there was no denying Dave's affection for Joe and his sisters. He might even die for them if it came right down to it...and it could.

Standing beside Carl, Allie cleared her throat and used her infamous older sister tone: "Now Joe, I insist you tell us where you've been. If you're in some kind of trouble, we have a right to know."

Joe knew that, unlike Sheri, Allie didn't care much for his overprotective style. In her opinion, he was always treating them like children, shielding them from the facts of their father's death, as if they were too immature to handle the truth. He would be working a lead, writing out some small detail, and right away cover his papers or photos if she walked into the room. She didn't like that, and had told him so on more than one occasion.

Now his conscience was at it again.

I could be a fool to tell this group what has happened. Yet I may be sorry if I don't.

You know it's against protocol.

Yeah, but instinct, not protocols, are what I trust. Mine tell me they're already in danger. They need to move to safety.

Maybe, maybe not. One thing's for sure, their running will make it look like they have something to hide.

He looked at his sisters. *If I don't talk, and they get hurt, I could never forgive myself.*

Is that what this is about? Protecting your feelings?

How stupid. I would die for any of them.

The question is, would you live for them? Would you give up this infernal pursuit and just live your life?

A bit late for that, isn't it? Or have you forgotten the last two weeks?

Suddenly Sheri's voice was interrupting the internal debate. She was saying, "Yeah, Joe. I'm with Allie. We have a right to know what's going on."

Conspicuously quiet for a moment, arguing internally, he surprised himself after a few seconds by blurting out, "A few weeks ago I received a phone call from Mom. She told me Dad's old shop was scheduled for demolition. Did you know about that?"

You just couldn't wait to spill the beans, could you, he thought as he spoke.

"We did. So? She told me she's going to have a new one built in its place," Sheri said.

Joe understood he was starting down a road from which he couldn't turn back, but it felt right to him now. It was as if he were only part of a larger plan somehow, something beyond his control.

"Well, I can tell you something you didn't know about that building," he continued.

"Such as?"

"Back when I was twelve or thirteen years old, I was working on my bike in the front yard one day when two men in dark suits pulled up and went into the house. I didn't pay much attention to them because we were always getting visitors from the base, you know. Then I heard them arguing with Dad. At one point it got so loud it scared me, so I ran and hid in the tall grass underneath the big swamp cooler. Pretty soon, Dad walked out onto the porch with the men. He was shouting something about his years of service and how they couldn't talk to him that way."

Allie cocked her head. "What the heck? Did Mom ever know about this?"

"I don't think so. You know how Dad was; he didn't like worrying her."

"Umm-hmm...that *was* Dad."

"Anyway, once the strangers drove off and Dad went back inside, I peeked through the water cooler fibers and spied on him. I saw him pull something out from under the couch. He just kept staring at it. Before long, I felt bad about watching, so I went inside and said, 'Dad, what's going on?' I must've really startled him because he jumped up and screamed, 'Don't you ever sneak up on me again!' I'd never seen him act like that, and it frightened me, so I started crying. Of course he felt awful. He hugged me and asked what I'd seen. I told him I couldn't tell, but I knew he was hiding something. That's when he showed me the strangest thing—an image, like a small head with a polished stone or crystal sticking out of the back of it. It had unusual markings on it that Dad thought were some sort of writing."

Sheri raised her palms, as if measuring an invisible item. "You mean like a statue?"

"Just a head. It was made of rock or something similar. For reasons I still don't understand, he showed it to me...and..."

He paused, his palms sweating. *This might be unwise.*

"He told me a weird story about where it came from."

Go ahead! Tell them everything! You can mop up the blood later!

"Yes?"

"A story..."

"Go on."

"A story...about a spacecraft...an alien ship."

The room grew quiet. Joe could read the questions in everybody's eyes, hear the doubts in their minds.

Finally, breaking the silence, Dave said, "A UFO? You mean...a flying saucer?"

"A flying object...a craft of unknown origin...it crash-landed in the desert, near Sedona, Arizona."

Dave turned and picked up a notepad, pulled a pencil from behind his ear, and jotted something down. "How do you know it was an unknown craft?"

"According to Dad, it was found intact, even though it apparently hit the ground at a phenomenal rate of speed. There was a military media blackout of the event, with an area several miles wide cordoned off."

Allie, looking flustered, studied his expression. "Joe," she said with a tone of suspicion, "this sounds like you're pulling a joke on us. Like one of those guys who disappears for a while, then reappears claiming alien abduction."

"I know it's hard to believe, but would I joke about something related to Dad's murder?"

Nervously twirling a band of her curly red hair, Sheri

said, "This has something to do with *that?*"

"I'm pretty sure it does. As a Lieutenant Colonel, Dad played a lead role in the crash site field investigation. He discovered the artifact during recovery and cleanup, and decided to keep it."

"But...why? Why would he do that? Keep this...whatever it is?" Sheri questioned, exchanging troubled looks with Allie.

"He must have had a good reason. Either way, he kept it and hid it in the shop."

"The building Mom's going to replace?" Allie asked.

"The very one. Dad wanted to hide it where Mom would never look, so he removed the paneling from behind the shop hot water tank, placed the object inside a leather pouch, and nailed the wood back over it. That's where it's been until now. He made me swear to leave it alone."

"Until Mom decided to bulldoze the building."

"Exactly. When she called me with her plans, I flew down under the guise of a vacation, and, while she was in town, took a crowbar and removed the paneling. I found the image right where Dad put it."

Joe seemed to grope for his next statement. "Together with this," he said, pulling from his wallet a faded, crumbled paper. The letter had nearly been ruined from being soaked in the Columbia River. "It's a note from Dad."

Sheri, letting go of her hair, said weakly, "What does it say?"

"It's brief. In fact it looks like it was scratched in a hurry." He straightened the paper and read: "Joe, if you're reading this letter, I'm probably not around anymore. If that's the case, please know how proud of you kids I am. You're such a perfect family....

As he read, Joe glanced up long enough to notice that

Sheri looked nauseous, as if she might throw up, probably drifting long enough to miss part of the note. A moment later, he finished, "...If General Nathan Webster asks for the object, give it to him. He can be trusted. But beware the men in black. You'll know them if you see them, especially their leader. He's an old snake. Trust God and family, and few others. No matter what, I'll see you again, either in this life or the next. Dad."

"That's all there is," he said, folding the paper and shrugging his shoulders.

Allie was nervously drumming her fingers against the caps of her knees. "I-I wonder when he put that note in the wall?"

"During my tour of duty, I suppose, just before his murder. He must've sensed some kind of danger."

"What do you think he meant about an old snake, and 'beware the men in black'?"

"I haven't got a clue."

Dave looked as though he did. "Hmm," he said. "So...you retrieved this object, huh? What then?"

"The first thing I did when I got back to Oregon was to call Uncle Amil. I thought if anybody knew about General Webster, Dad's brother would."

"Was he able to help?"

"He was. In fact, Nathan Webster is in a care facility not far from here. Mt. Hermon Convalescent Center in Oregon City."

"That's just around the corner from where I work," Allie said.

"I know...small world, huh?"

Joe drew his hand through his long brown hair and continued. "Anyway, I went to the Mt. Hermon center and asked to see General Webster. After some formality, they took me to his room. He didn't even know I was there. He has Alzheimer's or something and was unable to talk with me."

"So..."

"So I went back to my apartment, and then it got weird. Immediately after I returned home, a guy named Donald Pritchert of the Montero Research Facility, the military complex above the Columbia River, called me concerning my visit with General Webster."

"Sounds like you set off red flags," Dave said nonchalantly.

"What?"

"You had to sign in to see the General, didn't you? Did they ask to see your ID?"

For Pete's sake. Why hadn't I seen this before now? "Yes," Joe answered.

"Did you show it to them?"

"Of course." He knew where Dave was going.

"The care facility is subsidized. They obviously have ties to local government. With somebody like the General, they keep a record of visitors. Anybody whose name doesn't match a family or doctor's list is flagged. With the name Ryback, you might as well have sent a singing telegram. If this object your dad had was important enough to, well, die for, they're probably still looking for it. If they knew about your dad and General Webster's friendship, and that the two of them shared matters of, let's say, national security, the Ryback name showing up these many years later would definitely set off fireworks."

"You'd be right about that," Joe said bitterly.

"After this Donald guy called you, what then?"

"Donald seemed nice enough, just doing his job. He wanted to know why I had visited General Webster and if there was anything he could do to help me. As we talked, I told him that I had something I wanted to give to the general, and was curious if he had any living relatives I might pass a 'family heirloom' along to."

"Wha'd he say?"

"He said yes, and that I could drop it off at Montero Research, where he'd be happy to take care of it. At that point, my curiosity got the best of me. I wondered why a government contractor would be interested in helping a sick general with personal affairs. Later that evening, I put the image in my fanny pack and drove up there in my Ranger..."

"By the way, where *is* your pickup?" Garth said.

"As far as I know, it's still in the parking lot at Montero Research."

"Why?"

"If you'll stop talking, I'll tell you."

Garth studied him briefly, then said, "Sorry, go on."

"After I drove to Montero and checked in, I went to the lobby and asked for Donald Pritchert. The lady at the front desk led me to a waiting room, where she offered me coffee or something cold to drink. I told her I was fine. I sat there a few minutes looking at some strange magazines about the Earth being our mother or Gaia or something—the coffee table was covered with them—then this civilian with two Military Police walked into the room. The guy was a real punk. He immediately started questioning whether I was Clarence Ryback's son, what did I want with General Webster, what did I want to show Donald Pritchert. Finally, his belligerence cheesed me off, so I stood and said I'd made a mistake; that I'd be leaving now. That's when the MPs clasped their sidearms, and the civilian got in my face. He said something like, 'Listen up, *marine*. We believe you may have information of vital interest to national security. There's been enough dying over this thing. If you know anything about the item your father stole from the corps in Arizona, you'd better hand it over if you know what's good for you.'"

Sheri's eyes widened. "He said that about Dad?"

"Yeah, and it made me so mad that I pushed him...hard," Joe said with a smirk.

"You didn't!"

"I did. Then I told him he was out of line and that Dad never stole anything from anybody. That's as far as I made it, though. He ordered the MPs to search me."

Allie, sounding sympathetic, said, "Oh, Joe."

"Yeah, well, lucky for me Donald Pritchert opened the door to the room at that very moment. He said 'Here now! What's going on in here!?' I know it was Donald because the civilian said, 'Mr. Pritchert, please leave. This is a private matter and we have everything under control.' But I wasn't waiting around to see who was in control. I saw a large window across the room....'"

"You didn't!" Sheri cheered again.

"Afraid so. I charged toward the window, covered my head with my arms like this," he said, holding his hands on top of his head, "and cannonballed right through the plate glass."

Allie looked disgusted. "Joe Ryback! Have you gone nuts? You could have been killed!"

"I know it was impulsive, but I had the uncanny feeling that something worse than death was about to happen. Luckily, it had been raining all night, and the ground was soft. Muddy, but soft."

Allie shook her head in dismay. "I can hardly wait to hear what else you did."

"I headed for my truck, but somebody near the parking lot was yelling for security. So I scaled a fence and started home through the woods above the Columbia."

"You mean you headed home that night?" Sheri probed.

"Yeah."

"Then where've you been the last two weeks?"

Joe remembered his promise to Buck, to protect his identity, and deferred the subject. "I'll explain later...for now, let me show you what all the commotion is about. Maybe you guys can help me determine the significance of this thing."

He reached into the fanny pack and retrieved the small stony figure. It was blackish gray, polished in parts, with a thin, glasslike nodule sticking out of the back. He held it up in front of them. "What do you think?"

Except for Dave, the gang was nonplussed. As soon as he saw it, Dave's jaw dropped and he jumped up out of reflex, scooting his chair back in rough squeaks.

Joe was taken aback by the fear on the tough guy's face.

Dave was whispering, "Sweet Jesus...you've got to be kidding...."

Something in the sound of his voice sent a chill crawling through the room.

"What *do* you have there, my young friend," he finally said, walking over and grabbing the item, trembling as if holding priceless artwork. "If the government is willing to kill for this thing...then...whew, baby...it may actually be..."

When he hesitated, Sheri demanded, "Be what?"

"Part of the mother...of all conspiracies..."

"W-what?" Sheri repeated. "What is it? What's it for?"

"I don't know what it's for...but I know what it's modeled after."

"It's a model of something?"

"Not a model, per se," he sidestepped cryptically. "It's the face, Sheri."

"The face?"

"The face...from Cydonia...on Mars."

5—MANGLED SOULS

"Angels, both good and evil, take part in the spiritual battle for nations...we find clear evidence that angels have regularly participated in influencing world governments and in shaping human history."
Spiritual Warfare: The Invisible Invasion,
Huntington House Publishers, p. 123

July 24

Sheri focused on the highway as she followed the familiar landmarks. It was a gorgeous day for a drive. Less than twenty minutes had passed since she departed the Rose City, and the smell of the country was so exuberant that if it had not been for a restless night rehashing Joe's troubling story, she might have stopped somewhere along the way and picked a bouquet of wildflowers. Things being what they were, she couldn't wait to get inside the concrete walls of Mt. Hood Evangelical Seminary, where Joe and she were meeting a longtime family friend—Dr. Donald Jones—in hopes he could attach some significance to the image. Unlike Dave with his Mars-Face conspiracies, "Indy," which they called him after the lead character in the Indiana Jones films, was a Ph.D. in biblical history. He might have an expert opinion about the arcane object.

* * * * * *

Flying alongside, Justice and Swift watched as Sheri popped a gummy worm into her mouth and pushed the pedal down harder. She had no idea how grave their danger was, how high the stakes were in this cosmic contest.

* * * * * *

In the back of the car beneath a blanket on the floorboard, on pain pills she gave him but undoubtedly still sore from his recent physical exertions, Joe said, "Do we have time to drive through a Dairy Queen or a Taco Bell? I'm starving."

Sheri tossed a handful of gummy worms over the seat to him. "Absolutely not. You know how Jones is. If we're not there on time, he won't wait. Besides..." she added, biting her lip, "I think we're being followed."

Back at her apartment, she hadn't given much thought to the dark car parked across the road from her place. Her neighbors, the Gerlichers, often had visitors from out of town, and though this particular vehicle was not one she remembered seeing before, nothing about the shiny automobile had seemed out of place at the time. Even when she backed from the garage and started down Stark Street, she hadn't paid attention to the Lincoln pulling out.

"Somebody's following you? Why didn't you say so?"

"I don't know?"

"What does their car look like?"

"Big...and dark...with one of those funny antennas on top. You know, like an unmarked cop's car."

* * * * * *

Joe pulled the hot blanket from over his head and stared at the headliner. In the ceiling fabric above him someone had written "Sheri Loves Michael" with a marking pen. *The pastor's son, Michael*, he thought. *What a mischievous PK. The kid just can't get it through his head that she's too old for him.* "Where are you right now?"

"We just passed the Powell Street Chevy dealership."

He took a moment to visualize where he was, then said, "Up here a little ways you'll see the road that goes to Pastor Swanson's church; take that exit."

"Go to the church? Why?"

"Just do it and tell me if the car follows."

A minute later the Colt's turning signal clicked and the motor's rpm's lowered. "Yep," she said. "They've turned their signal on. They're going with us."

"Getting closer?"

"Staying about a block behind."

"But their car's big, huh...how wide?"

"I don't know, Joe. It's a battleship."

By now Montero might have sent investigators from the military and the FBI to look for him. That being true, this daytime trip to the seminary was unwarranted. Yet the uncanny feeling that he was on a quest pressed heavily in his heart. Somebody or something was guiding him, not against his will but influencing his decisions to the point that some unknown task was being accomplished. At the moment of his choosing, he could resist the invisible force and do whatsoever he wanted, though it would probably be unwise, especially given that, to this point, this power—God, he believed, *hoped*—had likely kept him alive. So what was he supposed to do now?

* * * * * *

Seeing Joe confused about his next move, Justice said inaudibly through the car's side window, "What about the old flood control canal where the kids ride their skateboards and go-karts?"

* * * * * *

"Hang on a second" Joe said to Sheri, "I'm getting an idea. Do you know where the old flood control canal is where the kids ride their skateboards and go-karts?"

"Yeah?"

"When you see the county road that leads to the canal, take it."

"Isn't that a dead-end road?"

"Not really. Remember the huge culvert at the end of it that cuts underneath the old Damascus highway?"

"You mean the tunnel thingy the kids ride their bikes in?"

"Uh-huh. We'll drive through it and lose these guys. Their battleship won't fit."

Sheri seemed bothered at the thought of it. "Bad idea. That thing's too small for my car."

"I don't think so. Amy Keller drove her Volkswagen Beetle in there during the Fourth of July party, you know."

"Yeah, but Amy's crazy. She doesn't care if she tears her car up. She's always doing loony stuff like that. Besides, my car's bigger than her bug, and there ain't no road on the other side of the tunnel, just a bunch of dune buggy trails."

"And one of those trails leads to the old Lewis farm. We can take their driveway back to the highway from there."

"How do you know that?"

"Trust me."

"Trust you? What if we get trapped?"

"We won't," he said, deciding to let her in on a secret. "Besides, I have a confession to make."

"What?"

"I've already driven your car through there."

"You what?"

"Sorry."

"When?"

"You remember that blind date you set me up with? 'Spacey,' or whatever her name was?"

"Tracy."

"Whatever."

"Yes?"

"We went on a picnic down there. When we left, I drove out that way."

"Do you mind telling me why?"

"It seemed like a good idea at the time."

"You think, show-off. See if I ever loan you my car again."

"You know you love me. So how far till we get to the county road?"

"Maybe a mile or two."

"Good. Here's what I want you to do. As soon as you see the exit, take it. There'll be a few seconds when the trees hide us from view. I'll jump over the seat and take the wheel from there."

"You're kidding."

"Trust me."

"Where have I heard that before?"

"You just be ready. Let me know when we're getting close to the exit because we'll only have a couple seconds to make the change. After you turn, don't stop, just jump into the rider's side and keep the steering wheel straight while I climb over. Once I have control, you crouch down. If we're lucky, these goons won't even know we've made a switch. Got it?"

"I guess."

"Do you or don't you?"

"Aye, aye, captain."

Two minutes later, maintaining her speed as she approached the hard right turn, Sheri said, "Okay, the exit's just ahead, get ready."

Doesn't she know to slow down!? "SHERI!"

Joe was too late. As she slammed on the brakes, he was pinned against the front seat while an avalanche of dirty laundry and snowboarding equipment came off the rear dash over the top of him. He yelled again, struggling to dig himself out, "Sheri! What're you doing!"

"Exactly what you told me to! And you'd better hurry, because they're coming fast now!"

Clambering awkwardly onto the backseat, somehow he caught his balance. Peeking through the rear window, he could see the dark Lincoln Continental bearing down on them. The pursuers obviously had more experience with vehicle maneuvering than Sheri did. He spun and began pulling himself headfirst onto the front seat, frantically trying to trade places with her while not ripping his wounds apart. His boot whipped against the center seat divider, slamming Sheri's hand and causing her to scream out in pain. Wrestling his body into the driver's position, half expecting to take a bullet in the back as he went, he shouted, "Sorry, Sheri, sorry! But hang on...we're gonna get wild!"

He smashed the gas pedal to the floor and fought to straighten the car in the road. As he turned into the slide, he could hear gravel from the Colt's spinning tires pinging against the Continental's expensive grill. They were right on top of him.

* * * * * *

Struggling to clamp her seat belt with her injured, throbbing hand, Sheri sensed the world around her shifting into slow motion. When the safety strap she was wrestling with finally locked in place, she looked across the cab at Joe, who was gripping the steering wheel like a race car driver. She heard the recently tuned-up but aging four-cylinder engine straining to carry them to sixty miles per hour.

When the Colt reached eighty-five miles per hour, it became nearly uncontrollable. The little dips in the road were like jump ramps that lifted the car momentarily before slamming it down with a thud. She could feel her spine crunching against her tailbone every time they bounced, tingling with the vibration of the gravel spraying up from under the floorboard. In her peripheral vision, the roadside trees and foxtails were becoming a blurry mural of greens and yellows zipping by. A high-pitched whistling sound, seeping around the windows, made it feel as if the shrubs were screaming to them to flee the nefarious, looming threat.

Suddenly, a strong male voice boomed from behind them, "This is the police! Pull the car over now!"

Sheri shouted to Joe, her voice vibrating as the compact's tires riveted along the ruts in the road, "Joe-oe, it's the po-o-lice! Pull over b-before we get k-killed!"

He stared straight ahead. "It's n-not the police, Sheri! The po-police d-don't drive Lincoln Conti..."

Without warning, the rear window exploded with a sputtering sound, followed by a series of small circular holes, which appeared as if by magic, cutting through the cab and breaking open the plastic dash.

GUNFIRE!

"GET D-DOWN!" Joe shouted to her. "GET DOWN N-NOW!"

* * * * * *

Just ahead, Joe could see the end of the gravel road and beyond that the tunnel opening leading into the abandoned culvert. His thoughts were racing. Was Sheri right? Was the space insufficient for her car to pass through *at this speed?* He too was no longer convinced of the idea.

As the Colt's tires flew onto the canal's concrete floor, the incessant roar of the gravel slapping beneath their feet gave way to the somewhat quieter sound of rubber against pavement as Sheri sobbed into the seat cushion, "Jesus, help us! Please, Jesus, help us..."

The automatic weapon's fire cut from behind them again. This time a bullet clipped the corner of the driver's headrest, sending fragments of foam and cotton into a particle cloud near Joe's left ear. He smashed the gas pedal down and aimed at the approaching culvert. He waited until the last possible second, then closed his eyes and braced himself for the real possibility of collapsing metal and physical destruction. As bad as it could be, this seemed to be the best chance they had under the circumstances.

A moment later, when the impact came, it didn't feel quite right. The tremor jolted his cheeks as the awful screech of fabricated metal slamming against solid concrete was heard, but for some reason the catastrophic force of inertia did not accompany the crash in the way he had expected.

Then it dawned on him. They were still moving. He opened his eyes and threw his foot against the brake pedal. The '89 Dodge slid in a soft circular motion that ended a moment later near a weeping willow tree.

Looking perplexed, Sheri stammered, "W-what happened?"

"It...it worked...we're on the other side of the tunnel," Joe said in disbelief.

It was the Lincoln Continental that had crashed. The little Colt had barreled ahead of the larger car through the concrete opening at nearly ninety miles per hour.

In the distance, smoke and fire billowed from the mouth of the abandoned canal.

* * * * * *

Inside the culvert, beyond Joe and Sheri's view, face down in the crumbled wreckage, the mangled bodies of two men assigned to track Joe down were burning in the rubble. Their mission had been to acquire the mysterious image at any cost. They had failed, and at more than this assignment. They had failed at life too, and now they would pay.

Around the would-be assassins, through the oak boughs, dark shadows began to accumulate. The demon of death, now calling itself Hecate, a black and powerful heathen goddess who enjoyed such fear in antiquity, led countless gleaming torches toward the confused, trembling souls. Horrible snakes wound about her head as hellish dogs and owl-shaped strigae emerged from the gloom and surrounded the killers. The men's eyes darted wildly as their fingers grasped frantically for a weapon. Beneath them, cold, bony fingers cracked through the ground, clasping their corrupted souls, jerking them down in a merciless earthen rend. Their senses, suddenly vivid beyond reason, filled with a burning sensation of sulfur as they burst into unquenchable fire. The mother they had so reverently obeyed during life couldn't and wouldn't help them now. What authority Gaia possessed was against these two anyway. Like Hecate, whose blood red eyes bulged now with murderous delight, Gaia felt only satisfaction as the doomed spirits screamed their way into the eternal torments of Thanatos and Hell.

6—THE NEPHILIM CODE

"As a trained chemist and a bishop of a sect that believes scientists from another planet created all life on Earth, Boisselier and other followers of the 'Raelian' religion say cloning is key to humanity's future."
"The God Game No More," *U.S. News & World Report*, 07-09-01

At Mt. Hood Evangelical Seminary, Dr. Jones was on the phone with his wife, Joyce, when his call waiting clicked. "Hang on, Hon," he said, "that may be Joe and Sheri now."

It was.

"Indy...I mean, Dr. Jones...is that you?" he heard Sheri ask.

"And where, may I ask, are you?"

"In the car right now. We're on our way. I'm sorry we're running late, but we should be there in about five minutes."

"You sure?"

"Positive."

"Okay, I'll wait a few more minutes, then you're in big trouble," he mused half-heartedly.

"Thanks. You won't be sorry."

"We'll see."

* * * * * *

Sheri switched her digital phone off and told Joe to speed up a little. They were both in shock and didn't know if they should tell Indy anything about what had happened at the culvert. The parts of Joe's story they felt were necessary to share were already so Machiavellian and unusual that giving the professor more information than he needed might stretch his credulity beyond his ability to absorb it.

"I'll just play it by ear," Joe said as he pulled into the parking lot a few minutes later. "Right now, I'm looking for answers, not speaking opportunities. Everything, including the Lincoln that chased us, will come to light eventually. If the guys in that car were killed, it'll be on the news by tonight."

As he spoke, Sheri looked for Indy's van and saw it parked in the staff area. She grabbed her purse, which held the image, and jumped out of the car as the engine shut off. She was already ahead of Joe, walking toward the main entrance, when Jones yelled from a side entry, "Hey! School's closed and the front door's locked!"

She waved and quickly joined the professor at the side of the twenty-year-old block building. Once inside, Jones, a middle-aged, ruffled-haired man with a teaching gig he thoroughly enjoyed, led them to a door where he joked, "This, my friends, is the blessed staff lounge...where the re-e-al thinking occurs."

He opened the freshly painted dark brown door with a key from his ring, went to what Sheri assumed was his favorite recliner, flopped onto its worn cushions, threw his arms behind his head, and said, "Okay, come in here and tell ol' Jones what's on your mind." A big and casual man, Jones was one of those kind of guys that had a hard time keeping his starchy white shirt tucked neatly inside his Wal-Mart dress pants.

* * * * * *

Entering and taking a seat on a floral sofa next to Sheri, Joe positioned himself so that Indy could look him straight in the eyes. After small talk, he rehearsed his father's amazing story, passing over the most fantastic elements and adding only an occasional twist when it seemed to interest Jones. At last he came to the end of his comments and waited for the professor's response.

Following a moment of silence, Indy rubbed his graying beard and said, "Did my students put you up to this?"

"What do you mean?" Joe said.

"This trick. Did they? Because I assure you, it won't work."

As if sensing some history behind the antagonistic comment, Joe reached for Sheri's purse and said, "I don't know what your student's have done in the past, Indy, but this is no joke. I need guidance and an expert's opinion. That's why I came to you. All I'm asking is that you look at the piece and judge for yourself."

Another pause, his eyes narrowing beneath his bifocals as he studied the youths, then Jones said skeptically, "Sure. Show me what you've got, but if this is a prank there will be Hell to pay."

Joe removed the item from the handbag and placed it on the coffee table in front of them. The professor's eyes widened as soon as he saw it. He studied the siblings, then turned his attention once more to the curious image. "May I?" he said, leaning forward and picking it up. After superficially inspecting the peculiar semblance and casting several inquisitive glances at Joe, he withdrew a microcassette from his inside coat pocket and, with the skills of a physician, began describing the details of the unusual stone, down to the cracks and crevices. Before long he focused on what he called "a headdress strikingly similar to those worn by Egyptian and Mayan royalty." He postulated the object's length, width, approximate weight, and pallid color. Finally flipping the image over, he noted the crystalline formation protruding from the back...and above it, the markings. "Well, well, what do we have here?" he said.

Cleaning his glasses with a handkerchief, then putting them back on, he stood, walked to a lamp, clicked it on, held the figure beneath the light, and instantly complained that he still couldn't "be sure."

"Come with me," he said, and ran out of the room. Joe gave Sheri a puzzled look before jumping up to follow him into the hall. Joe was impressed with how fast the big man was.

A few doors down and to the right, Jones opened a second door with a "Laboratory" sign on it. Once inside, he removed a small bottle of cleaner from a cabinet. "This should do the trick," he said, pouring its contents directly onto the shape. He held the object above a stainless steel sink and removed what looked like a fancy toothbrush from a drawer.

"Digger's brush," he said, noticing Joe and Sheri's curiosity. "My pupils use these when they participate in student archaeological digs. Don't worry, I'll be careful...just want to get a little of the buildup off the back of here...wouldn't want to jump to any conclusions..."

As Jones continued to mumble and scrub the back of the

item, he might as well have been talking to himself. Joe had no idea what he was so excited about.

After additional cleaning and a final close-up visual inspection, the professor placed the form on the laboratory countertop and said, "Well, Joe, you've either made a great discovery or found a brilliant fakery, I'm not sure which, yet. The facial image on the front appears to be adorned with a headdress similar to those worn by Egyptian pharaohs, but the writing on the back is definitely Sumerian."

Joe cocked his head. "Do you know what it says?"

"Just one word."

"Which is?"

"Annunaki."

Gazing at the marking, Sheri said, "What does it mean?"

"Depends on who you're talking to. I would say it refers to fallen angels. Authors like Erich Von Daniken and Zecharia Sitchin would disagree, of course. They believe the Annunaki were ancient astronauts from a planet called Nibiru."

Joe's senses heightened. His dad had found the image near a UFO crash site, and now Jones was talking about visitors from beyond.

"They believe the Annunaki were intergalactic scientists who performed genetic experiments on early hominids, changing their DNA and creating Homo sapiens."

"You mean us?" Sheri asked. "People?"

"According to the theory, yes. Primates had their evolution advanced, resulting in the human race."

"Kinda like Darwin on drugs?"

"I guess you could put it that way. They get the idea from misinterpreting ancient cuneiform tablets, specifically the Annunaki legends. Portions of the Sumerian folklore are viewed as records of aliens from a mysterious twelfth planet."

"This Nibiru?"

"Uh-huh, and that they came here and created the human race. They also believe the Nibiruans engineered the giants of the Old Testament."

Joe's expression became quizzical. He thought about what he was hearing, then said, "But I take it you don't agree?"

"Well...I think Earth was visited by creatures from heaven and that the giant Nephilim were produced by them, but I don't believe these were so-called 'extraterrestrial humanoids,' if that's what you're asking."

"But demons?"

Jones nodded. "If I understand the Bible and extrabiblical literature correctly, the Annunaki were fallen angels that left their assigned habitation and took women for wives. Nephilim were the mutant offspring of their unholy matrimony."

"Is this in the Scriptures somewhere?" Sheri asked, glancing at Joe, then back at the professor.

"I believe so, as well as other records. The Bible says that when men began increasing on earth and daughters were born to them, the Sons of God noted their beauty and took wives from among them. Are you familiar with that?"

"Somewhat."

"Well, many scholars believe these 'Sons of God' were angels that fell from Heaven. When we compare that interpretation with other books—Enoch, Jubilees, Baruch, Genesis Apocryphon, Philo, Malachius, and so on, an incredible tale emerges whereby we learn that the giants of the Old Testament like Goliath were half-human, half-demon offspring of fallen angels and humans. In fact the Old Testament term for *giant* is from the word *Nephilim*, meaning 'those who are fallen.'"

Jones motioned them to follow him back to the lounge. As they went down the hall, Joe was thinking Indy's story was getting wilder than the one he'd told. A moment later, as they resumed their positions on the couch and chair, Indy said, "According to the records I've studied, the Nephilim were built as part of a larger plan to destroy the children of God and to cut off the birth line of the Messiah."

"By crossbreeding humans and angels," Sheri said, leaning back on the couch.

"Sure. Satan understood the protoevangelium—the promise in Genesis 3:15 that a Savior would be born, the seed of the woman, and that He would destroy the Devil's power. So Satan's followers, the Annunaki, intermingled their DNA with Old Testament women in a conspiracy to stop the Messiah's birth."

"Something like a sex virus," Joe speculated, trying to grasp what Jones was saying.

As if already understanding the professor's point, Sheri added, "Something that would spread through marriage and end when humanity's DNA was completely corrupted. Under those circumstances, you're saying a spotless Son of God could not be born."

"Exactly. If the genetic makeup of man leading to the time of the Messiah was universally demonized, no Savior would be conceived, and mankind would be lost forever."

"So how come I never heard of this before?"

"I couldn't say."

Sheri bit her lip. "Well...obviously Jesus, the Messiah came in the flesh, so what foiled the Devil's plan?"

"A couple things. First, God commanded Israel not to intermarry with the heathen populations. This was so there might be a pure bloodline in Israel. Second, He ordered Noah to build an ark and to prepare for a flood that would destroy every living thing. The fact that God sent such a universal fiat of judgment like the flood illustrates how widespread the altered DNA eventually became. In fact, the Bible says only Noah, and therefore by extension his children, were found perfect in their generation."

"Meaning they followed the laws of God," Sheri continued.

"I'm sure they did, but that's not what the Hebrew word for 'perfect' in this case means. This is the same word that was used in Leviticus to describe an unblemished sacrificial lamb. The meaning here was not moral perfection, but that Noah was physically untainted; his DNA was not corrupted or altered by the Annunaki, as apparently the rest of the world had been."

Suddenly the light went on in Joe's mind. He had always wondered about the scope of the deluge, why it included children. "So God sent the flood because every human on Earth except Noah's family had been genetically altered over time?"

"Through a corrupted bloodline leading back to angels with women," Sheri added.

"According to some people, yes."

"But I thought Jesus said angels couldn't get married or have babies?"

"Actually, what He said was that in the resurrection we will neither marry nor be given in marriage, but that we would be as angels in heaven. Keep in mind, Jesus was talking about angels 'in heaven.' We're discussing fallen angels that, like Peter and Jude described in their epistles, abandoned their dwelling place and took up an alternative lifestyle."

Jones paused, adjusted his legs and added, "Another thing. Look at the angels that visited Abraham in the plains of Mamre. They looked like men; they walked and talked like men; they even ate food with Abraham. So as far as scholars know, angels can take human form and carry out normal human functions. It appears from the historical record that the fallen ones also engaged in sexual activity, or at least genetic manipulation."

Joe hunched his shoulders and looked soberly at the professor. Indy actually seemed to be making the case that fallen angels had mated with women, that these same spirits were involved in UFO activity, and that somehow this related to the image he was showing him. In order to bring the conversation back to his father's story, he said, "But if this disc my dad saw was the remains of a physical UFO, why would angels fly around in something like that? Spiritual beings wouldn't need spaceships to come to Earth in order to mate with women, would they?"

"Probably not, but fallen angels might create them for larger reasons."

"Such as?"

"To deceive mankind."

Joe scratched the top of his head. "First of all," he said, " how could fallen angels do that? Make physical ships? Second, how would that deceive us?"

Jones stood and crossed the room to a white refrigerator. He opened the door, withdrew a small plastic bottle of water, and offered one to Joe and Sheri. They took the Perriers as he returned to his chair.

"There's no doubt they could produce UFOs for their own nefarious reasons. The theology of transmogrification, where spirits take form, indicates ability by demons to manipulate energy and matter. And what about poltergeists and their unexplained noises—how else could spirits cause audible vibrations unless they have ability to make physical contact with tangible materials? This being true, maybe demons produce the phenomena known as Unidentified Flying Objects by manipulating energy."

Tapping his finger against his palm as if to emphasize the next point, Jones stressed, "And as far as how UFOs would be used to deceive us, this comes down to an argument of origins."

"Meaning what?"

"The ageless question—where did we come from? If people believe UFOnauts are advanced extraterrestrials scurrying about in spaceships, and that these same creatures visited the Earth in ancient days and tinkered with hominid DNA, that disturbs the Judeo-Christian doctrine concerning the age of the Earth and biblical creation. Satan would love people to believe we are nothing more than an alien zoology program. Of course," he said, rolling his eyes, "there's always Indy's Theory of UFOlogy."

"Indy's Theory? As in your own personal theory?"

"Mine and a few others."

Sheri smiled. "Tell us about this mysterious theory."

"I thought you'd never ask. According to the Bible, the End Times will be accompanied by fearful sights and great signs from heaven. The book of Second Thessalonians even says that, when the Antichrist is revealed, he will be accompanied by 'lying wonders.' Maybe these verses are talking about UFOs being used to introduce the Man of Sin. Wouldn't the world react to the sudden arrival of an intergalactic wise man with awe and wonder? The prophecies of Daniel seem to support this possibility."

"You're telling me the prophet Daniel talked about a Last Days invasion of UFOs?" Joe said, sounding incredulous.

"No, no. But he said the Antichrist will be a worshiper of Baal, and Baal was the lord of the sky. As Baalbamoth he was the lord of the aerial regions. As Baalzebub he was the lord of those that 'fly' or that flit about in the atmosphere. In the New Testament, Satan himself is referred to as the prince of the powers of the air. Therefore Scriptures lead me to believe that the aerial phenomena you and I interpret as UFO activity *could* be part of a Last Days delusion— something to trick humanity into accepting the appearance of Antichrist."

Joe took a deep breath and exhaled slowly. *UFOs could introduce the Antichrist, huh?* He stared at the image. "So when it comes to these Annunaki, you believe we're talking about fallen angels?"

"In a nutshell, yes."

"And somehow this relates to our little image here."

"In ways I don't understand. To be honest, I'm amazed to see Sumerian written on it. If it's not a fake, I would..."

"I already told you it's real," Joe said, defensive of his father's claims.

Jones picked the image up and turned it over in his hand. "Don't be offended, Joe. I'm just a professor. We're paid to be cautious, even skeptical. So listen. I have a friend who runs an independent laboratory. He does all kinds of subcontract work for the state and federal government, mostly crime lab stuff, but also a little radiocarbon and metallurgy testing. If you'd let me borrow this thing for a couple days, I could have him run a series of tests on it to determine its age and material makeup. We could even do a photo analysis and database search to see if any comparable artifacts have been discovered or described in the past. This is the best way I know to provide an authoritative answer. With your permission, I'd like to take it to him right away."

Joe looked at Sheri. "What do you think, Sis?"

She took a drink of her Perrier and said, "Indy's the expert. You wanted his opinion, didn't you?"

"I guess. I just need to be sure this lab guy doesn't submerge it in acid or something."

Indy laughed. "Joe, you crack me up. You worry a lot for a young man."

Jones might have understood Joe's trepidation if he had heard the entire story. Yet Joe didn't want to alarm him with all that ugly chase and gunfire business. Hedging, he finally said, "All right, go ahead and let your expert examine it. I'll contact you in a couple days to see what he thinks. In the meantime, it's probably best if you don't try calling me. And Indy," he added more solemnly than before. "Take care of this thing and keep it strictly between us."

Clearly elated with the prospect of further studying the artifact, Jones simply said, "Whatever you say, boss."

* * * * * *

At Maxamillion Video a hush fell over Allie, Carl, Dave, and Garth's intercessory prayer for Joe and Sheri, as a female reporter came over the radio:

> Gresham Police are warning area residents tonight to be on the lookout for two people that allegedly held up the Montero Research Facility in Corbett earlier today. They are described as Joe Ryback, a twenty-six-year-old male, and his accomplice, Sheri Ryback, a twenty-three-year-old female. The two apparently robbed the facility of a potentially dangerous experimental detonation device. The FBI have joined the Multnomah

County Sheriff's Department in search for the suspects. They warn that the brother-and-sister team should be considered armed and dangerous.

In what could be an unrelated event, a Lincoln Continental owned by Montero Research was destroyed on impact when it collided with a concrete wall at the Damascus Aqueduct near Troutdale shortly after the robbery. An eyewitness tells KETQ reporter Cindy Stormwell that bodies were removed from the wreckage. Investigators on location would not substantiate the eyewitness account or comment on the possible connection between the crash and the robbery earlier today.

KETQ remains at the scene, and will provide full coverage of the breaking story tonight on the evening news.

* * * * * *

It was fairly dark outside when Sheri helped Joe finish taping trash bags from the seminary's kitchen over the shattered rear window of her small car. As they pulled from the school's parking lot and headed east on I-84, the idea that people might be watching their homes had convinced her to avoid the Portland area. Returning to the Gray Hideaway was also out of the question, since Interstates I-84 and I-205 leading back into Portland could have goons lying in wait.

Finally Joe had come up with an answer.

It was 11:20 PM when she shut the engine off and coasted into Buck's gravel and pinecone driveway. Buck and Tater were gone, and Joe immediately concluded that they were probably sturgeon fishing. They liked doing that at night, he said.

"So what do we do now, Einstein?" she teased.

"Wait, I guess."

"You think it's safe to do that? Just sit here, I mean?"

"I think so. I have a good feeling about this place."

"What about my car? Shouldn't we try hiding it or something?"

"We can do it later, when Buck returns. It's dark enough outside, and nobody can see us under these trees anyway."

"Speaking of Buck, do you think he really has proof of...you know...Bigfoot?"

"I don't know, and I don't want to talk about it out here in the dark."

That was strange. Sheri had never known Joe to be afraid of the night. Creepy.

"I guess that was a dumb thing to bring up at the moment," she said to ease her own fears as well.

"At least we agree on something...Miss Einstein."

She punched him, rehashed their visit with Dr. Jones, argued about dating, dug through the backseat for the gummy worms bag, ravenously ate the last of them, and drifted to sleep.

* * * * * *

Joe watched Sheri rest while he, on the other hand, tossed and turned, trying every trick in the book to force the frightening events of the past few days from his mind, particularly the creature he might have seen and the alien stuff Jones had brought up. If that didn't give you the heebie-jeebies, nothing would.

Finally, around 2:00 AM, he slumbered off, dreaming of two magnificent angels standing post on either side of the car. They were like radiant sentries charged with guarding priceless treasure. Their swords were drawn. The taller of the two looked heavenward while speaking clearly to him in a powerful yet comforting voice:

> "Joe, be strong in the Lord and in the power of His might. Prepare yourself with prayer, and rehearse God's Holy Word. Don't be afraid of the terror by night, but draw close to the Father and trust Him. Do this, and He will bring you through the coming storm."

7—RENEGADE EXPERIMENTS

*"The footprints are there, deep in the muck on both sides of the creek....
[They] are about 13 inches long and 6 inches wide. They have a rounded
heel like a human's, but spread out into what looks like a set of five
dangerous claws."*
"Footprints: Prankster or Monster?" The Frederick News Post,
2-19-02

July 25

"Hey, boy, yeh gonna sleep all day?" Buck said as he
rapped the butt end of his fishing pole against the driver's
side window.

Both Joe and Sheri jerked straight up. At first, Joe didn't
remember where he was, nor did he appreciate the
unexpected interruption of what little sleep he was getting.
But then he saw the gentle eyes of the old man staring back
at him, and couldn't help but smile. The canine slobberfest
and part-time guardian angel "Tater" was beside Buck, his
upper body supported against the automobile by two
muddy paws and a wet nose pressed curiously against the
pane.

"Well, if yeh ever do get up," Buck continued, "let me
know and I'll fix yeh up a cup a' jo and some viddles, uh-

huh."

As the old man turned and hobbled off toward the cabin, Tater looked through the glass, woofed at Joe, then followed Buck inside.

"I wonder what time it is?" Joe moaned, scratching the top of his head and looking at himself in the mirror. Man, did he look bad.

Sheri said sleepily. "Not sure. But I have a question."

"Yeah?"

"What in the world is a *viddle*?"

"You're about to find out."

* * * * * *

At the Gray Hideaway, Dave cradled the back of his head and stared at the computer screen. After thirty-six hours of frustration, he'd finally found the impossible e-mail address. All the years of chasing disinformation and conning kooks in conspiracy chat rooms might have paid off after all.

He entered his online account and clicked on the "New Message" tab. He typed 1574654@tonagus.com in the recipient section, tabbed down to the message box, and wrote:

"Hello, Dr. Corsivino:

Pardon my lack of cordiality but time is of the essence. I must come straight to the point. If you are the Andrew J. Corsivino that worked in the field of genome mapping in the late '80's and early '90's, I need to speak with you. My name is Dave Pitzer, and I believe we share mutual convictions. A friend is in trouble. It involves the Montero Research Facility and the so-called robbery at the plant yesterday. I believe you once worked there. If so, contact me ASAP. Lives may depend on it.

Against the darkness,

Dave."

* * * * * *

Back at the cabin, Joe could tell Sheri was relieved about the "viddles." They could be potatoes, bacon, or anything else fried up in a liberal amount of grease, even sturgeon eggs, which the two of them diplomatically avoided. Not Tater. He seemed more than happy to have the extra share of scorched delicacy.

With breakfast out of the way, Sheri sat on the floor stroking Tater's floppy ears, apparently enjoying the warmth of the quaint woodstove, while Joe helped Buck with the breakfast dishes. He wondered why the old man hadn't been surprised by their visit. He wanted to ask about that, but decided to wait.

"Well, would yeh looky there," Buck said, pointing at Tater with one hand while holding a plate with the other. "He don't usually let strangers rub his ears like that, yeh know. He's kinda fussy 'bout being touched, uh-huh."

Joe looked at Sheri and said, "She's always had a way with dogs. She loves them and I think they know it."

Buck wouldn't get the double meaning, but Sheri would. Joe always called her boyfriends dogs. She glared at him from her position on the floor and feigned an oversized smile, then continued rubbing Tater's ears, launching him back into doggy la-la land.

"Yeah, well, Tater 'n me half expected yeh might show up perty soon, what with today's newpaper story, yeh know."

"What's that?" Joe said.

"Yeh know, the news, 'bout the robbery and the car crash and all. 'Course me 'n Tater knew it weren't true 'bout yer sister helpin' yeh rob the Trainers of that detonation device. We prayed fer yeh anyway, though, so's the thing wouldn't explode and that yeh'd see fit to give it back to em, uh-huh."

Buck's words brought Sheri off the floor and Tater right behind her. "What did you say? Joe and I were on the news!?"

"Oh yeah, little miss...sure have been, uh-huh. That's how Tater 'n me found out 'bout the two of yeh bein' t'gether. News folk 'round here been talkin' up a storm 'bout yeh robbin' the Trainers of an explodin' device. Said yeh used guns and ever-thang."

Bloody freaks. This situation was getting away from them. Joe placed his hand on Buck's shoulder and said, "In the first place, it isn't an explosive device. It's a stone image of a head or something. Second, we didn't rob anybody; the item was already mine. They're the ones that tried to take it by force, for crying out loud."

Buck shook his head. "If that don't beat all. I jest knew somethin' was sideways with that story. Yeh didn't say much 'bout what yeh was hidin last time yeh was here, but Tater 'n me just trusted yeh, figur'd yeh was the private type."

Joe carried a stack of dishes to the cabinet where Buck had removed them earlier, placed them on a shelf with some others, and said, "I appreciate that."

"Now when the news came out 'bout the robbery and all, well, we jest didn't know what t' think. So I told Tater, if I was a gamblin' man, I'd wager them Trainers was the ones what done wrong, uh-huh."

"I didn't tell you about the image because I didn't want to put you in jeopardy," Joe said. "I'm sure you've heard the old saying, 'what you don't know can't hurt you'?"

"Yep, I've used it m'self. Fact is, fer a couple days followin' yer last visit, I was downright a-feared. It was like a dark cloud was hoverin' over me. Then I dreamed 'bout two angels...bigguns too...and I ain't been a-feared since."

Joe remembered his similar dream from the night before. He took a deep breath. "But now I'm afraid it may be *necessary* for you to know what's going on, Buck. I think I need your help."

Buck wrinkled his nose. "My help? Yeh know old Buck loves yeh son, uh-huh. I've helped yeh b'fore! But I can't imagine what Tater 'n me could do in this sit-iation. Yer in a world-a hurt, no doubt, but don't yeh think yeh need some kind've highfalutin law man?"

"That may be true, but what I need from you is different. It's an idea I got after talking to Dr. Jones, a professor friend of ours. We call him 'Indy.' He's a scholar of biblical history."

"Indy Jones? That feller from that there movie?"

Joe was surprised. Buck knew something about the Indiana Jones films. "No. We named him Indy as a joke, because of the similarity of his name and credentials. Yet something he told us about the Old Testament made us want to take you up on your offer."

"You mean it made *you* want to take Buck up on his offer," Sheri admonished him.

"What offer yeh talkin' 'bout?"

"To see your Bigfoot proof."

* * * * * *

"You have mail!" Dave's computer squawked as he spun around in his chair. He wondered—could that be Corsivino already? He'd sent the electronic inquiry not even an hour ago, and wasn't altogether sure to whom. He clicked the minimized mailbox and watched the reply from 1574654@tonagus.com pop onto the monitor. The response read:

> "Mr. Pitzer.
>
> Greetings!
>
> Yes, I am Andrew Corsivino, the physicist you seek. Before I comment on my willingness to confer, please tell me something of your case. I look forward to your response.
>
> Sincerely,
>
> Andrew."

Dave's hands shook as he groped for the portable keyboard. Andrew Corsivino, though never willingly advancing such notions himself, was a legend among UFOlogists. Suspected of involvement with reverse engineering of exotic alien technologies and renegade experiments involving interdimensional time travel, Corsivino created a scientific uproar in the early nineties with his work and later condemnation of genome sequencing. Darren Copeland's award-winning 1993 Sci-World Magazine Investigative Report on Mutation

Cloning had made speculative connections between Corsivino's work as a physicist and the goals of mutation cloning. Yet the real controversy revolved around the journalist's conclusions that Corsivino abandoned his life's work with the United States Government following strong ethical differences with government project leaders. Following the conflict, Corsivino simply resisted public scrutiny and faded from sight.

Dave hardly knew how to start or finish his summary to the legendary figure. He recounted the necessary elements of Joe's story, added a few thoughts, then, satisfied with the portrayal, typed a bold request:

> "...so, Mr. Corsivino, perhaps you understand why I'm desperate for information. I haven't seen my young friends in a couple days. If ever there was a time for all good men to come to the aid of the righteous, this is it. Would you be willing to meet with me? I need to know everything you can tell me about the Montero Research Facility, the image, and, if possible, the protocols I need to advance.
>
> Looking forward to your response.
>
> Dave."

* * * * * *

Buck's feet shifted on the heavily worn throw rug as he rubbed his wiry beard.

"So...yer sayin' there could be a connection b'tween Bigfeet and the giants of the Old Testament?"

Joe smiled. "Sounds crazy, huh? Either way, I need

evidence to take to those highfalutin attorneys you were talking about, don't I?"

"Yeah...I guess. Let me show yeh somethin'."

Buck walked to the bedroom and began shuffling through the closet. Tater, following him through the doorway, disappeared around the edge of the bed and returned a moment later with a rubber sturgeon in his mouth. He sat in the entry on his hindquarters, tail wagging affectionately, looking at Joe. He bit the toy fish and it made a "squeaky" sound.

"Cu-u-ute," Sheri said, smiling at the dog.

"Knock it off," Joe said. Ever since being attacked by the neighbor's mutt as a kid, Joe generally disliked animals.

Tater cocked his head and crunched the fish again.

Squeaky.

Joe looked into the dog's soulful eyes. He wouldn't admit it, but if ever a dog *had* appealed to him, it was this one.

"I said quit it, that's annoying."

Squeaky squeaky.

Sheri smiled. Tater had thrown him a double-squeaky.

"He just wants to play with you," she teased.

"I don't care. It ain't my thing."

"Fine, brat. Tater, attack Joe."

Tater pricked his ears. *Squeaky...squeaky squeaky.*

Buck turned from the closet and walked slowly out of the room. He nudged Tater behind the ears and pretended to be upset. "Stop it, Tater, yeh dummy. Can't yeh see the boy don't wanna play."

"Where in the world did you get such a dog?" Joe said, trying hard not to sound attached.

"From a pertater sack."

"Pardon me?"

"I was fishin'. Saw a boat upstream throw somethin' in

the river."

"A potato sack?"

"Yep, the gunnysack kind. It was twistin' 'n sinkin', yeh know, somethin' in it, so I grabbed it from the water as it floated by."

"And found Tater?"

"He was jest a pup."

"So *that's* where he got that name."

"Yep. He's been my best friend ever since. I think the big Man upstairs spared 'em fer a reason, uh-huh. Now have a gander at what I got here, boy," he said.

Buck handed Joe something that looked like a wad of fur, maybe from a bear.

"Picked that up on the south shore."

Joe grabbed the fur ball unenthusiastically. If this was Buck's proof, he was wasting his time.

"I know it don't really prove nothin'. 'Cept I ain't never saw no fur like that b'fore, yeh know?"

"Well...I wouldn't know. Is this all you've got?"

Buck dropped his spit into a Folgers can. "Nope...but son, yeh realize to see the real proof I'm offerin', we'd need to cross the river at night, 'er in the early mornin', uh-huh. I don't think it'd be too smart to venture into Trainer territory in the daytime. On th' other hand, that's when they run the apes, after dark."

"Is there a different way to see the evidence?" Joe asked.

"Nope. But if yeh jest insist on goin', what I'm thinkin' is, they don't train the apes on weekends, yeh see. Prob'ly not enough workers those days. So this bein' Friday and all, early tomorrow mornin'd be the best time t' go. If the Trainers watch the river as I suspect they do, they're used to seein' Tater 'n me out there fishin early mornin'. Even if they see us comin' 'cross the water...they won't pay us no never mind."

Tater, hearing his name, offered a final appeal for playtime. *Squeaky.*

Joe looked at him, smiled, then said to Buck. "If these apes...as you call them...are not out tomorrow morning, how will we see your proof? Won't we be hiding, watching them through field glasses?"

"Oh, no, boy. I got differ'nt proof than that," Buck said, grinning. "Just wait. Yew'll see, uh-huh."

* * * * * *

Dave worked most of Friday night and Saturday morning posting his secret letter to Joe and Sheri. As usual, the message was located in a hidden link near the upper left corner on the front page of RaidersNewsUpdate.com. The file was inaccessible without the password—Joe's last name in lowercase letters. Similar links with invisible locations and access codes were hidden elsewhere at the website. These served as gateways to storage areas where classified and even above-top-secret information was being stored. Dave's hope was that Joe would remember this, locate a computer, and search the "ryback" link for the important information.

Sometime later that morning, a follow-up response from Andrew Corsivino entered Dave's mailbox. Based on information he had sent the physicist, the reply carried a sense of urgency about the need to meet face-to-face. Corsivino indicated an awareness of the late-breaking news concerning Joe and Sheri, and that he understood the ramifications far better than anybody else could. He wrote:

"Mr. Pitzer.

Greetings!

Reliable insiders verify your story. The situation concerning your friends is disturbing. I wish I had better news, but we are dealing with powerful forces.

Under the strictest anonymity I will meet with you to tell you what I know. The meeting should take place as soon as possible, and I insist on inspecting the item you spoke of. If you have family, you might want to think twice about involvement. Joe and Sheri may be targets of elimination. Everyone associated with them could be in danger.

Your friend,

Andrew."

Think twice? These kids were like family to Dave. He would do everything he could to help them.

"Hello again, Andrew," he typed without hesitation. "Yes, I recognize the risk and I appreciate your concerns. Now when can we meet?" He hit the "send" button and immediately altered Joe and Sheri's enigmatic message to include Corsivino's warning.

8—FISHING FOR BIGFOOT

"Up in the tree branches, they could make out a huge set of yellowish, reptilian eyes. The head of this animal had to be three feet wide, they guessed. At the bottom of the tree was something else. Gorman described it as huge and hairy, with massively muscled front legs and a doglike head."
"Close Encounters, Part Two," *The Las Vegas Mercury*,
12-1-02

July 26

By the time he hears the tree limbs cracking and the black lab barking, it's too late. Dozens of menacing sasquatches roar through the cabin door like an army of incarnated demons. Poor Tater doesn't have a chance. The first monster inside snatches him by the tail and instantly obliterates him. A moment later, a grotesque figure, a hybrid of no classification, flies through the window upright, it's sinewy arms and spindly fingers dicing the room with such electrifying force that Buck and Sheri are decapitated as easily as slashing overripe honeydews.

Now the mutation pauses, its gator face grinning, as if the first targets were so easy. Its chest wheezes angrily as honey-thick saliva drips from its distorted snarl onto the aged hardwood floor. In the shadows behind the being, Joe thinks he sees his father. Staying perfectly still, holding his breath, he watches as the alligator-man turns its blood red eyes on him.

The demon's jaw opens so widely that it seems to be coming unhinged. His dad, straining, struggles to reach forward, to grab and stop the beast, but is too late. Gurgling up from within the monster's warty throat, a high-pitch victory howl thunders across the room....

"Wake up, boy, wake up!" Buck was shouting, evidently trying to disengage him from a dreadful nightmare. The terrifying sound of his blood-curdling scream must have brought the old man to his side. "You okay, boy, you okay!?" he was saying.

It took a moment for Joe to snap out of it. "Y-yeah...yeah."

Looking uncertain, Buck said slowly, "Okay then. We need t' get goin'. It's a tad past three in the mornin' and we don't wanna be late, yeh know. Sheri 'n me been gettin' the boat ready."

Joe nodded and sat up on the edge of the couch. He wiped the sweat from his forehead. His heart was pounding like a hammer.

Man, what a freaky dream.

Outdoors, the thick dew dropped through the crooked doorway of Buck's cabin like miniature icicles. Something intangible was in the air, invisible, monstrous, chilling him to the bone. These were lingering figments of his dream state, the stuff of scary novels...right?

He sat there, quietly listening, as an overwhelming sense of apprehension convinced him otherwise. They were not alone.

Dread lingered nearby.

Eminent danger! his instinct screamed.

* * * * * *

It was 3:30 AM when the ringing of the telephone

snapped Dr. Jones from slumber. He fumbled and grabbed the wireless receiver. "H-hello?"

"Jones? This is Nathan!"

Looking at the clock, patting his mumbling wife, he whispered, "It's okay, honey. It's Nathan Reel; I'll take it to the living room."

A retired member of the Air Force's Special Photographic Unit, Nathan was the owner of PCD Imaging, the laboratory where Joe's image had been sent. To be calling this early was undoubtedly important.

Jones slipped from the comfortably worn mattress and strolled barefoot across the sculptured carpet, gingerly pulling shut the bedroom door behind his extra-large Garfield boxers. "Nathan," he yawned, "how you doing? What's up?"

"Maybe you can tell me, hmm? Your secretary delivered that artifact yesterday morning, right?" There was melodrama in his voice, a sense of impatience for idle conversation.

"Okay."

"Well, we started testing the darn thing right away, and I gotta tell you, we've made some unusual findings. You sitting?"

Jones leaned against the cold leather of his recliner, waited for it to warm to his skin, then rested on it fully. "Fire when ready."

"My biochemist calls me at home yesterday afternoon, right? Thinks I need to see something."

"And...?"

"And I go to the lab and luminescence has raised so many issues that we have to employ optical microscopy and X-ray diffraction to verify the morphology and crystal orientation..."

Maybe it was because he was sleepy, but Jones was already confused. "Nathan, wait," he mumbled. "I'm a doctor of theology, not metallurgy; talk to me in layman's terms."

"The bottom line, Jones, this sample you sent me?"

"Yeah?"

"It's Martian. You understand? Martian, and the crystallite is unknown."

Now he was awake. "What?"

"You heard me. This thing's not of Earth. The best comparison we have in our database is the Devil Canyon meteorite at the Department of Earth and Planetary Sciences in Albuquerque. But that's only part of it. The crystalline protruding from the rear?"

"I'm listening."

"It's made of unknown material and possesses unidentifiable properties."

"You examined it yourself?"

"Yes, and I think it's something like a computer chip. My guess is that it's supposed to plug into something."

"Any idea what?"

"It's a mystery, Jones, a mystery. But here's why I called. The photo analysis department ran into some serious pay dirt. You're familiar with the Viking pictures of the facelike mountainous region on Mars, aren't you? The Cydonia image some people call 'The Face'?"

"Sure, the face from Cydonia...favorite among conspiracy groupies."

"Well hold on to your hat. We produced digital versions of your artifact from various angles, and it fits the Mars Face like a glove."

Jones instinctively reached for his glasses, then remembered they were on the bedstead. "Are you sure?"

"Sure I'm sure. Our graphics people are the best in the world. They've looked this thing over from top to bottom. I'll fax you a copy of their report when it's finished, but the positions and asymmetry don't lie. It's objective, Jones, it's good science. Over ninety-six orientations line up. Whoever made this little image of yours had extensive knowledge of the face on Mars."

Suddenly Jones felt uneasy at what he was hearing and what it could mean. He looked across the living room at his library of cosmology books, listening as Nathan continued.

"Another thing. NASA's report on Cydonia, the one that claims the face is a natural formation? A mesa?"

"Let me guess. You don't buy it."

"It's unadulterated fiction."

"Says who?"

"A friend with NSA security clearance. Says the Mars Face is an artificial structure, a true representation of a humanoid. Evidently it's being studied by U.S. and Russian space agencies at this very moment. I hate to say it, Jones, I think you've taken possession of an above-top-secret piece of hardware, maybe even something crafted by...you know...sources...the ones that built the Mars Face."

* * * * * *

At his remote ranch outside Rio De Janeiro, Andrew Corsivino waved from his living room window at his teenage daughter, Shelly, as she rode by on the family's blue-ribbon Arabian. She was such a lovely girl. Proper, compassionate, naïve. If she only knew about her father's plans, she would be terrified. Operation Gadfly was moving forward. Rapid response teams from around the world were preparing to eliminate targets. Inside the family's

private airplane hangar, ten uniquely designed suitcase
nuclear warheads sat neatly in a row, waiting to be used.

* * * * * *

The wind whipping on the water's surface was freezing
Joe to the core. He rubbed his brittle face and stuttered
rigidly, "Br-r-r, Buck, I don't know how you stand being out
here all night. I'm so cold my ears are breaking off."

"Well, we'll be on the other side in a second er two," the
old man promised, pressing the throttle forward a bit. "Just
hang in there...it'll be werth yer while, uh-huh."

Buck pulled the throttle back and scanned through the
moonlight, past the beach to the trees. Joe looked too. No
sign of trouble...so far. Buck nosed the tri-hull in, shut her
down, and let her run ashore. As the engine quieted, he
faced Joe and Sheri and said, "Okay now. Take that gaff with
the rope on it, right there next to yeh, boy, and jump t' land.
Be careful and don't ferget to help the little lady."

Joe grabbed the equipment and stepped up from his seat
around the windshield to the front of the boat. He leaned
forward and leaped over the water, landing on the soft edge
of the sandy beach. Sheri didn't wait for his help,
independent as she was. Tater was next, then Buck, who
simply climbed off the boat and walked through the river in
his waders.

"Bring that hook and foller me," he whispered, turning
and starting toward the woods. "We don't have fur t' go."

Barely illuminated by the diminishing yellow moon, Joe
held the gaff above his head and walked behind them into
the trees. A symphony of wind sounds, like wandering
groaning spirits, filtered off the Columbia and enfolded the
would-be sleuths. In the distance, a coyote moaned for its

pack, while further downstream, a locomotive whistled the soft lap of the surf away, both sounds gradually absorbed by the thickening grove.

It all unnerved Joe. He wasn't sure about the wisdom of this mission anymore anyway. The fact that they were a mile east of the canyon where he'd jumped a few weeks earlier didn't help things, yet he couldn't back out now. The fearless foursome had entered the woods guided by the illumination of Buck's antique lantern and Tater's animal instinct. Plus he knew he'd never solve the mystery of what his dad had been onto—or murdered for—if he didn't stay the course.

Hiking away from the river, moving in a zigzag pattern, east, then west, a dozen yards at a time, he followed the old man into what soon became an abandoned State Park's trail. A little sign with Department of Forestry logos and some partially colored lettering were barely visible along the decaying fence line. Buck pointed to it and whispered, "See. That's the halfway point, uh-huh. We'll be there in no time."

In less than a quarter-mile they reached the second marker. Except for moonlight peeping through the treetops here and there, it was considerably dark outside. Images from Joe's nightmare lingered in his imagination, vivid and sometimes-monstrous interpretations made alive by every shadow and sound. Even the smallest scampering forest creature seemed potentially mutated.

Suddenly Tater growled and Buck stopped in his tracks. Blankets of shadows, a pirouetting cascade of blackness, resisted the probing lantern as Sheri bumped into the old man, stammering, "W-what's happening?"

"Tater, leave th' possum alone," Buck hissed, then stepped off the trail. He took a moment to explain that they would need to be careful from here on out, as the rest of the way was a bit rocky and "cluttered with moss-covered rocks and other slippery stuff."

The path was also getting steep, and Joe could hear Buck puffing, struggling to use his bad leg. Since neither Sheri nor he suffered similar afflictions, he suggested that they rest for a while, but Buck declined, saying he was determined to reach the destination before sunrise.

Not long after, they arrived at a plateau where Buck leaned over, set the lantern on the ground, and pointed to a pile of branches near the foot of a rock wall. "Here, boy. See these? We gotta move 'em away. Take this one...and this one...now this one...and those there...."

Joe did as Buck directed, and soon an opening in the clay began to materialize.

"I think it's a natural fermation. Prob'bly made by a quake...er maybe a thousand years of erosion," Buck said.

Either way, Joe found the pit oddly inviting. He pulled the last of the debris off and belly-slid to the fracture. Near the surface and along the sides, gray stones formed a polished border that phased into arrant darkness as it descended into the void.

"I can't see a thing," he said anxiously. "Somebody hand me the light."

Buck had different plans. "Hold on, boy," he countered excitedly. "I'm gonna show yeh something yeh ain't never seen b'fore."

Buck sat on a nearby log and scooted sideways until he paralleled the ravine. Leaning forward, careful not to slip, he began lowering the antique lantern over the mossy edge by a line tied to its wiry handle. The crevice was surprisingly deep and after six feet opened into a cavern of fifteen feet in width. The nylon rope slid smoothly while Buck's hand controlled the rate of descent with a back and forth, grip and release motion. The lantern fell a foot, then stopped with a jerk, another foot, then jerked to a stop. Shaking with what looked like uncertainty, Buck whispered, "Yeh know...I've been gonna fish this thing outa' here fer some time now, uh-huh...jest been waitin' fer the right moment...needed a little help, that's all."

As the light settled onto the cavern's floor, Sheri crawled to Joe and peered into the shaft. Joe heard her gulp as she saw it...whatever *it* was.

"How long's that thing been down there, Buck?" Joe said after a moment.

"Several months, near as I can tell. Tater was the one what found it, yeh know. I think he smelled the blood. Prob'ly hadn't been dead a day er two when Tater ran up here all frisky like, jumping 'round and barkin'. I was at the beach, and Tater wouldn't come when I called. So I decided t' get up here and have a look-see. When I did, I knew it was one of them apes. I covered it real good and Tater 'n me got outa' here quick. We didn't come back fer a month, and I wasn't sure if the Trainers'd retrieve it in the meantime, but it was here alrighty, and it's been here ever since."

"How big do you think it is?"

"Nine 'r ten feet, I'd guess."

Joe took the rope and carefully lifted the lantern. He swung it gently back and forth to illuminate the creature's striking features: a jaw lined with razor-sharp teeth, a skull as big as a lion's head, and biceps four times the size of an average human. Its dilapidated face still bore the imposing, devilish snarl of its lifetime. If Dr. Jones was correct, and Joe wasn't sure that he was, a similar brute had once stood before Old Testament Israelites and defied "the armies of the living God!" This one wouldn't be defying anything anymore, except maybe science, yet the big question was: How was it killed? Who put it here, or did it *choose* to die in this place?

Interrupting the silence, Buck said, "Grab that rope and hook, son...we need t' hurry now...it'll be daylight soon and we gotta get movin'."

Joe felt near his leg and found the gaff.

"Toss it in there and see if yeh can snag it...if yeh do, we'll pull it up together."

Wrapping the rope's free end around his wrist, he threw the tool into the hole and heard it thud against the monster's hip bone. He immediately pulled but didn't catch anything. He dropped it again, this time onto the giant's chest, maneuvering it until the point dangled against the beast's arm; then he tugged and caught a solid connection. He looked at Sheri and grimaced. Unsure about all this, he crawled backward, careful to keep the rope tight, and by the time he stood up, Buck and Sheri were beside him.

"Okay now, let's see if we can haul that thing outa' there," Buck said.

Clasping the line and moving together, Joe found the dead beast lighter than he had expected. Evidently rats and maggots had done their job. Mostly bones and fur remained. But two hundred pounds of decaying animal was still enough to test their footing, so he dug his heels in to illustrate how strong he was.

After ten paces the rope tightened to a confining stop. Motioning with his head toward the hole, Joe said, "You guys hold on while I see what's going on."

Joe ambled across the soggy rubble to the place where he'd been moments before, peeked into the abyss, and flinched. Two decomposing eyes the sizes of baseballs were glaring up at him through sinister sockets. Having reached the mouth of the crevice, the creature was too big at this angle to pull through. And what was that? Wire? A small tubular object connected to wire? It looked like a thermocouple...the kind hardware stores keep in stock for propane heaters.

"Buck! This thing's got something in its head!" he nearly shouted.

"Shhh! Be quiet!" Sheri blurted, as if she was thinking that if she got out of here alive, she'd never do anything so stupid again.

He lowered his voice and repeated, "But there's wire in its head! Wire! And it's connected to something!"

"Can yeh reach it?"

He tried. "No."

"Take hold of the cable and move it 'round. See if yeh can get it t' come outta there. Sheri 'n me'll keep the rope tight."

He struggled with the line, pulling left, then right, until finally a substance squeezed from the pulpy, rotten flesh that smelled so horrific he thought he would vomit. He turned his head, took a deep breath, and tugged again.

Something gave.

"I think it's coming," he said from the corner of his mouth. "Let me get a better angle."

He slid back, placed his legs in front of him, rolled the rope around his right arm, and grabbed on with both hands. Pushing with his feet, he felt it move again.

"I think we're gonna get it," he said. He instructed Buck and Sheri to lean back as well. "On my count, pull with all of your might. One...two...three...pull!"

When they lurched, stretching the line to its limits, something snapped and the hominoid's arm broke off. The raggedy appendage flew through the fissure's opening as Joe flailed backward, tumbling wildly, abruptly falling onto the ground.

Buck and Sheri lost their balance too and landed on their backsides.

The remainder of the corpse, dislodged from its restriction, dropped back to the bottom of the cavern and crushed Buck's rusty lantern with a reverberating *clang!*

Jumping to his feet, Joe whispered instinctively, "Everybody okay?"

Above and all around, daylight was breaking. The lantern had been destroyed, but now it didn't matter. The early dawn illuminated the only thing Joe needed. A log-sized arm with a fist the size of a soccer ball near his feet.

For a moment the hairy extremity mesmerized him. Then a lonely barge on the Columbia tooted, awakening him to the odd sense of the moment.

"That'd be Captain Majors making his weekly run," Buck said, standing up. "That means it's gettin' late, boy. We better get outta here while the gettin's good."

"Fine with me. I've got everything I need right here. What do you think, Sheri? You able to go?"

She stared at the mammoth arm, undeniable fear in her eyes. "Are you kidding? The sooner I get out of here, the better. No offense, Buck."

"None taken, little missy, but like I said, we'd better get goin' while the gettin's good." He helped her to stand, then hobbled over and spit into the crevice. He shook his head, as if disappointed. "I do wish I could-a seen the wire in that ape though, uh-huh."

9—THE HEXAGONAL ROOM

"Under the surface of Mars lies an ancient, nuclear-powered city left by Martian citizens. At least, that's what a group of space researchers think."
"To Spite the Face," *Phoenix New Times,* 12-10-02

Dr. Jones watched from a window inside the seminary's dining room as Joe and Sheri drove onto the parking lot in an old pickup he hadn't seen before. He didn't know where Sheri's car was, but a cellular call from her earlier had ended with him agreeing to meet them at the school. He too had unexpected news and was anxious to discuss his findings.

As he sipped from his coffee and watched the siblings jump from the '68 Ford, they raced to the rear of the pickup and jerked a bulky-looking object wrapped in a light blue blanket onto the tailgate. With help from Sheri, Joe wrestled the tubular item onto his shoulder and headed for the building's side entry. Scanning the parking lot as he went, he caused Jones to think he was watching for traffic. Jones was wrong.

* * * * * *

Thirty-five miles away, deep inside the reinforced walls of Montero's underground laboratory, the encryption translator on Apol's desk began downloading a top-secret communiqué from Security Chief Robert Donner's Instant Mobilized Encryption Fax. It contained positive news: The kids had been located and were under surveillance.

A demented smile crept over him as he read the dispatch.

TOP SECRET

Montero Research Security Division One
Level 10 communication
MEMORANDUM
TO APOL LEON
Special Agent to the Secretary of Defense
From: Security Chief Robert Donner
RE: Cydonia Enigma Confiscate and Target Delta Memo

> As you know, on Thursday agent Blair nearly pinpointed Target Delta's whereabouts using the subject's cellular phone. Before agency representatives could acquire a signal fix, the transmission ended.

> Earlier today, Blair intercepted a second cellular communication and successfully monitored a brief conversation between Target Delta and Donald Jones, a professor at Mt. Hood Evangelical Seminary near Gresham. The subject's conversation led Blair to believe the item may be in the

professor's possession.

Agents Blair and Whitestone are currently located across the street from the seminary in the HT Mobile Unit, and confirm the arrival of Target Delta. The subject's conversation is being monitored with Mach 4 Bionic Ears and parabolic boosters and can be patched to your office immediately. Both agents have been advised to stand clear of Target Delta until verification of the item's presence is made.

Please advise concerning any changes to the directive.

Security Chief Robert Donner

END TRANSMISSION

"Exsssellent!" Apol hissed forebodingly. "Soon the nations of the world will know who the god of thisss world is!"

* * * * * *

Back at the school, Sheri borrowed Dr. Jones' computer to send an e-mail to Dave and the gang. She briefly stated her and Joe's plans to be at the video store later that day, then added, "We've stopped to see the professor and to pick up the image. Boy, do we have something to show you guys! We should be there before noon. We're hoping Dave can help us retain a good attorney. I'll explain everything when we arrive...."

* * * * * *

Across the large complex in the dining room, Jones was astonished. Staring at the reeking specimen on the table, he asked, almost stammering, "Where on earth did you find this thing?"

Joe quickly rehashed the events leading up to the discovery—his visit with Buck, his trip up the mountain, the retrieval of the arm, the loan of Buck's pickup, and the details of Sheri's car—though Jones was too intrigued by the colossal extremity to hear half of what he was saying. An incredible proposition pressed in Jones's mind. It involved prehistoric cosmic war, the Annunaki, the Biblical "stones of fire," and the giants of the Old Testament. The call from Nathan Reel with the revelation of the head's Martian properties had got him thinking. If Joe's object really did come from Mars, NASA might confirm ruins of an abandoned city in the Cydonia region of the Red Planet during a future Rover landing. Did world governments already have proof of such and were covering it up? Would this support the theory of advanced extraterrestrials visiting precivilized Earth and creating Homo sapiens? Or was Joe's artifact a link to biblical stories of Creation, heavenly war, and the fall of men and angels? Jones preferred the latter but was unsure how the related texts matched the physical evidence. Rehashing it in his mind for several hours, he'd finally called his friend and Vatican scientist, Bishop Renaldo Banducci.

Though Jones was evangelical and Renaldo was Catholic, this fact had never impaired the professor's appreciation of the renowned scholar or his published works. Renaldo was a member of the Pontifical Academy of Sciences and was widely regarded as among the most progressive theologians in the world. Having met him years earlier during a lecture, Jones corresponded with the priest and on more than one occasion took him to dinner when he was in town at the local diocese. This was the first time he'd made a serious inquiry of the theologian's knowledge of cosmology and Scripture. He had not been disappointed.

As it turned out, Renaldo believed Ezekiel's citation of Lucifer moving "up and down amidst the stones of fire" was a reference to the once-glorious being's dominion of the planetary belt, including Mars. He had long thought the Cydonia Face and pyramidal structures near it were curious, potentially illustrating a past Martian civilization that, if proven, would provide physical support for the Bible's account of prehistoric war and the subsequent expulsion of Lucifer and his angels "from the heavens."

"Keep in mind," Renaldo shared over the phone, "Such evidence might also provide background for the building of the pyramids and similar structures on Earth—those monuments whose technical requirements seem far in advance of ancient man's comprehension, the physical construction of which may predate Adam and Eve. The astronomical features built into the Great Pyramid alone are startling: how the four corners face true north, south, east, and west; how the antechamber points to the center of the universe; and so on."

Jones, a history scholar in his own right, was fully aware of the pyramid's enigmas, yet now as he listened, he learned something he didn't know.

"Close to the Cydonia Face on Mars is a similar five-sided pyramid with detailed buttressing suspiciously positioned at $1/360^{th}$ of the Martian polar diameter from the Face. In the same area, other structures form a perfect equilateral triangle in what some experts at NASA are now calling 'the city complex.'"

Copiously scribbling the Bishop's thoughts as he spoke, Jones said, "I wasn't aware of the city complex, but the qualities of the enormous face are astonishing. Eyebrows over eye sockets with pupils. A parted mouth with lips and teeth. A nose tapered back toward the forehead. A crown strikingly similar to those worn by Egyptian and Mayan royalty." Jones had done his homework before calling the scholar.

Renaldo agreed. "Indeed. Mathematicians have postulated the chances of the face arising by chance at a thousand billion, billion to one, so it is significant."

"Significant enough to convince you it's real?" Jones had asked.

"In my opinion, if what we are seeing in NASA's photos represent intelligent engineering, not a trick of shadows and light, we may have no other alternative."

"But isn't that anethema? A challenge to biblical history?"

Clearing his throat, Renaldo had said, "Not really. In fact the answer to this riddle is found in the Bible, I'm sure of it, in such places as the book of Job, where the old prophet tells us that God destroyed the literal dwelling places of the angels that made insurrection against Him. Job specifically mentions the destruction of Rahab, a planetary body also known as 'Pride,' from which God drove 'the fugitive snake.'"

"So you believe, tenuously I take it, that cities on Mars might actually have existed, and that these were abandoned during a pre-Genesis war between Good and Evil?"

"I'd go a step further. If pyramids on Mars are confirmed in my lifetime, disclosed by reputable governments and scientific institutions, mind you, I'll present it to the Vatican as possible proof of such a war."

Jones considered the far-reaching ramifications of that comment, then reiterated, "Not to belabor the point, but wouldn't questions about the central doctrines of Christianity arise during such a discovery? Especially if the Martian buildings match the architecture of structures in Egypt?"

"Satan will use it to his benefit, undoubtedly," Renaldo confirmed. "People will point to Mars and then to the Egyptian desert and say, 'See! Here's proof! We came from aliens! The Bible is a hoax!' This could even be part of the strong delusion prophesied for the End Times."

Having agreed with this and other assessments made by the Bishop, Jones hung up and painstakingly reconstructed each element of the conversation before drawing his own conclusions.

Now, with a giant arm in front of him, he dared not say what he was thinking. Armageddon was swirling in his mind.

* * * * * *

Sitting in a phone cubicle at Portland International Airport, Dave impatiently asked his wife Sharon in hushed, low tones, "Well, where are they?"

"At the seminary," she said. "Sheri sent an e-mail this morning. It's obvious she hasn't checked the website or read your message. They're picking up the image and showing Dr. Jones some new thing. She didn't say what it was, but they're supposed to be at the video store in a couple hours. How about you? Corsivino arrived yet?"

"Nah. His flight was delayed in Denver."

"How long's the delay?"

Dave glanced at the illuminated flight schedules screen, then sighed, "An hour, and that was forty-five minutes ago."

* * * * * *

Before crossing the road to make a slow pass above Secure-It's Storage Company, Swift and Justice confirmed the situation with the newly assigned angel, Perfect Love, then drifted shadowlessly overhead, observing the fifty-plus armed men hiding behind the neatly lined orange and blue storage buildings.

"Blair and Whitestone are monitoring the conversation between Jones and Joe from the ordnance van," Justice said. "I'll keep an eye on them, while you make sure only five of those security force members make it into the seminary."

"It'll be my pleasure, Commander," Swift said with a tone of respect. "Which of us will go with Sheri?"

"Perfect Love. His strength is fear removal."

"But is he powerful enough to withstand the legions at Montero?"

"Not without prayer. Joe of course should learn to pray, as will Sheri, but obviously these kinds of demons will not be stopped without combined prayers and fasting. This is where the seminary students can help, by dividing and confusing the darkness through concerted intercession."

"Will they?"

"They must," Justice said sternly. "Otherwise the suffering that is to come will be in vain."

"It will not be in vain!" Swift exclaimed, his eyes suddenly fiery for battle. "This is our time, and it will be our victory!"

Raising his wings and grinning at his comrade, Justice

said, "So, you are ready for resistance? Good. For it shall be as strong as we've seen in four millennia."

* * * * * *

Back at Portland International Airport, the flight from Denver had arrived and Dave was standing outside the security gates with a crowd of others, observing the flight's passengers, when a short, unimposing figure said, "You must be Dave," and stepped from the line toward him. He wouldn't have recognized the little physicist if it hadn't been for the photos posted on the Internet. Thin and balding with black framed glasses over baggy, dark green eyes, Corsivino looked like a miniature version of the television detective Colombo inside his wrinkled overcoat.

"That would be me," Dave replied, sticking his hand out and receiving a strong handshake. *This must be how it feels to meet a celebrity*, he thought.

Corsivino nodded. "It's my pleasure to meet you. I apologize for the delay. Something mechanical on the plane had to be double-checked before leaving Denver."

"Better safe than sorry, huh?"

"Oh, my, yes."

"How was the flight other than that? Pleasant, I hope?"

"Very nice. Of course I was involved with some last-minute work on the laptop. I hardly paid attention to the view until descent. Then I took a moment to appreciate the scenery. My wife and I always love the Rose City. We come here whenever possible. Do we have a car or shall I secure one for us?"

"Mine's outside...if that's okay."

Corsivino scanned the room, then said, "Certainly...and we don't need to wait on luggage as I'll not be staying overnight. My departing flight leaves this afternoon. The youths, Joe and Sheri, they are prepared to meet us?"

Dave looked at the floor. The renowned physicist had responded to him the day before with news so important that he had agreed to meet him face-to-face. In exchange for information, Dave was to allow the scientist to inspect the artifact and to determine its value to the Montero Research facility.

"Not exactly," Dave said, looking embarrassed. "But I know where they'll be in an hour or so."

Corsivino stared at him blankly. "You do understand the imperative nature of my visit, don't you, Mr. Pitzer? That I must examine the image?"

"You will, I guarantee it."

"Wonderful."

* * * * * *

In a secret corridor deep beneath Montero, a hooded figure drifted silently along a gore-encrusted hall. Six burgeoned-headed aliens known as "Grays" floated behind him, chalices filled with human blood and eyes in each of their three-fingered hands. Most of the government scientists, project directors, and mutation caretakers working nearby were unaware of the chamber. Those who did know of it were too afraid to say.

With motion like that of a python, the specter undulated to the hexagonal room at the hallway's end, coming to rest on one knee before a bronze image of the Greek goddess Hecate. The smell of brimstone wafted around the idol, as two candelabras, each bearing candles made of human fat, cast faint, quavering shadows against her three-dimensional form. Light from the burning wicks and smoke from the same provided amorphous motion, as though Hecate herself had emerged from the pit to meet her devoted priest. To her left were the eyeless heads of recent victims, impaled on iron spikes jutting randomly from the wall. To her right was the emaciated shell of a young woman, driven mad with pain, chained and staring down pleadingly for the shadowman to help.

The hooded figure, dedicated to the goddess since birth, only chanted, the evil spirit inside him growing stronger with each reverently uttered word. The accompanying demons formed a semicircle behind him. They were swollen with malignancy, humming a monotone vibrato as they poured their goblets onto the towering goddess's feet. They listened as the hooded one prayed.

"Oh great Hecate Brimo, daughter of Persss-es, thou who possess-es power over eternal dessstiny, receive my offerings and grant me victory over the enemies of my lord. Sssend forth your demonic hordes, your hounds and horrible serpents, to diss-comfit the children of light. Ssseize their hearts, oh Great One, cause them to tremble before our terrible power. Make them stumble, dreaded goddess, these ignorant children; make them fall down and deliver the Master's key into my hands. Do this, and I will lift you on high. I will exalt your throne above the ssstars of heaven."

As the final eye fell from the medieval cups, the Grays moved to embrace the shrouded phantom. He alone could control them, so dead and white, their cackling voices whining repulsively, "Ma-ast-er, we fear yo-ou! You're the ki-ing of the Men in Bla-a-ack!"

Suddenly he seemed to them to be in transcendence, cheeks twitching as if metamorphosing, eyes fluctuating as brilliant as molten steel, gazing through them to somewhere beyond this dimension, to the lower world, no doubt. He was becoming a creature of the night, a powerful consociate of the Master of Darkness.

Since 1987, when his fateful visit with the UFO pilot fulfilled the course of his life, he had understood that the gods were returning, that he would become one of them. Now, as the *appearing* drew nigh, his eyes turned as promised, integrating the reptilian's beautiful arch. His human form was but a cocoon these days, an incubator of his new, special self. His parents had foreseen this possibility when they named him, for a name could be a powerful invitation, they believed, even when abbreviated, like Apol.

10—ABDUCTED

"Unbelievable as it may sound, some bioethicists...explicitly endorse engineering animal DNA into human embryos as one method of producing the 'post-human' race."
"The Transhumanists," *National Review*, 9-21-02

Swift watched from above them as agents Blair and Whitestone sat in the HT Mobile Unit van across the road from Mt. Hood Evangelical Seminary listening to Dr. Jones and his fantastic speculations. The highly sensitive equipment inside their van was simultaneously monitoring every sound inside the school.

"Just look at the size of these fingers...." the agents heard Jones say. He had been talking about Old Testament giants and marveling at a large arm. The beast's hand was evidently gnarled and angry looking, terrifying in its savage qualities. Its razor-sharp claws rooted deep inside its horrendous digits, while decaying muscles, twisted and tortured, revealed the chimera's design for magnificent strength.

"If something like this got hold of a man...well, he just wouldn't have a chance! No wonder the Israelites were paralyzed at the sight of Goliath!"

"You really think this could be a what-you-call-it...a Nephilim?" Joe responded from somewhere near Jones.

It sounded like Jones choked, then, "Ughmmm...ahh...excuse me. Well, certainly...I mean...this arm, combined with your Martian artifact...yeah, it could represent the unfolding of biblical prophecy."

"Couldn't it simply be an unknown primate? A sasquatch?"

"That would make it the zoological discovery of a lifetime, but of course. Either way, it might explain the so-called Big Foot sightings we've had in the Northwest."

As Swift watched Blair, the agent whispered to Whitestone, "Have you ever heard such bunk? These guys haven't got a clue what they're dealing with."

Whitestone snickered and rolled his eyes, whistling a descending melody.

Now they heard Jones making a request. "You'll let me send this to PCD Imaging, won't you? That's the lab where the analysis of your image was done."

"I will, because there's more where that came from...and I plan to get it...the skeleton, that is," Joe agreed.

There was a scuffling noise, then Joe added, "For now I need my dad's image. I'm taking it to see Dave."

Whitestone raised a finger to his lips, "Shhh...this might be what we've been waiting for."

"No worry," Jones said. "Here it is, and here's a copy of Nathan Reel's report too. I kept a copy for my records...."

Whitestone glanced at Blair, then gripped his handset and shouted into it, "GO, ALL TEAMS! GO, ALL TEAMS!"

Fifty men in camouflage BDUs immediately began cascading around Secure-It's steel buildings, their clothing swooshing and their boots *clomp, clomp,* clomping as they moved over the road toward the seminary's parking lot. Five squad leaders, tense with anticipation, came through the ditch onto the pavement first. They made quick hand gestures toward the other soldiers, sending Alpha team behind automobiles onto the main parking area while Bravo team positioned near the north and rear of the building. Charlie team took the larger south-side area while Echo and Fox assumed primary assault stations with plans to enter the facility through the front and rear doors.

Gracefully, Swift unfolded his broad wings and descended from the school's roof, lighting at the main entrance. Considering the soldiers, he decided whom he would allow inside, then prompted them.

"On my command," Whitestone whispered into the radio. "Wait until everyone's in position...."

One by one the squad leaders checked in until Whitestone, sounding solemn, ordered, "All right...let's do this thing."

Swift's lightning-quick movements had earned him his unusual name, and today would be no different. He spun from his position, then shot like an invisible tornado through the building, jetting past humans and passing through walls until he arrived at the rear emergency door.

Just as he calculated, he was right on time.

CLUNK!

A utilities expert popped the lock bar off the emergency exit and pushed the rear door open from the outside. Swift slammed it in his face and held it there.

The soldier, jerking his fingers away, cursed in surprise.

CLANK! RUMBLE! BLAM! CRASH!

Each member of Fox team pointed his weapon at the rear door. It wouldn't matter. Nobody was coming through that room for a while. Swift had filled it with desks and furniture, floor to ceiling, wall to wall.

In an explosion of energy Swift reappeared at the front

of the school. Three soldiers were in the foyer now, and two more were entering the doorway. He gazed into their souls. All were the good men he'd prompted, just soldiers doing their job. He stepped beyond them through the wall and stared down the hallway. Jones was sticking his head through the dining room doorway a little ways away. "What's going on out there?" he yelled. "You drop something, Sheri? You okay?"

The morning sun, shining through the windows, cast the unfamiliar shadows of the soldiers along the lobby. Swift made sure Jones saw them.

"Hello?" Jones said with concern. "Somebody there?"

Three doors down, Sheri bolted from the office into the corridor. "Did you hear that!? Sounded like the building was falling down!"

Jones stared past her. A rifle barrel was retracting behind the curvature of the wall.

"Sheri, come here, girl," he said calmly.

She took a step forward, heard something at the end of the hallway, and started to turn around.

"Keep coming," Jones said firmly.

Now Joe was at the dining room door with the giant arm on his sholder. It was wrapped in the blanket again. Before he could speak, Jones placed a hand over his mouth and motioned with his finger for the two of them to follow him. He turned and walked away from the intruders, down and around the corner toward the rear of the building where the emergency exit was.

A second later the front lobby filled with scuffling. Someone was shouting. There was dashing, doors slamming, sounds of hurrying.

Swift prompted Jones to pick up the pace and momentarily they arrived at the exit room. Jones pulled the door open and looked inside. He was stunned at the amount of furniture stuffed into it from nearby classrooms, wall to wall, floor to ceiling.

"What in the..." he blurted.

"What's the deal?" Sheri interrupted.

"I've absolutely no idea," Jones replied under his breath.

* * * * * *

At Montero, Apol Leon plowed through his office and grabbed the command center's microphone. "Whitestone! Let'sss have it! Do I have my item or don't I!?" Apol knew Whitestone was terrified of him, especially when he spoke with that gruff reptilian modulation.

He heard Whitestone say, "N-not yet, sir...but...but...we're very close...we're closing in on it now, sir."

"What do you mean you're closing in on it? Do you know where it is or don't you?"

"No, sir...I mean, yes, sir, I do... I mean...we'll have the item any second now, sir."

"You will if you know whatsss good for you," Apol seethed. "And I want those idiot kids, especially the girl! I have *ssspecial* plans for her. And dispose of that useless doctor of theology! You understand, Whitestone!?"

There was silence, then, sounding confused, Whitestone said, "S-say again, sir? You w-want me to leave the boy and the professor alone?"

Apol stiffened. His eyes drew down to a razor's edge. "Are you senile, Whitessstone!? I sssaid *terminate* the doctor and bring me those kids! Kill him, and bring Joe and Sheri to me! Understand!?"

On the other end of the line what Whitestone heard

was, "Are you senile, Whitessstone!? I sssaid leave the boy and the doctor alone! Bring me the girl and the item! Understand!?"

Justice was sitting next to Whitestone in the van, changing the words as they came through the speaker.

"Y-yes, sir! I understand! I wouldn't dare question your authority, sir, never...and...I apologize if I sounded disrespectful, sir, " the agent stammered.

"Shut up, imbecile!" Apol snapped. "I don't need your apology! Repentance is for women and cowards! Do as I sssay and you will be blesssed. Fail me, and even the goddesss will be unable to help you!"

"Yes, sir, I understand perfectly, sir. I will not fail you," Whitestone cried in response.

* * * * * *

As the angels watched, they saw Jones contemplating his options when he remembered the school's library. The room had once been used as a girl's dorm, and a collapsible fire-escape ladder existed just outside the west window.

Simultaneously, in the HT Mobile Unit, Whitestone was surprised again, this time by his *own* voice sputtering over the radio. "Sergeant Jacobs," a voice that sounded just like his said. "Move your team to the front of the building!"

The real Whitestone shouted, "What!?" and keyed his handset. "Jacobs! Delay that order!"

Yet his radio seemed to have a mind of its own.

Near the west side of the building, Jacobs responded, "Yes, sir. We're moving out." The sergeant motioned with his hand, and Fox team fell into position, rapidly moving east. As the soldiers headed away from the library and disappeared around the side of the building, Jones entered the room and ran to the windows above where Fox team had just been. Jones peeked through the mini-blinds and found the parking area clear. He slid the window open near the escape and motioned for Joe and Sheri to climb outside. "Be very quiet," he whispered as they stepped onto the aging scaffolding. He followed, gently closing the glass behind them.

He put his finger to his lips to emphasize stealth, then gently tested the ladder's spring-loaded mechanism. The old escape had never been used, but the seminary's staff was trained to operate it in an emergency. The contraption's springs creaked like an amplified box springs mattress.

Jones froze and looked at Joe. "No way this is going to be quiet. I'll let it down as gently as I can, but if somebody comes, you kids jump on it and run for your lives. Go that way," he said, pointing to the end of the parking lot. "There's a steep hill back there and it's a long way to the bottom, so be careful. Once you're at the base you've got a clear shot to Damascus. Just keep running that way, got it?"

"Yeah," Joe said, sounding impatient. "Let's move."

Jones tightened his ironlike grip on the collapsible ladder and pushed down hard. It sounded like a ship's hull being ripped by an iceberg. It was certain to give their location away, Jones thought. Of course, he couldn't see Perfect Love's enormous wings wrapped like draperies around the trio, absorbing the clattery sound.

* * * * * *

Across the road Justice flew up and out of the HT Mobile unit with an explosive surge of energy, etching the midmorning sky with luminous ribbons of light. The ground beneath him passed with the haste of an electron as he materialized beside Swift in the middle of the complex. "It's time," he said, and the two of them shot upward and banked right toward the front of the seminary.

* * * * * *

EIAOOO CLANK CLUNK!
As the fire ladder touched the ground, Sheri stepped around and out onto it. She didn't waste any time moving briskly rung by rung down the rusty device to the bottom. Joe, equally agile, adjusted the large arm on his shoulder and followed her. Jones came next, and soon the three of them were running across the asphalt toward the hillside.

Leaping over the shrubbery at the edge of the driveway, Joe and Jones were safely at the bottom of the embankment within seconds—one hundred twelve feet away.

Sheri wasn't with them. She had turned to see if they were being followed and caught sight of something resembling the Martian artifact on the ground near the escape ladder.

* * * * * *

Joe saw Sheri at the top of the hill. Before he could ask what she was doing, she cupped her hands and hollered over the bank, "Joe! Do you still have the image!?"

Checking his coat pocket, he discovered it was gone. It must have hit a rung and fell out during the climb down. The rotten thing had brought him nothing but trouble anyway. Maybe losing it was fate. "No! But leave it, Sheri. Let's go!"

Her hardheaded response didn't surprise him.

"Wait...I can get it...hang on..." she said as she turned and disappeared from view.

"No, Sheri! Come here now, or so help me you'll get what you deserve," Joe yelled. Immediately he regretted the statement. It was a bad habit, telling her she'd get what she deserved. He always said that when she dated men without his approval. He knew he shouldn't have said it here, under these circumstances.

Now, out of his line of sight, he heard scuffling, maybe Sheri, objecting and resisting. A moment later, tires from several vehicles screeched across the pavement. Doors opened, boots rushed on the pavement, a door slammed, engines revved, and tires squealed again.

He had already thrown the monster arm aside and was clambering on the gravel to get back up the mound, his heart pounding so hard it felt like it would explode, when frenzied determination filled his thoughts. *If anything happens to Sheri, I'll kill everyone involved!*

He pushed with all his might, disregarding the sharp stones and hidden debris cutting against his ankles from the sand. Going up the steep hill would be much harder than coming down had been. His fingers ripped into the grit while every step forced gravel into his shoes. He didn't care. He'd willingly sacrifice his feet or ankles or anything or *anybody* to save his kid sister.

He fought like a wildcat against the crumbling edge, clawing the dust and finally making it to the halfway point. Soon he found the ground getting firmer. He'd be at the top any second now. He glanced back at Jones. The good doctor was dragging the arm, sweating profusely, but following close behind.

Above him, through the sagebrush and azaleas lining the parking lot's edge, he could see the tip of the seminary's roof materializing. No cover existed between here and the bushes. If somebody approached them now, they'd be sitting ducks.

A second later a sound returned, an automobile moving past the building toward the rear of the parking lot.

He froze. They *were* sitting ducks.

The vehicle slowed to a crawl, then eased to a stop. A door opened and somebody got out. He could hear steps crossing the pavement their direction. Then a rope unfurled over the bank's edge and landed beside him with a *flop!*

"Grab hold of the rope, Joe," a familiar voice called out. "The soldiers are gone, but they'll probably come back."

Dave Pitzer and a man in a gray overcoat stepped through the bushes and peered over the edge. They looked nervous, surveying the surroundings as they held the nylon line.

"Do you see Sheri!?" Joe yelled to them.

Dave's eyes were wide and anxious. "She's gone, Joe; they took her." He shuddered.

Without hesitation, Joe began desperately pulling toward them. Soon he reached the top, and, after going a few feet beyond Dave, froze in his tracks. Sheri was nowhere. He couldn't believe what had happened. Dazed and in shock, he muttered, "How did you know where we were?"

Dave simply swallowed and jiggled a well-worn set of field binoculars.

The Martian image was gone.

And so was Sheri.

11—SHADOW MAN

"Details in the patent do not make it clear what use these mixed-species embryos would be put to, but experts are in no doubt that the potential is there to create a hybrid creature."
"Patent Allows Creation of Man-Animal Hybrid,"
The Observer, 11-26-02

In the time that passed from leaving Dr. Jones at the seminary to arriving inside the Gray Hideaway, Joe watched as Andrew Corsivino talked on a cell phone. He spoke with two people, one in French and the other in German, for approximately thirty minutes. From the sound of things, he was giving orders and making plans. Finally, folding the phone closed, he leaned on Dave's computer desk and said, "Okay, Joe, I've made some arrangements that will help you."

Joe's original idea hadn't diminished. He wanted to drive straight to the police to report Sheri's abduction. The little physicist was barely keeping him from it.

"I still think I should go to the police," he said.

"What would you tell them, Joe?" Corsivino pressed. "That a respected government contractor abducted your sister? They'll laugh you all the way to your jail cell. Don't forget, Montero claims the two of you robbed them."

"They can't prove that, because it didn't happen."

"I understand, but I've seen the news reports and watched the security video depicting Sheri holding a gun on Montero personnel while you stuff what appears to be a detonation device into a fanny pack. It's followed by a very convincing clip of you jumping out of the window with it. The video's blurry and contrived, but it's probably enough to lock you up for a while."

"You'd better listen," Dave said. "I'd stay away from the police if I were you."

That was always Dave's position with regard to law enforcement, Joe believed. But computer hacking gave him reasons to feel that way.

"Besides," Corsivino said. "I know where she is. Local police have no jurisdiction there."

"And that is?"

"You know, of course. Montero."

Joe's brow dropped. He clenched both fists and kicked a chair across the room. Storming toward the door as if he was headed for a fight, he heard Corsivino caution behind him, "She's in a very high security area below ground, and if you want to see her alive again, you need to pay close attention to what I have to say."

He turned, walked over and shoved his flush-red face an inch from Corsivino's. He didn't know this man from Adam, but if the physicist were being anything but forthright, he'd pay for it. "Then why don't you tell me what I'm supposed to do, huh? And how do *you* know where she is!?" The tone of his voice was a stone-cold threat.

Corsivino didn't batt an eye. "To begin with, I have friends on the inside. Secondly, I need some room to breathe. Please?"

Joe studied his reaction to intimidation, then backed off a little. "You got something to say, spit it out. My sister's in this situation because of me." *And the last thing she heard me say was that she'd get what she deserved...*

"I'm aware of that, but are *you* aware that the people you're dealing with reach to the highest levels of global influence, politically and otherwise? They'll stop at nothing to possess what they want and to guard their identities. You've breached their protective shield."

"And?" he said, crossing his arms over his chest.

"And your sister could be irreparably harmed by them. Her only chance is that you do as I say."

"Tell me what you have to say, and I'll tell you what I plan to do. And by the way, why would you risk helping me anyway?"

"My motives will be clear soon enough. In the meantime, I've made some arrangements for you. It's not much, but it's what I can do under the circumstances. You'll be contacted within the next twenty-four hours by a man code-named 'Phobos.'"

Corsivino handed Joe his encryption-enabled cell phone. "He'll reach you on this."

Joe took his coat off, slipped the phone into one of the pockets, hung it over a chair, and said, "What's he calling about?"

"Detailed explanations as to why we are helping you, including information and equipment you can use to get into Montero, to hopefully rescue Sheri. If you succeed in getting her out, friends will be available to transport the two of you to a safe house where you can remain as our guests for a while. Your identities will need to be changed, and we can handle that, too."

Joe looked at Corsivino and grinned slightly. *This could be a setup, a diversion for his own purposes. What he doesn't know is that I'll be using him.*

"But you must understand, if anything goes wrong, there are larger issues than the rescue of your sister."

Aha. There it is. "Larger issues." "Not in my mind," Joe said flatly.

"I understand your feelings, but believe me when I tell you, millions of people are in similar danger. We must think in terms of global responsibility."

"You have your priorities and I have mine."

"Yet our enemy is one and the same."

"Maybe, but our objectives are not. My father was murdered. My sister won't be."

Corsivino looked at Dave, who was slumped on a crooked green recliner, then back at Joe. "Let me explain something. When I came here today, I intended to confiscate the key ingredient, the Martian artifact. Obviously that will be impossible now..."

"Confiscate!" Dave huffed, rising onto his elbows. "What in the world?"

"Yes, well, my colleagues and I believe the image you had in your possession is the cosmic equivalent of the Missing Link. If it's what we think it is, it dates back to 1987 when a saucer-shaped object crash-landed in the desert near Sedona, Arizona. The craft and three alien bodies—one of them alive—were recovered. The ship was intact, but the salvage team was perplexed. The ignition key, for want of a better term, was missing."

Joe recognized the dates and details as elements of his father's story. "You believe the object my dad retrieved was this key?"

"It's very likely."

"What makes you think so?"

"Three circular plates, called Dropa discs, were also recovered from the crash site. They contained microscopic verses in a language similar to primitive Sumerian. Among other things, they served as the ship's logs. They identified the occupants as the 'Annunaki of Nibiru,' and the key as integral to facilitating the vessel's astounding ability to travel interdimensionally."

"You're saying the UFO my father saw could travel through time?"

"Evidently through multiple dimensions, and forward in time, yes."

If this were even remotely true, Joe understood the image's importance now. Needless to say, the key to such technology would be worth killing for, and he thought he knew by whom. He glanced at Dave, who appeared to be thinking.

"Shortly after the Sedona crash," Corsivino went on, "your father, Lieutenant Colonel Ryback, became the focus of an internal investigation by military intelligence. The subject investigation centered around the paradoxical technology's missing element, this key of sorts, which your father was believed to be hiding. The object was never recovered...and your father was found beaten to death some time later."

"So he was murdered for the artifact?"

"His death was probably a mistake."

"You got that right!" Joe grumbled. "Definitely a mistake for those who did it."

"Well, we think he was tortured by a rogue military element in hopes of forcing him to surrender the Nibiruan Key's whereabouts."

"Is that what these dead-men-walking call it? The Nibiruan Key?"

"That's what it became known as. It's a reference to the distant home of the Annunaki. Yet to the military, it's the holy grail of interdimensional time travel—the ultimate weapon—an instrument of unlimited power supposedly developed by no less than advanced alien intelligence."

* * * * * *

The treeless parking lot outside the Gray Hideaway offered little covering as a shifty-eyed man ambled across the north walkway with a small black box. He looked left and then right and back again. His senses told him that nobody cared what he was up to. But here in this quiet neighborhood, with its community watch program and matching warning signs, they should have been concerned.

* * * * * *

Dave held his hand up like a kid wanting a chance to speak.

"Yes, Dave?"

"You couldn't figure out the technology without this key? You couldn't jump-start the spaceship's motor?"

"It turned out that way," Corsivino said. "By the time I came to Montero, the research staff was trying to work around the key, to hot-wire the motor, if you will. They were reverse engineering the exotic technologies, without much success, although some astounding conclusions were being made along the way."

Joe thought about the conspiracy theories Dave had run on his website over the past year. He couldn't remember any as far-fetched as this, not even among the infamous Roswell files hidden on page two. "Such as?"

"We learned that the most important characteristic of the alien technology centered on a distortion pulse, a puzzling technology, which existed between four columns in the middle of the ship. We called it the Enigma."

"As in a riddle?"

"Of sorts, technically speaking. The Dropa described it as being able to manufacture a vortex in the space-time continuum. Not warp drive technology or wormholes mind you, but a multidimensional gateway to Heaven...or Hell...or anywhere else. We came to believe the device would help us breach our three-dimensional membrane. We broke open the champagne bottles and celebrated. Man was about to make his nest among the stars."

Joe loathed what he was hearing and mused sarcastically, "What happened on your way to becoming gods?"

Corsivino frowned. "We found our dream disintegrating. No matter how we tried, we couldn't replicate the Nibiruan Key's effect on the Enigma nor obtain the vortex described by the Dropa discs. To make matters worse, the project took an unexpected turn when advanced human DNA labeling was discovered in the Dropa. It illustrated genetic manipulation done by the Annunaki thousands of years before, including specific formulas for improving the human species."

Maybe Dr. Jones knew what he was talking about after all, Joe thought.

"The formulas called for introducing animal, and, in at least one case, alien DNA into human genome. Experts at the Pentagon quickly determined humanity had been the subject of unknown mutation experiments. They convened a black operations panel and concluded that regardless of what else the Dropa texts represented, the discovery provided a unique opportunity for human enhancement studies."

"So this is where you got involved, I take it," Dave said.

"Following the panel's above-top-secret report, genetic engineers like myself were given unprecedented resources, and the genome sciences were born."

"Sickening," Joe slipped.

Corsivino looked into his deep green eyes. "I understand. Not everybody was enthusiastic about our research back then, either. There were project scientists—those of religious persuasion—that came to believe the spacecraft and its contents were a remnant of forbidden technology, something cast down from heaven, perhaps a leftover of Lucifer's rebellion against God."

"Did they express these views?" Joe knew in the military that you usually keep your mouth shut, even when you disagree.

"A Jesuit named Malachi Malina did. He openly cautioned about dark forces he thought were trying to initiate Armageddon again, to unleash the Antichrist."

"What do you mean, trying again?"

"You know, another Hitler or Antiochus Epiphanes, except this time a very high-tech one. The Jesuit based his conclusions about the Nibiruan Key and its devilish connection on similarities between ancient history involving the Nibiruans, or Annunaki, and the genetic experiments growing out of our research."

This was really starting to sound like Jones now.

"He showed us where the Annunaki offered weapons technology to Israel's enemies in exchange for women. The antediluvian females became hosts to genetic experiments, resulting in a breed of giants called Nephilim."

"Like Goliath," Dave said.

"According to Malina, yes. Goliath was one of an army of giants, created to destroy God's people and to take over the world. God thwarted the original plan by eliminating the ancient Nephilim."

"And that was that." Dave said.

"I wish it were that simple. Malina believed history was repeating itself—that the disc recovered from Sedona was a Trojan horse—something to trick world governments into joining forces with Satan in preparation of Armageddon. Malina even speculated that the alien bodies we had recovered were demonic concoctions."

* * * * * *

Outside, the shifty-eyed man returned to his car, got inside, and pulled the snub-nosed .38 revolver from behind his belt. He watched the parking lot behind the video store and in a perverse sort of way almost hoped somebody would ask him what he had been doing. When an elderly woman pushed her grocery cart a little too close to his vehicle, he winked at her and whispered, "Kill ya next time, Granny."

* * * * * *

"Sounds like something a friend told me recently," Joe said to Corsivino.

"What's that?"

"Dr. Jones, a friend of the family, he believes aliens and demons are one and the same."

"Father Malina was convinced of it, and he claimed it was illustrated in history books from civilizations around the world."

"History books? You mean mythology, don't you?" Dave corrected.

"Both. I remember Malina discussing the Greek Titans, how their legend began with so-called gods mating with earth women. He compared that story to Genesis where the Sons of God took women for wives and their offspring became mighty men of old. He also showed us how the word Titan equals 666 in Greek and means 'gray, whitish, or chalky gray,' fitting the skin coloration of the bodies recovered at Sedona. He certainly felt we were opening the gates to an ancient perdition by tinkering with this alien technology."

"So...he's the one that convinced you to quit?" Joe asked, refering to Malina.

"What started me thinking we scientists had been duped was a meeting between Major General William H. Layton, the secretary of defense, and Montero's top genetic researchers."

Joe recognized the Major General's name. He had heard him speak while he was stationed in Hawaii. He was definitely a command presence, not somebody to second-guess.

"He told us that Special Agent Apol Leon—a military expert of some kind—would be in charge of genetic research in our department from there on out. We were becoming an All Black operation. No information concerning our undertaking was to be divulged to any military or government departments outside our own. This was now a top-level national security issue. Of course we voiced our allegiance and reaffirmed our oaths, but the ethics of our work certainly changed after Apol Leon, and Hell, came to Montero."

It suddenly dawned on Joe that Corsivino was talking about the man on his answering machine at home. He froze and listened carefully.

"Mr. Leon was on special assignment from Wright-Patterson Airforce Base where the alien bodies were kept.

After formal introduction of him, General Layton disclosed top secret information related to an advanced race of humanoids, which supposedly visited Earth some ten thousand years ago."

"What proof did they offer of that allegation?" Dave said smartly.

"What proof did they need to offer? We had the alien bodies and their ship."

Dave opened his hands, palms up. "I mean that Earth was visited ten thousand years ago?"

"According to General Layton, the aliens left evidence of their visit everywhere—the pyramids, Nazca Lines, even an ancient city on Mars where excavations were underway by joint U.S.-Soviet stealth expeditions. We were told in no uncertain terms that these aliens were our creators. Homo sapiens was the product of their genetic handiwork on apes."

Joe stared across the room at Dave's computers again. He was familiar with many U.S. political and military figures. This was astounding information and probably confirmed Dave's worst conspiracy fears. He returned his sights to Corsivino and said, "General Layton actually said that?"

"Not only that. We were told of a second, more aggressive breed of creature called Anakim. The aliens made them to rule over the newly created people. Each Anakim had the strength of ten men. They were ruthless, but outnumbered by the humans. Eventually they were killed by hordes of men after the aliens, who were also known as 'flying geniuses,' departed for outer space. According to General Layton, the death of the Anakim was recorded in the mythos of every ancient culture, including the Bible, where the Hebrews called them Nephilim."

"But why would a Major General get involved with all

this mythology?"

"A newly deciphered portion of the Dropa had caught his attention. It provided the genetic formula for recreating the Anakim-Nephilim. Needless to say, the military was profoundly interested in it. This represented the ultimate soldier, a perfect killing machine, and Apol Leon was at Montero to introduce our researchers to the technology we would use to manufacture them—the cutting-edge science of transgenics."

* * * * * *

Standing next to Nathan Reel at PCD Imaging, Jones was visibly unhappy with Corsivino's instructions not to contact the authorities. Like Joe, he worried that Sheri was in extreme danger and that he should call the police immediately. He needed a trusted advisor and considered Nathan Reel to be his man. Jones wanted Nathan to see the giant arm anyway, and since Nathan was ex-military and a good friend of Portland's police chief, he thought he could kill two birds with one stone.

"So what do you think?" he said, watching Nathan as he carefully examined the giant arm.

"Heck of a thing, Jones, heck of a thing. Offhand I'd say it's a mutation of some kind, a freak of nature. Probably a carnival escapee, a gorilla afflicted with gigantism..."

Jones tapped him on the shoulder. "I'm not talking about the arm, Nathan. I'm worried about Sheri. What do you think about me calling the police? Isn't that the right thing to do?"

"Not necessarily. If this guy you met *is* Andrew Corsivino, you better take it slow."

"What difference would that make?"

"Maybe a lot, Jones," Nathan said, sounding derisive, as if Jones should have known better than to ask. "Corsivino was involved with the highest levels of shadow military research at one time. The blackest projects."

"You mean stuff like the Manhattan Project?"

"Beyond that."

"Above top secret?"

"Certainly. The government isn't limited to known clearance levels, especially not white ones—confidential, secret, top secret."

Jones was nonplussed. He thought the onion layer was only three levels deep. "They're not?"

"Of course not. Black and above-black levels exist. This is where special access projects, sometimes called SAPs, are funded. The above-blacks, the ones called waived SAPs, these are the scary ones."

"And that's where our friend Corsivino worked?"

"Where even congressional oversights are removed."

"So if Corsivino says to wait on calling the police, we should? Where does that leave Sheri?"

"Trust me, Jones. If her abductors plan to kill her, they most likely already have. But tell you what I'll do. Give me a couple hours to contact a friend at the city's crime lab. I'll ask him to nose around a little, see what he can dig up. Maybe he's heard something. While he's doing that, I'll have a look at our big friend here, try to figure out who or what he was. Maybe then we'll both have a reason to call the authorities."

* * * * * *

Joe realized he was clenching his fists again. His head was

tilted down, his eyes fixed on Corsivino. He needed to calm down, think about his plan, glean as much information as he could from this man before making his move. He bit his lip and said, "So, Apol Leon came to teach you about transgenics, huh, the technology you would use to re-create the Nephilim. What does that actually mean?"

"Simply stated, transgenics is the science of altering the genetic structure of one species by introducing the DNA of a different species into its genome. Under Apol's watchful eye, transgenics at Montero developed in the form of male human embryos having their molecular biology altered through inserting animal and alien DNA into their genome."

"Just where does one get alien DNA? I assume you don't run to the corner market for it."

Corsivino grinned. "From the specimens we recovered at Sedona. Those strands produced the most fascinating and horrific results."

Dave shook his head. "I hate to think what *that* means."

"Mutated embryos aggressive inside their mothers' wombs; highly intelligent, brutish creatures after birth; babies with phenomenal growth rates; an unequivocal thirst to rule, conquer, and dominate."

"You must have been so proud," Joe smirked again. *Remember! Diplomacy!*

"Actually, we were flabbergasted. At six months of age the real problems developed. The chimera—or *Nephilim* as Apol insisted we call them—became uncontrollable. Due to their size and physical strength, special cages had to be designed to hold them. A few months after that we found it necessary to implant control chips directly into their brains."

"Evidently those chips were not foolproof at supervising

your babies."

"What? Why do you say that?"

"Because at least one of them escaped," Joe said. He took a moment to fill Corsivino and Dave in on the recovery near Montero. He described the appearance of the carcass, the arm that was now in Dr. Jones's possession, and the wire inside the beast's head. He speculated that Jones was having the specimen tested at Nathan Reel's laboratory.

Corsivino's reaction was one of astonishment. "That's what he had in the blanket at the hillside? This arm?"

"Affirmative."

"Well, when and if that arm's DNA is analyzed, a fifth and sixth nucleotide will be discovered. It's unlike anything ever seen in animal or human DNA before. It could really open a can of worms."

Good. "And the wire in the giant's head? That was one of your control devices?"

"It's called AngelStar. It too was a product of reverse engineering, actually designed for human implantation. The aggressive nature of the Nephilim forced us to interface the neural chip with the beast's brains, in order to control them. From what I remember it caused the creatures to become lethargic when set at one hundred sixteen megahertz."

Dave, sounding like his contemptible old self again, said, "But did it satisfy naysayers?"

"What do you mean, naysayers?"

"The scientists that were uncomfortable with the project...the Malina guy and the others who thought this might be an Antichrist thing. Were they willing to go along with the research once they saw the ape-men could be controlled?"

Corsivino looked confused by the question and said,

"The fact that we learned to control the beasts was a separate issue to Malina and his colleagues. Questions about the ethics of our research grew regardless, even among the nonreligious types. Eventually, I found myself among them."

Joe raised an eyebrow. "I thought you said you were a project leader?"

"I was, but you must understand, Joe, even though I knew I was breaking my own values, there was something alluring about our work. It was as if a beautiful Siren stood somewhere in the distance, bidding us to come to her. It drew us back day after day with promises of discovery and immortality. Indeed, we believed our work would immortalize us in more ways than one."

"But you were finally convinced otherwise?"

"It all came to a head one day during a casual conversation with Malachi Malina. He'd been removed from the research program at Montero a week before. The official reasoning was ambiguous, but we all knew Malachi was terminated as a result of his challenging the ethics of Montero's research. In the days following his departure, Malachi contacted several team members, including myself. He couldn't speak publicly, so he chose to address his former co-workers privately, to challenge our moral apathy. In my case, he specifically wondered why as a professing Christian I was not concerned with my role at Montero, why I couldn't see it as an affront to the divine order."

Joe was incredulous. "You're a Christian?"

"Is that so hard to believe?"

"With the work you were involved in? Yes, as a matter of fact."

"Then you and Father Malina would have agreed. He came right out and asked me. 'Andrew,' he said, 'the Bible tells us that God commands humans, animals, and plants to reproduce after their own kind. If God requires species integrity, how do you reconcile what you are doing? Your research at Montero not only violates Scripture, but could open a Pandora's box to a molecular biological nightmare.'"

"He was right," Joe said, not that he understood the science.

"I know, in many ways, I see that now. By introducing animal and alien DNA into human genome, we were breaching the species barrier and producing unclassified mutations beyond imagination."

Joe couldn't help himself. Even though he wanted to play this guy, he scoffed, "Yet you remained. I sure hope the pay was good."

"Actually, I left the program not long after Malina did."

"I remember that," Dave said, raising his finger. "It was big news."

Joe was more interested in what motivated him. "Was it a conflict of conscience, or were you just protecting your butt somehow?"

"I'd say a mixture of both, although my conscience drives me these days, believe it or not."

"That's not an answer."

"Okay, in particular, the problem for me was this: The molecular biologists at Montero classified the functions of the alien genes supplied by Apol Leon. Yet none of them knew how the gene's coding would react from the alien species to human. There were strong possibilities that interspecies differences would measurably effect the gene's protein interactions, thus modifying the human hereditary traits in the mutations. That represented a potential catastrophe beyond measure."

Joe hoped he would rephrase the comment so he could

understand the important point.

As if reading his mind, Corsivino said, "Let me put it a different way. Since interbreeding between humans and Nephilim was now theoretically possible, it was reasonable to believe the mutated DNA would get out of the bottle someday. When that happened, alien and animal characteristics would be introduced to our own species, altering the human genetic code and eventually eliminating humanity as we know it. Malachi Malina believed this was not only possible, but also perhaps the whole idea. That was something I could not be part of."

Joe was contemplative, then finally said, "Sounds like a Dr. Jones theory."

"Meaning?"

"Something the professor told me about God having to destroy the human race during Noah's flood because giants had interbred with humans. According to Jones, by the time Noah and his children came along, they were the only ones left with DNA not corrupted by intermarriage with Nephilim and their offspring. In order to preserve the human species, God had to eliminate everybody but Noah and his family."

"Jones is a smart man," Corsivino said. "What would you say if I told you a similar plan is unfolding as we speak, right beneath the world's nose?"

"I'd hope you were kidding. A plan to annihilate mankind by interbreeding humans with Nephilim? Why would anybody want to do that?"

"They are deceived. The government and military are deceived. They believe their research is leading to a super army that will police a New World Order—a better world system. Those of us in Operation Gadfly think differently. We believe Montero's work is part of a larger scheme to force Armageddon and to enslave mankind."

Dave raised his hand again. "Operation Gadfly?"

"It's a consortium of scientists dedicated to the destruction of Montero, its research and researchers, and similar factories around the world."

"You mean there's more than one factory!?"

"Oh yes. Nine others in the Alliance of Nations. Ten in total."

* * * * * *

Beep...beep...beep...beep...

Slowly emerging from what felt like a drug-induced sleep, Sheri felt a piercing white light cut knifelike across her retina, creating a miserable, nightmarish ambience that galvanized the memory of a man jumping from a dark automobile and grabbing her by the throat. The car mirrored the Lincoln that had chased her before, deluxe and sleek with overtinted windows.... The thug was holding her arms...then her mouth...until she bit him...and he punched her and cupped her face with a cloth.... Suddenly the strong odor of chemicals rendered her helpless against his nasty wet tongue...licking along and into her ear...the third of the unwanted "feels" he had copped before throwing her into the car.

Now somebody else was talking, telling her to be still, jabbing her with something that smelled of alcohol. A nauseating substance tinged her mouth. Her lips were dry and hurting, her throat parched. She struggled to focus; to sooth the burning sensations.

"I said be still, child," a corpulent woman spat with an unfamiliar, maybe Jamaican accent. "Don't move ya het, we-ah be done in a minute."

Sheri stretched her face and got her eyes open. Bleary objects crowded the room around her: a beeping monitor anchored to a stainless steel cabinet; a series of lights and attachments from an overhead multidirectional arm; bizarre images of winged women on the walls here and there; a Medusa-like idol staring down at her from the corner of the room.

"A-am I...in a hospital?" she whispered, straining to rise.

A shadowy presence in the corner of the room was watching, as if waiting for her to respond. "You *could* sssay that," it hissed. "But it isn't the Portland Memorial, Blue Eyes."

The fiendish voice delivered the words with such emptiness; it felt as if they had been flicked at her from a snake's forked tongue.

She looked toward the presence, then at the nurse. Realizing she was strapped to the bed, she tried to scream, but could only whimper, "W-hat are you d-doing?"

The large lady with the icy stare held up a hypodermic needle filled with her blood. "I'm done wit yew," she barked unsympathetically. She placed the specimen on a tray and waddled out of the room.

A sick uncertainty engulfed Sheri as she returned her gaze to the shadow. Resonant evil lingered there. And something else around her, observing, no, *examining* her.

The presence nearby groaned and what sounded like a chain dragged over the floor. "Sssooo...you ask why you are here? It's really quite ssimple, dear. Since you seem so fond of *The Book*, allow me to quote a verse that will clarify everything. It's one of my favoritesss, from Genesis, chapter six."

Edging toward the light, the pale silhouette of a tall man in a dark suit emerged. Now his voice became eerily bright and melodious, like an angelic child. "There were giants in the earth in those days; and also after that, when the sons of God came in unto the daughters of men, and they bare children to them, the same became mighty men which were of old, men of renown."

Who, or what, was she witnessing, and why was it quivering like that!?

The darkman hissed, and the dragon's voice returned. "You sssee, dear. Your purpose is to serve as a kind of, shall we sssay, mother?" He made a gurgling noise, trembled, and answered her next question before she could ask it. "Oh, did I fail to mention? It'sss your big day, Hon. But don't get excited yet. Before you can conceive, we've got to tessst your blood for compatibility. We can't have nasty human virussses messing things up for us, can we?"

The words, delivered so bare of human sympathy, sickened her. Instinctively she knew she needed to get away. She struggled against the straps, heaving and grunting and jerking fruitlessly.

The presence, sounding amused by her fear, snorted, "Well look on the bright side, sweetness. If everything checksss out, you'll be the new virgin mother. Imagine how your friends will envy you then! On the other hand, if you're not ssselected to bear the special child, you'll at leassst get to be Rahu's bride. You'll love him...you'd be number...what is it now, six? Seven? Oh, I do lose count with Rahu, he goes through females ssso fast, you know."

Sheri clutched the bed rails and clenched her eyes tight, telling herself she was in a dream. Such madmen's houses of terror could not exist in the real world. The fact that her abductor seemed anything but human and possessed no apparent capacity for caring was certain proof that she would wake up at any moment to find herself wrapped in the warmth and familiarity of her bedroom. Even the cruelest nightmares came to an end if she cried! This one would too. She burst into tears, sobbing, "W-what I k-know is that you'd better let me g-go!"

She opened her eyes to see if she was at home now. The darkman took a step toward her. Something darted from his mouth and slipped immediately back inside, "But, my dear, you've only just arrived," he hissed.

With the man's demented eyes glowering at her through the shadows, she screamed as loud as she could, "GET AWAAAY! YOU'RE POSSESSED!"

"You might sssay that!" Apol boiled, swaying to her bedside. As she tried in vain to draw back, he wiped her tears with his scabrous hand and licked the salty moisture from his fingers. "But I wouldn't ussse such obsolescent language, or that tone of voice, Sheri. Your ssspeaking to the possessor, not the possessed. My host is way past the point of thinking for himsssself."

12—PRIVATE NIGHTMARE

"We have, indeed, been contacted—perhaps even visited—by extraterrestrial beings, and the US government, in collusion with the other national powers of the Earth, is determined to keep this information from the general public."
Victor Marchetti, former Special Assistant to the Executive Director of the CIA, *Second Look*, Vol 1, No 7, May 1979

Admiral John Stark punched his number into the security keypad and watched as the elevator gate opened. He stepped inside, followed by Apol Leon, and the doors to the oversized room closed. To initiate the voice-activated security cab on its rapid descent to seven hundred twenty feet below ground, he simply demanded, "Level thirty."

The stoutly framed admiral was a no-nonsense soldier, his graying hair cut short around his stern bulldog face, his demeanor serious, his jaw set for confrontation. Staring straight ahead, he said roughly, "Agent Leon, I cannot overemphasize the need to follow regulations on this matter. Some in the Pentagon are concerned things may be moving too quickly. There are unanswered security questions. There are fail-safe questions."

Apol stood against one wall of the elevator looking at the admiral. It was no secret the two men didn't get along. He smirked caustically, "Begging your pardon. You know that every question was answered in the military appraisal. Furthermore, the commander in chief has authorized each move persssonally, has he not?"

"I'm sure he has. But the president's concern is with NASA's budget appropriations and his campaign promise to keep the United States at the lead in space exploration. I'm worried about public safety."

"Level ten," a female voice uttered softly over the elevator speaker.

"Some would think such language could get a man relieved of duty, John," Apol challenged.

The veins in Stark's neck swelled. "First of all, you will address me as Admiral! Second, oversight of this project is in my purview. I'm darn well going to see to it that nothing goes wrong here. If I don't like what I see, your precious research will be stalled indefinitely. You understand what I'm saying?"

"Sssertainly, *Admiral*, but need I remind you of the separation of powers? I have responsibility for the project's integrity. There are deadlines, and frankly we've had our share of setbacks. I insist we go green. Safety measures have been checked and rechecked, as was verified in the appraisal. You'd know that if you'd read it. There's no reason to wait any longer."

"Level twenty."

"I read your so-called military appraisal, every page, and truthfully, I'm unimpressed. It was measurably ambiguous. We don't even know what this vessel will do when she's fired up. Will we be able to contain the situation once the key is in place? Are we 100 percent certain? We're talking about national security here. We're talking about American lives."

"Nothing I haven't thought about a hundred times myself, but ssso far everything we've gleaned from the Dropa has been accurate. The army of giants is nearly finished, the monuments on Mars were discovered right where the discs said they would be, and there's no reason to think the Enigma is any different. If anything—you should be eager! We're ssstanding on the threshold of our next big evolutionary step forward."

Stark didn't care a whit about evolution. "I'm glad you're excited about it. Now let me reaffirm my position. I'm not about to let anyone commit this country to an unknown course of action until I'm satisfied with the safety issues. That includes you...you got me?"

Apol's face was turning red, illustrating difficulty at hiding his rage. He looked at Admiral Stark as if he wanted to slit his throat from ear to ear. "Then what *would* it take to sssatisfy you, Admiral?" he seethed, sounding barely able to contain his need to kill him.

"All that I require, Mister Leon, all that I require. Now show me what you've got."

With that, the female voice said, "Level thirty," and the elevator bumped to a stop.

As the doors to the room opened, the two men marched out into a colossal hangar filled with white-robed technicians. Both of them looked as small as ants beneath the Reindeer—the largest extraterrestrial vehicle ever captured.

* * * * * *

Joe followed behind Andrew Corsivino as the three men walked from the Gray Hideaway toward Dave's car. He knew it would be naïve to accept everything the physicist had offered—especially the unearned favors—for in his experience, nothing in life was free. Everybody wanted something, only in this case he didn't know what the "something" was. Yet if only part of Corsivino's offer to help was truly a gift, he owed the man a word of appreciation. Pushing aside his suspicions for the moment, he said, "I guess I should say thanks for setting me up with Phobos."

With the same serene expression he had seen earlier, the no-nonsense scientist simply responded, "We're happy to do what we can."

Corsivino opened the passenger door and paused. "Keep in mind," he said, "the rescue of Sheri will be difficult even with the assistance of Phobos. Although," he added, "I'm sure my enigmatic friend will have a couple tricks up his sleeve...something to help level the playing field."

Corsivino sat on the front seat as Dave opened the opposite door and got in. It was a beautiful afternoon in the Rose City. Children were riding bicycles. Senior citizens were gathering at the Community Center across the street for bingo. Next door to the Center, an elderly man and his wife were having a garage sale while the grandkids waxed the car...and next to Joe was an angel.

Justice whispered to him, "You left your coat with the cell phone upstairs on the chair."

"Oh...just a sec, Dave," Joe said. "I have to grab my coat before we leave."

Dave unclipped a key from his keyring and threw it to

him. "Make it quick. I need to get Andrew to the airport on time."

Joe nodded and headed for the building as Dave turned the ignition to start the car. It made a *clickity...clickity...clickity* sound.

He twisted the ignition again, grumbling.

Suddenly Corsivino's eyes widened and he screamed, "GET OUT!"

It was too late.

The vehicle exploded with such ferocity that a large part of the framework disintegrated at once. Other pieces shot burning debris dozens of feet into the air as the energy wave created by the blast catapulted Joe across the parking lot and against the store's block wall. Blood began gushing from his nose as he collapsed onto the pavement. The building rattled as store windows and automobile glass turned to shrapnel against the scrambling retail customers. Almost instantly the airborne sections of the mangled wreckage returned to the parking lot with a slamming squall of collapsing metal. Fire engulfed the burning fragments as people ran screaming into the street.

Blocks away, others heard the horrific boom and saw the showers of flame. Car alarms blared, dogs howled, a dark-skinned five-year-old on her tricycle tumbled onto the road screaming, "Momma, Momma," as slowly, a collective human drone evolved into a symphony of weeping in and around the Gray Hideaway.

A few hundred yards away, a lone vehicle eased down the street and away from the store. Corsivino had been the shifty-eyed man's target. Dave was collateral damage. Mission accomplished.

* * * * * *

Allie was on the phone with Dave's wife, Sharon, asking about Joe and Sheri when, for a split second, she thought she heard a bang and an alarm of some sort, then the phone at the video store went dead. Something unexpected had occurred. She shouted into the cell phone, "Sharon!? Sharon!?" When nobody responded, she shoved the gas pedal down and began nervously praying the Lord's Prayer.

* * * * * *

Confused and watching a golden-skinned man walking through the flames toward him, Dave found himself in the middle of the road, standing among the burning remains of what at one time was his automobile.

He looked at the glorious person and said, "W-what's going on? Who are you?"

"My name is Justice," the man responded. His voice was as cool as silky running water. "Don't be afraid. Come with me."

Now Dave was off his feet and ascending into the clouds. A little ways ahead, another man, equally shiny, was carrying Andrew Corsivino.

"Why an explosion?" he heard Corsivino ask calmly, as if somehow he understood that they were on their way to an appointment.

"The Lord has many ways," the swifter being said. "His chariots are fifty thousand."

* * * * * *

As the orderly wheeled Sheri along the brightly lit

corridor into the observation room, Perfect Love walked beside her. Sheri was fast asleep, unaware of the chemical taste metabolizing inside her mouth, the result of the powerful sedative given her. The male nurse removed the straps and lifted her limp body from the gurney, placing her on a bed next to another young woman named Katherine, then pushed the gurney back out into the hall. The door closed and locked automatically, and a guard positioned next to it pulled on the handle to be sure. This was level twenty, an area unavailable to anyone not cleared by Apol Leon.

The room was pastel blue, accented by a silver-gray border at the ceiling, with no windows, no phone, no television, and no amenities except for a place to sleep and a small sink and water closet in an open corner. The bed was standard size, mounted to a stainless steel frame, which in turn was bolted to the floor. When lying upon it, a person could see a mural on the ceiling of a winged goddess surrounded by six adoring gray aliens. The artistry was captivating, but evil lurked within the image. The goddess's eyes followed you wherever you went, recording every move.

Katherine, the seventeen-year-old sitting up on the bed, wore a standard medical gown, the same as Sheri. She was pleasantly thin with beautiful blue eyes. Before running away and living on the streets in Portland, she had kept her dishwater blonde hair stylishly down to her shoulders. Her cheekbones were among her most striking features, high and defined like a runway model's. She was curvaceous and flirty in an innocent way, attributes that undoubtedly contributed to her abduction. She was allowed one hour in the morning to bathe, to put on makeup, and to do her hair. Her physical beauty was obviously important to Apol Leon, as were other parts of her, like her ovum. Fortunately her eggs had not been needed yet. Soon they could be.

* * * * * *

Katherine stared at Sheri, thinking how much she resembled the emerald angel from her dreams. Every night for the past week, the night vision had been the same. She was precariously balanced on a dirt ledge overlooking the ocean. She didn't know how she got there, only that somehow she had slipped over a cliff's edge and was holding on to a tree root for dear life. The sea beneath her was inundated by millions of apelike monstrosities, swimming about, feeding on legs and heads and other mortal remains. Farther away, a great monster, a dragonlike devil impossible to look at for very long, wanted her. Its eyes were a burning lamp of fire, its tongue deeply forked, and when it breathed, the ocean bellowed before it, swirling and churning out a blood-soaked foam. The earth shook when it exhaled, and when it inhaled, millions of souls were swallowed deep inside its dreadful bloody gullet.

It watched her, waiting for her to loose her grip, spewing tidal waves of fury in its effort to consume her. Each time the water crashed against the mountain face, she'd scream and pray to the unknown God. Then the root would dislodge, and she'd start to fall, but a redheaded beauty with green-tinted skin would reach over the cliff's edge and grab her in the nick of time. "Don't be afraid," the angel would say. "Follow me, and I'll show you the way." That's when she'd awaken in a frightful, desperate sweat.

But this was no dream, and the girl on the bed next to her—although bearing an amazing resemblance, minus the green skin—was no angel. Just another female, young like the others, a potential donor to their captor's mysterious plan.

* * * * * *

What the young woman named Katherine didn't know was, as with her, physical beauty and especially virginity had been mandatory in accepting Sheri. Unscreened eggs from fertility clinics were good enough for Montero's regular embryo needs, but the Super Nephilim's body needed to come from Apol's DNA and the purest female contributor. Virgins were therefore selected, preferably with blue eyes, then injected with hormones and sucked dry of eggs. Afterward they were considered as candidates to host the impending child, or given to the Nephilim as food.

As this was Apol's private nightmare, the formula for the New Messiah project was unknown by other scientists working at Montero. The genetic blueprint for creating the alien god had been provided by the sole survivor of the Sedona UFO crash before its death at Wright-Patterson Airforce Base. Apol was the altered result of the first stage—the most manlike Nephilim ever mutated from a living human specimen, a virtual ambassador of the Annunaki of Nibiru. His offspring would be the result of the second stage, a deity by mythological standards.

For reasons unknown, the second phase of the New Messiah project had been unsuccessful thus far, and Apol was getting nervous. Every moment he could use was spent gazing through a microscope into a petri dish, making minute adjustments on the micromanipulator and inserting restriction enzymes and strands of his DNA into the abducted eggs.

He'd never run short of such material. A typical woman

supplied thousands of eggs, and the process for multiplication, unlike at other government-funded cloning labs, had been solved at Montero thanks to the Dropa, which explained the process of cell division in humans and primates using a combination of egg fertilization to jump-start spindle formation. After that, it was a simple process of replacing the human DNA with Apol's. As the alien cells divided into two cells, then four, Apol would manually separate the cells and allow the replication process to start again. By dividing cells in this way, he had created as many as sixteen single-cell embryos at a time. All but one were typically frozen, while the remaining embryo stayed in the petri dish, dividing, specializing: transforming into Homo nephilim.

Yet unlike regular Nephilim code, which had been highly successful, every embryo made of Apol's special DNA had degenerated into worthless cell matter before developing far enough to be implanted, or died shortly thereafter.

Yet any day now, with blessings of the goddess mother, he told himself, he would triumph. His son, the son of perdition, would inevitably be conceived. It had to. The Enigma was about to open, and the Master would step through it. *He* would expect a body, a host for his transmigration; the biblical seed of Satan depended on it.

* * * * * *

Speeding was not something Allie usually practiced, but this was different. She pressed the accelerator, swerving around cars and trying not to vomit as the nausea in her stomach reacted to her worst fears. Her spirit told her that something unspeakable had occurred at the Gray Hideaway video store, something involving casualties. She could see a black cloud in the distance, a few blocks away now, and she was starting to smell the smoke. She flipped her scanner on and found the police band abuzz.

"Unit twelve, unit twelve, this is base, do you copy? Over."

"This is twelve, base. Over"

"The chief is en route. ETA is two minutes. Set up roadblocks and advise the bomb squad that the Anti Imperialist Liberation Army is claiming responsibility for the explosion. Block press and civilian access. Other explosives may be in the area. You copy? Over."

"Copy, base. No press or civilians. It seems awful quick for AILA to claim responsibility, doesn't it, base? Over."

"Chief will explain on arrival. Over."

"Roger that, base. Over and out."

The smoke was billowing from the rear parking lot where a crowd had gathered, but Joe was on the front side of the store holding Sharon on the curb when Allie slid to a stop beside them. His face was covered with dirt and blood. It scared Allie enough that she jumped from the car screaming, "Joe! You okay!? You okay!?"

Grabbing him by the arms and quickly looking him over, she found him blackened with soot and smelling of gasoline. Blood from a cut behind his ear was trickling down his neck, mingling with ash, forming a tiny black pool near the base of his shoulders. His hair was slightly singed and matted as if he'd slapped at it to put out a fire.

He wheezed through his blood-stuffed nose, "I-I'll be okay. Help me get Sharon into the car...I think she's fainted."

Allie could see a battalion of emergency vehicles coming down the road toward them. "Wait...here comes the ambulance now."

"We're not safe here," Joe snapped. His tone was a flat-out order to move. "*She's* not safe either, now help me," he said, picking Sharon up and walking quickly toward the car.

Allie ran ahead of him and opened the rear door as he laid Sharon on the backseat and crawled over her to the front. He doubled over as Allie jumped in, started the engine, floored it, and nearly hit a police officer pulling a ribbon across the road.

* * * * * *

Twenty minutes later the phone rang at Dr. Jones's residence. Allie's husband, Carl, was panicked and wanted the prayer chain to intercede in prayer. Mrs. Jones picked up the receiver.

"Hello?"

"Hello, Joyce!?"

"Yes?"

"Joyce, this is Carl, Allie's husband?"

"Oh, hi Carl, what's up?"

"I needed to speak to Indy. Is he there?"

"Afraid not. To be honest, I'm not sure where he is. He called earlier and said school had to be cancelled due to a break-in. Seems the thieves were after the school's computers again. Anyway, I don't know where he is. You want me to have him call you when he gets home?"

From the sound of things, Joyce was unaware of Sheri's abduction. Carl would have been too, if Allie hadn't called and filled him in, telling him to be ready to leave for Granny's farm as soon as she arrived. "But call the prayer chain first and tell them to pray," she had said in an urgent shout. "Especially for Sheri!"

He had packed in a rush and dialed the number to start

the intercession circle, mostly because he said he would. Now he wondered if he should be the one to tell Joyce about the abduction and explosion. It was obvious she was uninformed. Dr. Jones had either lied about the cause of the break-in, or Joyce had assumed the facts. Either way, the truth would come out eventually, wouldn't it? He determined it would and spilled the beans to get the chain started.

13—THE REINDEER

"These 'waived SAPs' [Special Access Programs] are the blackest of black programs. How many of the SAPs are unacknowledged, and how many are waived, is a question which only a few people can answer: eight members of Congress, the members of SAPOC (including the Deputy Secretary of Defense), and the Secretary of Defense."
"In Search of the Pentagon's Hidden Budgets,"
International Defense Review, 5-18-01

Admiral Stark stood next to Apol Leon with a puzzled look on his face. The Nibiruan Key—as the Martian image was called at Montero—was on a table in front of them while across the room the extraterrestrial vehicle (ETV) hovered silently between the lab's ceiling and floor.

This was a new development, and Stark wondered if the ETV was somehow reacting to the image.

Previously the seventy-five-foot-wide vehicle had nested on a titanium cradle, which in turn was mounted to a crawler similar to the two-tracked transporter built by NASA to move the space shuttle and mobile launcher platform, but on a smaller scale. The disc had been airlifted to Montero at night by a giant military freighter and lowered into the bunker using an express Otis cargo elevator with a concealed trap. Once positioned with the crawler transporter, it had remained motionless, until now. Floating spectrally above the hangar's floor like this was an unexpected and astonishing event, even to a man like Admiral Stark.

He observed how the ship glistened with a greenish hue, as if the air around it was being cooled to a misty fog. It made no noise other than the crack of static electricity on his hair and skin. The hull, a ring-shaped dome defined by a crest, had a transparent section circumventing the entire midsection at the rim. The translucent panel itself measured fifty inches from top to bottom, providing a window through which the ship's crew originally looked out. Admiral Stark considered it, and thought how terrifying the reptilians and grays must have appeared staring from that portal. It took his mind back to his childhood, to a time when he was just a boy on the farm.

It was Halloween night, October 31, 1938, and young John Stark had just come in from playing in the wheat field when his mother held her hand up to shush him. His parents were beside the radio, faces blanched, listening to an animated reporter talking about a UFO in a field near Grovers Mill, New Jersey.

At first the reporter thought it was a meteorite. Then the top of the crashed object began rotating like a screw. The reporter moved in for a closer look as the threaded section pushed off from the top.

"Ladies and gentlemen," he had exclaimed, *"this is the most terrifying thing I have ever witnessed.... Wait a minute! Someone's crawling out of the hollow top. Someone or...something. I can see peering out of that black hole two luminous disks.... Are they eyes? It might be a face. It might be.... Good heavens, something's wriggling out of the shadow like a gray snake. Now it's another one, and another. They look like tentacles to me. There, I can see the thing's body. It's large, large as a bear*

*and it glistens like wet leather. But that face, it...ladies and gentlemen, it's
indescribable. I can hardly force myself to keep looking at it. The eyes are
black and gleam like a serpent. The mouth is V-shaped with saliva
dripping from its rimless lips...."*

Stark remembered how frightened he had been that
night. Seeing his parents disconcerted for the first time,
watching them hold hands and stare at the radio while the
announcer described the malevolent scene. Of course
neither Orson Wells nor the Mercury Theatre actor who
played the reporter was aware of the public's
misconception. The radio dramatization of H. G. Well's
classic *The War of the Worlds* had been meant as a Halloween
stunt. It created mass hysteria. Now Stark couldn't help
wondering if Wells had based his fiction on an unknown
record or source. Perhaps he was just a visionary, but
portions of his description had been uncanny.

As he reminisced, Apol stepped toward him and
introduced the Montero engineer that had been on duty
when the Nibiruan Key was first brought to the hangar.

Stark harnessed his thoughts and said, "Yes...hello, now
let me get this straight. I understand the ship moved to its
current location of its own accord...the moment you carried
the key into the room? Does that sound about right?"

"Yes, sir. Just as you see it, without warning."

"Has it done anything else? Any signals, transmissions,
anything?"

"Not to my knowledge, Admiral. It simply lifted off the
pedestal and stopped in midair."

"What about the key, notice anything different about
that?"

"Yes. Both it and the ETV seem to be interacting in
some way with the baseline energy field."

"Explain," Stark demanded.

"I cannot, sir, not yet anyway, but the ETV's propulsion system seems to be functioning as a result of the ambient electromagnetic and quantum energy field, the baseline energy state from which all matter is alternating. It appears the ship is tapped into mother nature somehow."

The engineer paused, perhaps to see if the Admiral understood. When Stark didn't indicate one way or the other, he said, "What I can say is that the vessel is airborne by generating its own gravitational field."

"You mean the propulsion is based on antigravity?"

"Of course gravity is the least understood of all forces of nature, but I'd say that's correct. It also seems to function in proximity to the key. Whenever the key is moved beyond sixty-six feet of the ship, the propulsion system shuts down and the ETV returns to the cradle. When the key is returned to within sixty-six feet of the ship, it immediately taxies to this default location."

"How accurate are the movements, assuming you've tried it more than once. Does it return to the same place? Any variations?"

"No variations whatsoever, sir, it's an exact positioning each time. Even the rate of ascent and descent are duplicated perfectly. Would the admiral care to see a demonstration?"

"Not now," he said decidedly. "Can you speculate what will happen when we actually insert this key into its slot inside the ship?"

"It would be pure hypothesis, sir. Of course we hope to learn something about the Enigma. Perhaps an answer to the superstring and M-Brane theories too...the idea that we live in one of many dimensional membranes, surrounded by other unseen universes."

Stark pulled his cap off and ran his hand through his hair.

"Yes, I'm familiar with the theory about parallel universes. Supposedly we can't see them because their light photons stick to their dimensional membranes, just as ours do. Beyond such conjectures, what do you believe is happening to the ship itself?"

"We're assuming the onboard systems have come online. Of course we can't be certain, can we?" the engineer questioned.

Either this response was not the kind Apol wanted from a supervisory member of his team or he was worried it would fuel the Admiral's pessimism. In either case he raised his scaly finger and began pointing out the environmental benefits such free energy systems could provide to the New World Order. He didn't get the chance to finish. A sultry African-American approached them from behind and articulately informed the Admiral that a call was waiting for him in the Blue Room. It was Air Force One, and the president of the United States was on hold. Admiral Stark didn't need to be reminded that a person doesn't keep the leader of the free world waiting. He gave Apol and the engineer a look as if to say *wait here*, and turned on his heels to follow the assistant. As he moved toward the office, he could hear Apol in the background scolding the man for his inappropriate answer.

"Mr. President," Stark said after closing the door and picking up the receiver, "this is John Stark."

The president responded pleasantly through the phone, "Admiral Stark, how are you doing. How's the wife and daughter?"

"They're fine, sir, and you?"

"Fine, Admiral, just fine."

The president seemed to make a calculated pause, then the tone of his voice changed. "Listen, John, General

Layton received a call from agent Leon earlier today. Seems the two of you are having some kind of disagreement over the launch date for Santa's Reindeer."

Stark wondered why the president was using coded language. Air Force One and Montero both employed unbreakable communication systems. *Maybe it's just a habit or good discipline*, he thought. Either way, he'd play along. "I'm not convinced the Reindeer is in good health, sir. Could be diseased."

"General Layton disagrees, John. He assures me that Apol is correct, everything is healthy and there's no need to stall."

"Sir, with all respect, General Layton is echoing his advisors. They all see budget cuts on the horizon, and they're feeling the pressure to produce something spectacular. You know how it works, sir, the right breakthrough or technological discovery could renew public support for the space program and make it difficult for budget cutbacks during appropriations. This equals dollars for Pentagonees like Layton to siphon into their Special Access Programs. Layton's reaching, sir, he's reaching. As for Apol, well, that man's a megalomaniac. He could care less if he blew the whole world up as long as he gets what he wants."

"Now, John, let's not get carried away here. The Reindeer is in the stable," the president said, meaning the disc was bunkered below ground in an impenetrable fortress. "The animal can't go anywhere until we're ready for it to, you know that. So let's not worry about the beast escaping. For Pete's sake, a dozen hydrogen bombs wrapped in cobalt couldn't blast that thing out of the barn."

"I'm not worried about that, sir, I'm worried about the unknown, the things we haven't contemplated. This is an exotic animal, and I have a feeling we haven't begun to comprehend it. In my opinion, we should order a full and thorough review. Who's to say what Hell this thing will unleash?"

"Or Heaven, John, it could unleash utopia!"

"Okay, maybe utopia, but I don't think we should be so foolish as to jump from the plane and *then* check for a chute."

Stark immediately regretted that comment. A man of his position didn't speak condescendingly to the president of the United States. Quickly he added, "It's just that I fear for the community, sir, that's all, the beast could be rabid."

The president continued on an even keel. "John, you're a vice admiral, you can't afford to make decisions based on fear, and you certainly can't afford to second-guess me. The flight of the Reindeer has been reviewed and approved at every level. Everybody is signed off, including General Layton, and he is the secretary of defense. Now if you've got credible reasons to delay, let's have it. Otherwise, I'm afraid we're on course for the holidays."

"I don't have the evidence yet, sir, but remember, this SAP was waived," Stark pressed, meaning that the project was so sensitive that the Senate and House management oversight protocols had been waived. "If I can just have a few months to report back to SAPOC, I might be able to get the status of the project changed."

He heard the president sigh. "It'll never happen, John. All you're doing is forcing me to make you stand down. You understand? I'm trying to be civil here. I appreciate your heart, really I do. But I think you're overreacting. What I need from you is a firm commitment to expedite matters at Montero. All right, John?"

Knowing he would get nowhere by exasperating the

president, Stark finally said, "All right, Mr. President, I understand your position."

"Good, John. I knew I could count on you. You're a good man. Remember to say hello to the wife and daughter, will you? Give 'em my love."

As the President hung up, Stark knew what he had to do, even though it would represent incalculable cost. Otherwise the War of the Worlds might play itself out after all. He set the receiver down and rejoined his thoughts to that Sunday night in 1938, trying to recall the chilling words of the actor and hoping they would not prove to be prophetic.

"Ladies and gentlemen. I have a grave announcement to make. Incredible as it may seem, both the observation of science and the evidence of our eyes lead to the inescapable assumption that those strange beings who landed in the Jersey farmlands tonight are the vanguard of an invading army from the planet Mars."

14—PHOBOS ON THE FERRY

"Fifty years ago—on Feb. 20, 1954—President Dwight Eisenhower interrupted his vacation in Palm Springs, California, to make a secret nocturnal trip to a nearby Air Force base to meet two extraterrestrial aliens."
"Ike and the Alien Ambassadors," *The Washington Post,*
02-19-04

July 27

The sun was not very high when Granny Coe, her hair weaved back into a long white braid, noticed her Rhode Island Red being chased from the dog's bowl again. She pulled on her smock and grumbled to herself, "One of these days Princess is gonna catch that stupid chicken. She's gonna bite 'im and shake 'im and leave 'im for dead."

She pushed the seasoned window open and hollered at Big Red. "Get on now, silly bird, get away before you get yourself ate!" The golden retriever, hearing her voice, gave up the chase and strutted back to her bowl.

Every critter had its place here on Granny's farm. The cows and one retired horse grazed in the field near the barn, the chickens scratched around the fenced area by the coop, the ducks nestled quietly by the creek, and Princess meandered wherever she pleased.

Although the ranch, once the model of country charm, had fallen into disrepair since Grandpa Tony's death, Granny had done her level best to maintain the hospitable ambience of the old homestead. No one, perhaps not even Granny herself, knew how she kept up with it all: feeding the animals, minor tractor repairs, fixing little things around the farmhouse, and the garden, it was simply more than a body could do. But she was a wiry old gal and it had earned her the nickname "Granny Gadget."

"Princess chasing Big Red again, Granny?"

She turned and saw Allie coming through the living room toward the coffeepot. She had her hair pulled up in a sloppy bun and was wearing the flannel nightgown Granny loaned her the night before, her eyes puffy, her face haggard, as if she'd been crying. Granny didn't ask.

"Ohh, that dumb bird ain't got no sense," she said. "One of these days Princess 'ill catch 'im. Then she'll learn that ol' rooster a thing er two."

Even though Allie smiled, it looked to Granny as if she was hiding an unknown heaviness. She watched as her oldest grandchild sat on the Queen Anne sofa by the woodstove, careful not to spill her coffee on the braided rug, and stared down at the first edition of the *Portland Times*. It was spread on a coffee table in front of her, right where Granny left it earlier, sometime before Big Red broke the morning's silence with his natural alarm. Allie seemed to be weighing the paper's words carefully as she leaned over and clutched the front of her gown. The article in front of her read:

CAR BOMB KILLS TWO, INJURES SIXTEEN IN PORTLAND

A car bomb killed two men and injured sixteen others at the Maxamillion Video Store in Montavilla on Monday. It was the deadliest attack since the Anti Imperialist Liberation Army began claiming responsibility for such assaults in the United States last year.

Young children and senior citizens, as well as store owners, were among victims of the explosion that sent pieces of twisted metal and glass through the air at the popular business.

Police said military-style plastic explosives indicative of the kind connected to AILA in the past were used. The charge was detonated by a timer that had been wired to a car's ignition switch.

The Anti Imperialist Liberation Army wasted no time claiming responsibility for the bombing, and said it was in response to the arrest of Carlos Lorenza in Mexico City, a member of the militant group that fled to Mexico after being placed on the FBI's Ten Most Wanted list last spring.

FBI Spokesman David Martin said a special task force was being formed to investigate the crime scene, but that evidence so far supported the AILA claim. "It was a brutal and cowardly act," he said.

Later in the day Chief Martin called on Congress to pass tougher antiterrorist laws....

* * * * * *

While downstairs Allie was reading the paper and hiding

from Granny what had happened to Sheri the day before—her husband Carl's orders—a muffled chime in the upstairs guest room woke Joe. At first he didn't know what he was hearing; then he remembered the cell phone Corsivino gave him. He stumbled from bed and rifled through the dirty clothes he'd dropped on the floor the night before. Sugar ants fell from the garments as he uncovered the coat with the phone, unzipped the pocket, grabbed the communication device, and gently placed it over his tender ear. The swelling in his nose had gone down overnight, but it was still sore, not to mention how puffy his eyes were from crying about the death of his good friend, Dave.

"H-hello," he mumbled into the receiver as he stomped to kill the ants. Dust from the crusty rug immediately convinced him that this was a bad idea.

"To whom am I speaking?" a gravelly voice said.

After what had happened to Corsivino the day before, he had doubted the call from Phobos would come. "This is Joe."

"Get a pen and take down these instructions."

Right to the point...usually the way Joe liked it...but since yesterday his mind was a flurry. "H-hang on," he said, reaching into a nearby desk drawer and finding a pencil and a discarded receipt. "Okay, I'm ready."

"From your current location you will drive south on old Interstate 99 until you see the Brooks Market near Salem. Are you familiar with that area?"

Joe tightened. How did the man on the phone know his location? He walked to the window and peeked through the curtain to the driveway leading into the farm. He couldn't see any unfamiliar cars, but that didn't mean he wasn't being watched. "I know the intersection. How do you know where I am?"

"Global Positioning Satellite and the chip inside the phone. Now pay attention. At the Brooks Market intersection you will turn right. Continue due west until you see a sign that says 'Wheatland Ferry.' Got that?"

He relaxed a bit. "Yeah...I got it."

"Follow that road to the river. Park your car on the ferry at exactly 10:00 AM today, and exit your vehicle. Walk to the north safety railing and wait. You will be contacted there. Bring the telephone with you. Do you understand these instructions, Mr. Ryback?"

"I do, but how can I be sure that you are Phobos?"

"You can't."

"Then why should I trust you?"

"It's simple. I know your exact position at this very moment. I believe you call it Granny's farm? If I wanted to harm you, do you think your army of chickens could stop me?"

Joe was starting to like this guy already. "I'll be there."

"Good. Don't be late."

As the man on the other end of the line hung up, Joe looked at the cell phone. Encryption *and* GPS. He wondered what other cutting-edge toys Phobos had at his disposal.

* * * * * *

Fifty miles from Granny's farm, a top-secret meeting was concluding near the little town of Amity. Nine members of Operation Gadfly, including Phobos and a female mathematician who subscribed to chaos theory, were talking.

"Did he take the bait?" the woman said, her voice sounding sour.

"If that's what you want to call it," Phobos said.

"Of course that's what it is; we *are* using the boy for a diversion, aren't we?"

Malachi Malina seemed agitated by her comments and pressed, "Listen, Beth. We're giving Joe the only chance he has. If in the meantime we use his distraction for our purposes, I don't see anything wrong with that."

"Now see, that's what I'm talking about. You and your 'ends justify the means' ideas are no different than the enemy we're fighting."

"Oh, for Pete's sake. There's a great deal of difference between us and them, and you know it. We're fighting for righteousness..."

"Righteousness!?" she blandly interrupted. "And using deception to do it!?"

"It's not deception if we do everything we told the boy we would!" he countered.

"Uh-huh. Tell that to his mother at the funeral."

"Ahem." Phobos feigned clearing his throat to resume control of the meeting. "Okay, ladies and gentlemen, your points are taken. But let's all keep in mind that Joe is a marine and that this is his sister. He's young, yes, but he's motivated, and that may make the difference. Besides, like it or not, we've gone too far to turn back now. So we'll help Joe, and in the meantime his distraction may help us. Timing will be crucial. We'll only have a few seconds while the guards are focused on his activity. That's when we'll make our move."

Phobos glanced across the table at Donald Pritchert. "Your department ready, Donald?"

"It is. The DNA bombs are in place and await further orders," he affirmed, meaning that Operation Gadfly's bio-assassins were in position. The soldiers Donald referred to were unlike any other. They carried no visible arms and were trusted members of the scientific community. Yet the weapons they possessed were frighteningly lethal. Over a five-year period they had met casually with Montero's chief supporters, in the fields of science and defense. In each case a simple handshake or pat on the back yielded the fleck of skin or single strand of hair needed for a genetic sample. These specimens were then studied with the individual's particular vulnerabilities being identified. Later, pathogen-loaded viruses, or DNA bombs as Donald called them, were engineered from the samples to deliver infectious agents lethal only to the original donors. These viruses could then be injected harmlessly into the assassin and carried invisibly to their mark. In the target's presence, a simple cough would release the magic bullet, killing the victim within a few hours or days.

Referring to Special Atomic Miniature Munitions, or SAMM suitcase nuclear warheads, Phobos continued, "All right, what of the SAMMs?"

The one-kiloton bombs, although small comparatively speaking, would be smuggled into the bottom levels of each Nephilim factory where they would annihilate the giants' army, leaving the civilian population overhead untouched.

"The men are prepared to go in when you are, sir. The snipers are also prepared."

"Good. Operation Gadfly will commence on my orders. Advise everyone to stand ready."

* * * * * *

The powerful sedative was doing its job, perhaps too well, for in a twisted sense of justice Sheri was receiving the kind of deep rest she actually needed.

Katherine, already intrigued by her striking similarity to

the angel in her dreams, brushed Sheri's curly red hair to one side, exposing her partially open mouth. Even her pouty lips, though not tinted green, were identical to the angel.

* * * * * *

It took less than an hour for Joe to go from Granny's farm to the Wheatland Ferry. As he drove down Route 99 past Woodburn and then west on Brooklake Road, it was like visiting a different world. The air here was fragrant with fruit blossoms and cooled by irrigation mist. On both sides of the street, loam covered with vegetation and tree groves stretched for miles over the gently rolling hills. It was a sweet taste of American farmland and people who were not in a hurry, families and neighbors who were committed to each other and unaware of the blackness growing around them.

As he paid the dollar-fifty toll and drove onto the aging shuttle, he could hear the Willamette River beating rhythmically against the ferryboat's side. The watery hum reminded him of the movie *Jaws* with its splashy maritime soundtrack. As the ferry pulled offshore, he stepped out of Allie's car and stood next to it, catching his balance.

Cautiously, he surveyed his surroundings, then let go of the door and teetered over the moving platform to the north safety railing. Next to the banister, his back to the river, a barrel-chested man with a military haircut was looking down at the water. He was about seventy years old, dressed in Armani jeans, Bruno Magli shoes and a Ferre polo shirt. He had a cell phone matching the one Corsivino gave Joe in his left hand and a set of truck keys connected to an oversized ring in his right. He twirled them on his index finger, stopping occasionally to palm them.

Joe leaned on the railing a few feet away, pulled the special phone from his pocket, and held it up conspicuously.

Without greetings, the stranger said, "Follow me," then walked away toward a dark green Suburban at the front of the ferry. As he went, he motioned with his hand for Joe to enter the passenger's side of the vehicle. Joe recognized his voice as the same gravelly one from the phone call earlier that morning. Joe opened the door, and by the time he was inside, the man was seated across from him.

"Close the door," the big fellow ordered. "We don't have much time."

Joe straightened himself and pulled the handle, being careful not to disturb a large briefcase on the seat's center console separating the two of them. Atop it was a standard issue Negev light machine gun, Israeli Special Forces issue.

"Joe Ryback, I assume?" the man with the gruff southern drawl said.

His voice reminded Joe of his dad's, country but authoritative. "That's right."

"You may call me Phobos. Of course it's not my real name, but I need to maintain anonymity for the time being." He hit the power-lock button and both doors clicked. "What's important for you to know is that our friends did not die in vain. Andrew and Dave were good men, and I believe they have gone to a better place."

The comment startled Joe for some reason. It seemed so abrupt. "So you know who is responsible for Dave and Corsivino's murder?"

Phobos stared at him in a way he'd seen on senior officers, the kind of battlefield expression typical of a career soldier's ability to separate personal loss from duty. "Of course," he said. "In time, you will too. However, we need to discuss the issue at hand. First, I understand Corsivino filled you in on the activity at Montero. True?"

Joe returned a deadpan stare. "Yes."

"What did he tell you?"

"I know about the aliens, the ship recovered from the crash, and the transgenic research on giants."

Phobos pursed his lips as if he was unhappy about Joe knowing that much. "I hope you appreciate the need to protect this intelligence, son. Guarding the knowledge you possess is far more important than either of our lives, or that of your sister. Over the next forty-eight hours you may acquire even more sensitive data. If anything goes wrong during that time, we will disavow any knowledge of your actions. Furthermore, members of the consortium are monitoring your movements and are prepared to take you out...kill you, if that becomes necessary to protect our interests." He paused as Joe considered that, then added, "On the other hand, if you follow orders, we stand ready to help you in the extraction of your sister."

I'm getting a little tired of people telling me which family member will die next if I don't do what they say, Joe thought. "So why *are* you willing to help me?"

"Let's just say I owe your dad."

Joe's thoughts raced. What did this man know about his dad? If Phobos had been involved with his father's murder, he'd kill him where he sat. He made a calculated glance at the machine gun, wondering if it was loaded and if he could get to it in time. Otherwise a lightning-quick fist to the throat was possible from here. He'd crush the man's esophagus and break his freaking neck. "What do you mean, you *owe* my dad? What do you know about his death?"

"Your father, Lieutenant Colonel Clarence Ryback, is remembered with high esteem among our group. If it hadn't been for his insight and willingness to hide the Nibiruan Key, there's a good chance none of us would be here now. So we're doing this for him. As for you, you might say we've accepted destiny's induction of you into our private army."

Joe had the feeling he wasn't hearing the whole truth. He wanted Phobos to fear him, to think he was under post-service battle stress, which in many ways he was. "Then you can count on me to guard the information I've received," he said. "But I warn you. If I find that you've misled me, or that you or your associates had anything to do with my dad's death, I'll hunt you down with extreme prejudice and kill you like a dog."

"I can live with that," Phobos surprised him by saying. "Now let me bring you up to speed. It appears the Nibiruan Key—the image you had in your possession for a while—will be inserted into the extraterrestrial ship within the next seventy-two hours. That means time is of the essence. You *must* get your sister out of Montero's Level Twenty right away. I'll help you, but make no mistake about this; the mission is perilous. You need to ask yourself if you're up to the challenge."

Joe was prepared to die for Sheri if necessary, but this was the first he'd heard of Level Twenty. "I'm up to it. But the area you mentioned is not something Dr. Corsivino advised me on."

"That's because nobody's supposed to know about it. Thankfully, we're not as dumb as the lead agent, Apol Leon, thinks. In fact, we're very much aware of his scheme. But the Level Twenty project, 'New Messiah,' is on a need-to-know basis, and frankly, son, you don't need to know. Your immediate concern will be to get Sheri out of Montero at the time we set during the next forty-eight hours."

"Why not go in now?"

"You'll have to wait until I say."

"Can you explain why? What we are waiting on?"

"Sorry, that too is on a need-to-know. What I can tell you is that the intelligence we require to determine when the operation—called Operation Gadfly—can begin, will be acquired within the next two days. It would be a mistake to move prematurely, but when we do go in, Sheri cannot be there. The survivability rate at Montero will be zero."

Joe turned to face him. "Corsivino didn't say anything about a zero survival rate. He mentioned Operation Gadfly, but nothing specific about the title or particulars."

Phobos looked through the rearview mirror, probably checking to see if anyone was watching them, then grinned slightly. "Operation Gadfly is the code name adopted by the consortium for its mission. It's from Greek mythology. It refers to the gadfly who stung Pegasus on the butt."

"Meaning...?"

"One of the heroes of Greek legend was a man named Bellerophon. He tried to fly into heaven on Pegasus. To stop him, Zeus sent a gadfly to sting the winged horse. When it did, Bellerophon was bucked off. The consortium sees a paradigm in the myth. The Alliance of Ten Nations might try to use the extraterrestrial vehicle as a high-tech Pegasus, a way of conquering heaven. If they do, and if the consortium believes this in any way represents public endangerment, we'll be the gadfly that stings the UFO's butt. Get it?"

"Yeah, okay. So what about my sister? How do I get to Sheri?"

Phobos picked the machine gun up and placed it on the floorboard. He opened the briefcase and pushed it toward Joe. "Getting in will be easy, I'll take care of that. It's getting you and Sheri out that will be difficult. To succeed, you'll need all or part of these."

Inside the luggage was a neatly folded schematic of the interior of Montero and several other objects. Joe picked up the map and laid it aside. He pulled the briefcase closer and made a mental inventory of the contents—a Ka-Bar fighting knife, flash grenades, pineapple grenades, chemical light sticks, trip wire, and other standard issues weapons, all conveniently attached to a tactical load bearing vest. Next to that was a microcassette player, a Montero employee uniform, and two unknown particulars; a device that looked suspiciously like a Star Trek phaser, and a thin blanket made of highly reflective material. He pointed at the phaser. "Looks like something out of a Star Trek movie."

"You're not far off. That's a P-22 Hand Activated Laser, also called a PAL, and it's lethal."

Joe carefully picked the weapon up. It was unlike anything he'd seen in the corp. It looked like a DustBuster, only smaller. The handgrip was rubberized and curved slightly downward, a novel design for easy forward firing. On top of the grip was a thumb button trigger. Ahead of that, two sets of transparent lenses ran along the main body. One lens went left to right with the words *Power Indicator* below it. The other aligned from front to back with *Beam Intensity* in red. He stared quizzically at the big man as he held it.

"It's simple to use, really," Phobos said, apparently noting his curiosity. "First, turn the safety off. That's on the back of the handgrip. It looks like a miniature safe dial."

"I see it."

"I've programmed it so that all you have to do is dial Andrew Corsivino's initials—left to the letter 'A' and right to the letter 'C.' Think of A/C electricity if that helps. Once you've done that, push the dial inward and the laser will come on. After that, simply point and push the trigger button."

Joe rubbed his finger along the dial to get the feel for it, but didn't turn it on.

"Now this is important," Phobos stressed. "The trigger is like a spring-loaded toggle. Push it left and the PAL will emit two nonlethal ultraviolet beams. They will immobilize any target within thirty-three yards. The beams form a positive conduit and a negative one that tetanize muscle tissue. In short, the target will be disabled by a sustained contraction of the skeletal muscle mass."

"Like getting hit by a police Taser," Joe surmised.

"Exactly, except this little beauty will drop an elephant at a hundred feet away. It uses UV radiation to ionize photon particles like an electric wire leading to your target. And it also has a lethal setting. Toggle right, and your mark is dead. The diaphragm and heart muscle movements will freeze. They'll die before they hit the ground."

Although he hoped it wouldn't be necessary, Joe thought such a weapon could be useful, quiet and deadly. He set it aside and pointed at the reflective blanket. "And this?"

"I'm especially proud of this little beauty," Phobos said, pulling the cover out of the briefcase. "It's an Active Camouflage Shield, or ACS for short. You can literally disappear behind it."

Joe looked stumped, then Phobos added, "Like the Arnold Schwarzenegger movie *Predator* where the alien hunter is invisible to the human eye except for slight distortions in the space around him."

Joe had seen the film. "I guess I know what you mean."

"The science presented in that movie was based on Active Camouflage research. Of course the technology has only recently been perfected, but the film's depiction of the invisibility created by the science is fairly accurate."

"Then you're saying the Pentagon has actually developed invisible soldiers capacity."

"The hardware is not deployed yet, but it will be, in different battlefield applications. In this case, switch the ACS on and throw it over you, and there's a good chance nobody will even know you're there."

Joe shook his head. "We sure never had anything like that in Fox Company."

Phobos agreed, although it no doubt had been a long time since his platoon days. "Not in my squadron either. The technology is ingenious in its simplicity, though. It's just a marriage of low-powered microprocessors, fiber optics, and liquid crystal display technology. You're familiar with the Texas Instruments wristwatches that display time and date by projecting numbers onto a watch's screen, aren't you?"

"Sure," Joe said, looking out the window and noting the ferry was about halfway across the river.

Phobos glanced in the same direction, then said, "It's a simple microprocessor that transmits information to an LCD skin, effectively projecting imaging data upon it. Active camouflage does approximately the same thing. See this here," he said, pointing to a dime-sized lens on the edge of the material. "This is a camera. There are dozens of them...see here, and here," he continued, pointing out several more along the edge. "These little cameras pick up the surrounding images wherever you are. They transmit that data through fiber optics to the microprocessor...that's this little bulge back here." He tapped a raised section approximately one inch wide on the back of the material. Joe noted an On/Off switch on it. "This microprocessor displays the data in real time on the blanket's skin and curves the facsimile around you, effectively rendering you invisible. Only when you move are mirror distortions created, as in the *Predator* movie."

"And if necessary, I could use this to hide from the giants, is that your plan?"

Phobos' brow dropped. "No way, son...the Nephilim are highly sensitive to smell. They're Hell's bloodhounds, I'm afraid...they'd find you in a heartbeat. The ACS will only be helpful where humans are involved. As far as getting past the giants, that's the good news. They're kept in an area we call the Dungeon. It's the lowest level, isolated from all but minimum personnel. You'll never see the Nephilim out of their cages...unless..."

I knew it. There's always a catch. "Unless what?"

"Unless you get caught, then you might...but let's not think about that. You're a marine, right? You make no plan for surrender or defeat."

"I was also trained to prepare for the unexpected."

"In that case, use the PAL, and remember to toggle right."

Joe perceived the comment as a brush off of his "giants" concern. Maybe the big man was hiding something. He watched as Phobos reached into the briefcase and removed a small box from the top pocket of the tactical load bearing vest. "Last but not least, you'll need these," he said, opening the lid and sitting it down where Joe could see inside it. The box held something like a credit card and a transparent container filled with liquid. Inside the liquid was a human finger and an eyeball.

Startled, Joe took a long, deep breath. Who had surrendered to such agony? Whether alive or dead, it was inconceivable that someone's eye had been cut out and their finger wrenched off. What kind of people was he dealing with? Mercenaries without conscience? An elite group of specialists doing what they believed was good for the many? Would he join them in anything, no matter how inhumane, to save his sister?

Phobos seemed to read his mind. Slowly and solemnly he said, "War is hell, son, a sorry obligation to survival that causes otherwise sensitive men to regard culture, ideology, and even compassion as luxuries. Don't even ask how I got these. Just take them. You'll find them indispensable to the plan for extracting your sister."

15—SPINDLY SPIDER LEGS

"Behind the scenes high-ranking Air Force officers are soberly concerned about the UFOs. But through official secrecy and ridicule, many citizens are led to believe the unknown flying objects are nonsense...."
Former CIA Director Vice Admiral Roscoe Hillenkoetter, in a signed statement to Congress, August 22, 1960

Returning to Granny's farm, Joe parked Allie's car and entered the farmhouse through the weathered back porch door. He carried the suitcase with its cargo to the guest room upstairs and laid it on the bed, then exited the house and found Allie in the field, helping Granny with the chores. After hugging Granny, he led Allie to a familiar place alongside the barn where as children they crawled through the loose red boards and magically transformed the straw-strewn theater into Hulk Hogan's wrestling ring and Nancy Drew's study. Leaning on the aging wood, he described the details of his meeting with Phobos, the rescue scenario, and the need for outside coordination. When he was done, Allie agreed to be part of the plan, and to be ready for him and Sheri if the recovery was successful.

* * * * * *

Apol raced into Section A of the main laboratory and grabbed his scrawny lead geneticist and particularly devoted crony. Drawing him to one side of the room, he whispered briskly, motioning with his hands while cloaking his voice beneath the hum of the second-generation Cray supercomputers. The information he needed was somewhere beyond this room, in Section B, lost in the isles of transparent polymer jars where preserved specimens— gorilla-humans, octopus-humans, lizard-humans, and some bulbous-headed ones resembling alien Grays—were labeled sequentially to match corresponding computer files.

Somehow the crony knew where to find what Apol was looking for. On aisle ten, section six, a fifty-gallon container held the experiment. It was made of Apol's DNA and had lived two full years before its head exploded.

"Get the reference numbers and bring them to my lab," he ordered. "Hurry."

"I will, my lord," the crony said, turning away to get a pencil and paper.

Returning to his workroom and shoving past the invisible Grays, Apol stared into the petri dish. Normal embryo development of his cell matter to the 128-cell stage. He'd watch it overnight, and if all went well, he'd hurry to implant it. *This could be the one that will live forever*, he thought. *But who should be its host? Sheri the voluptuous, or Katherine the younger?* He'd have to pray about it. The goddess would guide him. She always did.

* * * * * *

Joe spread the schematic out and popped the cap off the

highlighter, tracing his course from entry to end as Phobos had instructed. Mission time from incursion to extraction: forty minutes, the Lord willing.

He would wear the Montero uniform over the blanket and load bearing vest and ride through the research center's security gate with Phobos sometime within the next forty-eight hours. According to the nametag, the uniform once belonged to a large man named Michael Williams. Joe knew nothing about him, only that his finger, eyeball, uniform, and a recording of his voice saying, "Level Twenty," "Level Ten," and "Level One," were to be used in the rescue attempt. Joe wondered how Phobos got these, and why he could get past Montero's security protocols. The man smacked of double agent.

Once inside the compound, he would separate from Phobos and enter the service elevator alone. He would operate the cab like Phobos explained, removing the employee shirt once inside. He would exit on Level Twenty, immobilize the guard, and use the security card to gain access to Sheri's room. Using necessary force, he would acquire her and reenter the elevator where he'd cut the bracelet from her wrist and leave it on the floor. The bracelet had a locator chip in it.

Stopping on Level Ten, he'd exit and command the elevator to resume movement to Level One. The bracelet's beacon would hopefully mislead security to the southwest side of the complex while he and Sheri followed the map through Level Ten's low-security area.

On the northeast side of the facility they'd meet up with Phobos and ride a second elevator seven hundred fifty feet below ground to the Dungeon. Nobody would expect that. From there they'd move through the Nephilim Training Access Tunnel to the forest outside, then to the boat where

Buck and Allie would be waiting to transport them over the Columbia River.

Joe pulled the load bearing vest across the bed and reinspected the weapons load. He understood how many ways this plan could go wrong. It could get very, very ugly.

* * * * * *

It all happened so quickly. One moment Nathan Reel was cruising thousands of feet above New Mexico at one hundred twenty-five knots in his new Cessna 182; the next, he was staring out the cockpit at thousands of giant bugs.

Before leaving Portland the weather had been nice; the sun was shining with just a few clouds gathered around the mountains. After filing his flight plan with Flight Services, he loaded the giant arm with two boxes of reports and stole out of Troutdale without incident, maintaining altitude and tracking straight for Albuquerque with a manageable crosswind component of twenty knots.

Stopping in Nevada long enough to refuel, he contemplated turning back, but finally decided against it. He knew it was wrong to steal the appendage, but he simply couldn't allow his friendship to Dr. Jones to cloud his better judgement. The giant arm was his ticket to recognition at the prestigious Los Alamos National Laboratory.

Ten minutes from his destination, however, something unexpected captured his peripheral vision. A moment later Albuquerque Control Tower noted his movement off course with sudden descent and radioed to ask if he was okay.

Without saying what he saw, Nathan nervously identified himself. "Albuquerque Tower, this is Cessna three one one echo, over."

"Cessna three one one echo, maintain VFR at five thousand five hundred, heading one six zero, report fifteen miles out."

Nathan was confused. "Yeah...ah...I don't know what I'm looking at up here, Albuquerque. Looks like bugs of some kind...giant bugs..."

He heard the controller, sounding hesistant now, say, "Roger that...just got dots from primary radar. You say these look like bugs?"

That was what he had said, and at first the mysterious things did look like bugs, locusts to be exact, very large ones, perhaps mutations or even an optical illusion. Then, as the plane neared the swarm and he got a closer look, the furious roar of leathery wings and undulating abdomens revealed a ghastlier sight—the freakish insects bore human-size thoraxes tipped with stinger tails and spindly spider legs.

"Cessna three one one echo, traffic twelve o'clock, one mile, unknown?"

Nathan narrowed his eyes and looked closer. "What the..."

One of the creatures hovered, its hairy legs dipping up and down against the cloudless sky, then it focused on Nathan and in a flash was on him. The monstrosity's coloration was blended yellowish green with tumorous nodules pulsating with the rapid flapping of its wings. Its eyes were sharp and threatening, its thorax quivering with anticipation, as if hungry to inject its life-extinguishing poison into the helpless human prey. Snarling and growling like a vicious rabid dog, the monstrosity attached itself to the aircraft's window and thrust its stinger-tail swiftly against the tempered glass. When the window didn't break, the hybrid cocked its head and leered at Nathan, emitting an eerie, otherworldly howl. Nathan stared at it in disbelief.

The demon was wearing a Mayan-like crown, and looked identical to the face from Cydonia on Mars.

He keyed his mike and stuttered into the radio, "A-ALBUQUERQUE, B-BE ADVISED..."

Striking the cockpit again, harder this time, the flying hybrid cut him off, its bony stinger ricocheting off the rounded glass. Another strike and then another until the transparent shield cracked. The arthropod glared at the break, then at the Nephilim arm in the backseat. A snarl stretched over its face. Its pupils narrowed and hardened as its wicked mouth dripped yellow-green saliva from its deranged mandible.

With unnatural speed, the demon struck the glass again, this time splintering the crack outward into dozens of random jagged lines. A high pitched whistling sound began rushing in along the windshield's seal, and Nathan knew the cone was about to collapse.

He dove for the emergency parachute beneath the rear seat, grabbing at it frantically, his heart pounding like a hammer, but he couldn't reach it before the plane slammed against the buzzing madness of a million powerful wings. The plane, spiraling out of control, flung him around the narrow cab as helplessly as a rag doll until he crashed through the shattered window into the open air. In the background he heard the Cessna's emergency locator transmitter begin whoop-whoop-whooping.

Now he found himself surrounded by flying demons and facing a noxious, vacuous chasm, a shaft directly ahead resembling an open furnace door. It was glowing with embers and billowing out sulfurous smoke and ash. Gagging on the fumes, fighting to remain conscious, he watched as the vicious bug that attacked his plane surged across the sky and plunged its stinger deep into his belly. A burning sensation like red-hot steel shot through him, suspending him aloft. In the background, other creatures snatched the boxed reports and the giant arm drifting through the air. They dragged the materials like amorphous shadows into the roaring blaze.

As quickly as it had entered him, the demon pulled out, shot into the prodigious oven, and disappeared, leaving a fire spreading through his belly, down his legs, paralyzing him. He wondered if the entire scene was as real as it seemed or if he was dead already and imagining the Devil's mouth. He focused his attention on the oven as darkness enclosed the anomaly on both sides. And then it was gone, together with the evidence of profound genetic engineering that would have made him famous. The unknown nucleotides and gamma-amino methionine hydrolase reports were also taken, as were the locusts.

And somehow, he understood. That was the way it was supposed to be.

Swallowing hard, he said good-bye to his wife and kids as he plummeted toward the earth.

* * * * * *

At Montero, Apol sensed the opening and closing of *Kosmos*, and smiled. The flying minions had found the giant arm. His power over them was growing. Prophecy was being aligned.

He spat on the floor and continued toward Genetics, homicidal sociopath that he was, exhaling a jubilant rattle through his distorted lips. "And they had tails like unto ssscorpions, and there was stings in their tails: and their power is to hurt men five monthsss. And they had a king over them, which is the angel of the bottomless pit, whose name in the Hebrew tongue is Abaddon, but in the Greek tongue hath hisss name Apollyon. Revelation, chapter nine, verses ten and eleven."

* * * * * *

As thousands of unclean spirits writhed from the soils and into the trees and alleyways near Montero, seminary students gathered with faculty members for the emergency prayer council. Jones, walking to the podium and greeting the small group, said, "Let us enter His gates with praise!" He was proud of the students for assembling so quickly. He motioned them to join him as he began singing out, "All hail the power of Jesus' name, let angels prostrate fall..."

Across the street from the seminary, a phantasm watched as other students arrived late at the school. The specter's outline was of a bull-headed man, a vaporous Minotaur with an ornamental rod in his hand. Two yellow eyes, barely discernable, seethed with hatred of these Christians. They were too Christlike, not religious enough. Near his hooves a volcano of smaller shadows pushed through the sediment, clawing across the lowlands, heralding the arrival of the Gray army.

The Minotaur raised its scepter as a voice from deep within the earth echoed through its lips. "Come forth great serpents! Prepare the way before me! Come Quetzalcoatl! Come Agathodemon! Come Damballa and Midgard! Assemble the Gray legions, for the day of battle is at hand! Thus will we ascend above the heights of the clouds! We will exalt our thrones above the stars of God!"

Overhead, Justice and Swift amassed the gathering legions of bright, majestic warriors, readying for the opposition. Six-winged angels, four-winged angels, others with two wings and no wings at all, some warmly humanlike while others too terrifying to look upon flew in, cherubim, seraphim, and other servants of Yahweh Sabaoth—The Lord of Armies—each expert in spiritual warfare.

"There's a storm brewing outside." Jones said to the students. "And it reminds me of Psalm 104:3–4: *'He makes the clouds his chariot and rides on the wings of the wind. He makes winds his messengers, and flames of fire his servants.'"*

Closing his Bible and patting it reverently, Jones said, "One day Martin Luther read this scripture following a particularly bad storm. You know what he said about it," he asked before answering his own question. "He said, 'The devil provokes such storms, but good winds are produced by good angels. Winds are nothing but spirits, either good or evil. The devil sits there and snorts, and so do the angels when the winds are salubrious.'"

A student, raising her hand, asked what Martin Luther had meant.

Jones answered, "In his own way, Luther was telling us that the cosmos is teeming with angels, and that they are involved with everything from weather to astronomical phenomena to interceding in the lives of God's people and protecting them. They fought for Elisha in 2 Kings 6, they engaged the prince of Persia on behalf of the prophet Daniel, and they helped our Lord and His disciples in the New Testament. While we don't pray to angels, we rest assured that they are riding on the clouds and watching over us this stormy night. That goes for Sheri, too, wherever she is."

Several students and faculty members solemnly said amen.

"So let us pray," Jones continued. "That God will send forth his mighty angels to intervene in Sheri's circumstances. We don't understand why God has allowed Joe and Sheri to go through this storm, but He has, so there must be a reason. We must believe in the end that they will come forth without so much as the smell of smoke. We pray that Jesus will be glorified through a miracle of deliverance."

More amens.

Now Jones raised his voice. "How many times have we stood in this chapel, singing, 'We've got the power, in the name of Jesus. We've got the power, in the name of the Lord! Though Satan rages, we will not be defeated. We've got the power in the name of the Lord!' Let's practice what we preach, and do what we've been appointed to do. Let's storm the gates of Hell with prayer. Let's bind principalities and powers and let loose those angelic influences over our city."

To that, even the angels said amen.

Yet as the faculty and seminary students gathered around the altar to pray, the murky blackness outside continued unabated.

* * * * * *

On the north side of the Columbia River, Tater lay next to the cabin deck, his ears low to the ground, whining eerily.

"What's the matter, boy?" Buck whispered through the screen. "Somethin' up with bigfeet?"

Tater glanced at the old man. His big, inquisitive eyes speaking volumes.

Under his breath, Buck said, "Yeah...I'm worried 'bout them kids too, uh-huh."

* * * * * *

At Montero, Perfect Love stood next to the girls, his sword drawn.

16—THE HOARY DEMON

"NASA scientists and engineers [have verified] that man-made structures and objects have been discovered on the Moon."
Russian newspaper *Vecherny Volgograd*, 10-05-02

July 28

It was midnight at Montero and Secretary of Defense William H. Layton stood beside the joint chiefs of staff and the secretaries of the army, air force, and navy. Like the others, he was here to witness what promised to be the definitive step in the future of warfare—the insertion of the Nibiruan Key and the flight of the Reindeer. In addition to United States Government and military officials, representatives from the Alliance of Ten Nations with special Pentagon clearance as well as several members of NATO and the United Nations were in attendance.

* * * * * *

Meanwhile on Mars, a celebration was about to begin. The joint U.S.-Soviet stealth archaeological team Outpost

Alpha—named as such to represent the planet some now believed to be the original home of man—was preparing to commemorate the flight of the Reindeer by breaking open a case of Okhta vodka and getting drunk. A crude banner hung just inside the Mars Inhabitable Support Structure (MISS), announcing: "День нашего спасения прибывает!"

"Hey Nikolay," a well-built American named Kevin said. "Where's the booze?"

Kevin Thompson was the least-educated but most athletic member of Outpost Alpha. His job was to maintain the sophisticated equipment that created breathable air, rover fuel, and electricity. His pride and joy was the OGS, which among other things produced oxygen and mixed carbon dioxide from the Martian atmosphere with hydrogen from underground rivers to produce methane. The fuel was stored in metal bottles and used for generating electricity and fuel.

Nikolay pointed to a table in the corner of the MISS and replied in a heavy Russian accent, "They took it there. Have patience, my friend, I will join you."

"Okay, but tell me, what's the banner say?"

A Russian colleague named Abram had made the banner. Nikolay looked at it and said, "It is...how you say, a prophecy? I think it means the time of our salvation is come, something like that."

"What's that supposed to mean?"

Abram was across the room, writing in a journal. Nikolay waved to his comrad and shouted, "Абрам, что Вы подразумеваете баннером?"

Abram glanced at Nikolay and then at the American. He smiled a toothless smile. "Наш Христос собирается возвращаться! Наш создатель - в пределах досягаемости," he said.

"Ah, he says the Nibiruan Key heralds the return of our Christ...our creator is within reach."

Kevin smiled and waved back at Abram. "Oh...yeah. Good thinking, Abram!" Then, under his breath, he added, "What a bozo."

* * * * * *

At Montero a technician climbed off the hydraulic scaffolding and carried the Nibiruan Key into the huge ETV. He walked past project leaders near the Enigma to the cockpit where Apol Leon was waiting. Apol took the key and turned regally toward the console. This was the moment everybody had waited for, the moment of truth.

A hush fell over the staging area as the atomic clock reached t-minus ten seconds and counting. Apol glanced at the scientists and military brass around him. *These ignorant humans have no idea what's going on,* he thought. *They stand here foolishly watching, as if some magic Santa sleigh were about to be turned on. Well Santa's coming all right, and he knows who's been naughty and nice. He knows, and the nice are going to die.*

With the insertion of the key, Apol's plan to compel a New World Order would begin. The "alien invasion" was only hours away, and with it a global crisis brought on by mass panic and fear of the unknown. The Federal Emergency Management Agency (FEMA) would suspend the constitution, and martial law would be imposed. Then the UFO presence would thrust upon the world's leaders the need for representation. That's when Apol would emerge as the *alien's* ambassadorial choice. His prominence and power would become universal, undisputed.

It was the perfect setup—the making of a global police state in which he would become a god. It was the kind of great deception he imagined Henry Kissinger had envisioned, when at the 1991 Bilderberger Conference in Evians, France, Kissinger reportedly said, *"Today, America would be outraged if U.N. troops entered Los Angeles to restore order. Tomorrow they will be grateful! This is especially true if they were told that there were an outside threat from beyond, whether real or promulgated, that threatened our very existence. It is then that all peoples of the world will plead for deliverance from this evil. The one thing every man fears is the unknown. When presented with this scenario, individual rights will be willingly relinquished for the guarantee of their well-being granted to them by the World Government."*

It was a good plan. A perfect plan. One that was about to become reality.

Suddenly from the hangar floor, General Layton, watching the atomic clock, signaled that the time had come by motioning to a soldier standing on the hydraulic platform, who nodded to a technician standing just inside the ETV, who gave thumbs up to Apol Leon at the console.

Apol lifted the Nibiruan Key and kissed it pontifically, then slid it into the ancient receptacle and joined his hands to his lips, as if in a prayer gesture.

The assembly on the hangar floor froze, contemplating every possibility.

A presence moved through the ship and licked the side of Apol's face.

He blushed.

Then the ozone charged with static and crawled over the officials, raising the hair on the tops of their arms. A faint sound, barely discernable, began bowing and thumping like a kettledrum in the distance.

Those in the ship thought they saw something, then moved back, as slowly a throbbing blackness, pulsating like an ebony ball, materialized between the four columns of the

Enigma. The orb swelled and collapsed in sync to the pistonlike sounds, its skin undulating like a soap bubble, rolling and swirling as if it were alive, breathing and dancing to the echoing rhythm of some unfathomable universe.

* * * * * *

One hundred and twenty miles away, a senior technician on duty at the U.S. Air Force's top-secret Satellite Control Facility was glancing over his *Outdoorsman* magazine when he unexpectedly caught sight of something unusual on his SCF monitor. Whatever it was, it looked ablaze. He dropped from his reclined position and rolled his chair toward the screen. "Somebody find the colonel," he said a second later. "Tell him to get in here...quick."

The sergeant tossed the magazine aside and readjusted the cameras to optimize mapping sensitivity. An early-warning satellite was reporting anomalous changes both inside and outside Earth's atmosphere, unlike anything the senior tech had seen before.

He changed the RTC settings and raced outside to look at the sky.

Nothing unusual could be verified visually.

He returned to his station and stared at the monitor again. The huge flare was growing, indicating incredible temperature increases.

Why the instruments were reporting what his eyes could not substantiate was a mystery. As far as the computer was concerned, the sky was on fire, burning through and coming apart like a rip in the fabric of space.

"Dadgummit!" he said impatiently, "Where's the watch commander!?"

Just then the colonel raced into the room. "What is it, Sergeant!?"

"We've got unknown acquisitions, sir...take a look at this."

Quick-stepping to the remote tracking computer, the colonel leaned over the sergeant's shoulder. The screen was detailing a rapidly expanding redness.

"Are you mapping this?" he questioned.

"Yes, sir."

"Is it monochromatic? Oriental bird flashing?" he asked, insinuating that the Chinese might be pointing a laser at the satellite to confuse the Americans.

"It's no laser, sir."

The colonel stepped backwards, still watching the screen as he picked up the hot-line to NORAD.

The commander-in-chief at the North American Aerospace Defense Command Center answered. "CINC-NORAD."

"This is Cricket Control," the Colonel said. "KH-20 is picking up massive energy readings. Do you have unscheduled thermals?"

"We have activity from terrestrial to celestial."

"To celestial?"

"Yes."

"How wide?"

"From the blue to the red planet."

"Are you certain?"

"Yes."

"What is it? Heat?"

"Negative."

"Solar flare?"

"No."

"What, then?"

"We cannot substantiate the cause at this time, Colonel, but whatever it is...it's growing exponentially. Cricket is to continue coordination of SGLS auto-tracking and range/range data to Mission Control."

"Roger that," the Colonel said, and hung up.

At the computer, the senior tech was mumbling under his breath, "M-maybe Hell opened its mouth to let us peek inside."

"What?"

He looked at the Colonel apprehensively. "Something Grandma told me...something from the Bible."

"What's your grandma's Bible got to do with this, Sergeant?"

"She said in the last days Hell would open and a great furnace with bug-headed demons would crawl out of it...or something like that..."

"Hell! Bugs! Stop acting stupid, Sergeant, and readjust those satellite settings!"

"Y-yes, sir."

* * * * * *

Three hours later OGS Maintenance Director Kevin Thompson stumbled from the MISS air lock and fell flat on his face in the Martian terrain. He was drunk as a skunk and evidently thought it was funny. At least he'd remembered to put on his Extravehicular Mobility Unit (EMU) spacesuit before venturing outside the Inhabitable Structure.

Managing to get back on his feet, he began singing a song by Don McLean.

*Did you write the book of love...and do you believe in God
above...'cause the Bible tells you so?...And do you believe in Rock
and Roll...can music save your mortal soul...and can you teach
me how to dance real slow?...*

Inside the MISS, the sound engineer who was watching
Kevin turned his helmet-cam and microphone off. Kevin's
singing was awful, and the cam's recording of the
prehistoric Avenue of the Dead passing erratically beneath
his feet was as boring as it could get. Kevin had taken his
turn at perimeter check a thousand times before and hadn't
needed any help. He could do it this time without being
monitored, even if he was as drunk as everybody else
planned on getting.

*Jack be nimble, Jack be quick, Jack Flash sat on a candle stick,
'cause fire is the devil's only friend.... And as I watched him on the
stage...my hands were clenched in fists of rage...no angel born in
hell could break that Satan's spell...*

* * * * * *

Moving silently near the south side of the Great Mars
Pyramid, the ground responded to the *human* insertion of
the Nibiruan Key by gliding open and spewing acrid smoke
into the Martian atmosphere. Quetzalcoatl, that hoary
dragon that had relished the sacrifice of tens of thousands
of ancient earthlings, peered menacingly up from the abyss.
It had been imprisoned there during the Great War with
Michael, the chief prince of Israel. Now it detected an
approaching heartbeat and smiled demonically, warmed by
the notion that business was about to resume. Heartbeats
were such a delightful thing, especially when ripped from

the chest and offered in sacrifice to the Feathered Serpent. Quetzalcoatl heard singing.

And as the flames climbed high into the night...to light the sacrificial rite...I saw Satan laughing with delight...the day the music died...

Spontaneously he raced from his prison, his vast serpentine belly slithering along the ancient stone-way so meticulously aligned with the Dog Star Sirius, honing in on the vulnerable lush.

* * * * * *

Kevin thought he saw something moving in the middle of the ancient city, near the Well of Sacrifice. Was it a set of eyes? Crouching, sliding along the ground? Nah, couldn't be. Too big! Plus nothing could survive outside an EMU anyway.

And in the streets the children screamed...the lovers cried and the poets dreamed...but not a word was spoken...the church bells all were broken...And the three men I admire most...the Father, Son, and Holy Ghost...they caught the last train for the coast...the day the music died...

* * * * * *

Quetzalcoatl waited until Kevin floundered inside the City Center, to the area near the prehistoric flat-topped Pyramid and the gigantic Chacmool altar where human abductees were brought by the Grays and sacrificed to the god. He waited and remembered the sweet taste of blood, thick and satisfying like summer honey upon his forked tongue.

> Bye, Bye, Miss American Pie.... Drove my Chevy to the levee, but the levee was dry.... Them good ole boys were drinking whiskey and rye...singing this'll be the day that I die.... This'll be the day that I die...

Quetzalcoatl circled Kevin, closing to within several yards before charging him. The demon raised its ten-foot-wide head and leered into the inebriated eyes. Kevin teetered as if trying to decide what he was looking at, but was too late. In a flash Quetzalcoatl clamped his razor-like incisors around his right arm, biting through the tender meat and cutting off the appendage at the shoulder, knocking him to the ground. Kevin reacted as if he was so drunk he didn't realize what had happened.

"H-hey! Whad's goin' on?" he slurred, trying to sit up and attempting to use both arms. He flailed sideways as the poisonous atmosphere began seeping in around the missing arm's stub, taking his breath away.

Quetzalcoatl leaned forward and smiled, allowing Kevin to focus on the arm piece dangling from his mouth.

Kevin looked confused, then burst into screaming as he began kicking at the demon, bouncing rocks and dust off the monster's scaly hide.

Trembling with delight, Quetzalcoatl laughed and chewed the mouthful of arm, grinding it in his teeth. His nocturnal eyes, dead and predatory, rolled up like a great white shark's as he lurched forward and slurped the rest of Kevin's body into his hyperextended jaws.

Turning violently, he dragged Kevin down the Avenue of the Dead, over the rough pathway toward the Chacmool, shredding his waist with his fangs as he went, deep enough to torture but not enough to kill him. Seconds later, near the ancient altar, he thrust his forked tongue into Kevin's chest cavity and scooped out his heart, slapping it on the Chacmool with a crimson splash. Flipping the remainder of Kevin's carcass into his hideously large gullet, he ground the human remains into oblivion.

* * * * * *

An hour later, at Area 51's Mission Control, a male voice crackled over the radio. "Omega Control, Omega Control. This is Outpost Alpha, do you copy?"

"This is Omega Control, Alpha, we copy."

"Omega, this is a level-ten message. Repeat, a level ten, coded high priority."

"Acknowledged, Alpha. You are clear to proceed with level-ten transmission."

"Omega, we've got unknowns. Kevin Thompson is gone and we have mass tango movement near the city center."

"*Tango*, Alpha?"

"Mass tango movement. Betty Lou indicates one hundred sixty-four thousand dots and climbing," the man said, meaning the MISS computer was picking up unknown life forms on the Martian terrain.

"Have you checked Betty Lou, is she operating correctly?"

"She is...and we have visual verification from the Great Pyramid cameras."

"You're sure the dots read organic...not mechanical or electrical?"

"Yes, sir. Looks like lava flowing out of the ground near the pyramid's edge. Flowing up and breaking into organic strands. Cameras twenty-three through twenty-eight near the Face are also picking up ground movement, but no dots there yet."

"And what about Kevin? You said he's gone?"

"Nobody knows what happened to him, He simply disappeared. He was conducting a perimeter check when his tag went straight line. We're still looking for his signal...thought we had a heartbeat earlier...could've been...eh...wait a minute.... Betty Lou says we're at three hundred sixty-seven thousand dots at the pyramid now. Gains seem to be doubling every few seconds."

"Do the signatures indicate random or intelligent movement?"

"I would say intelligent. Dots...eem to be oving toward the Face, the Cit...nter, and ...oming...ward the MISS."

"Say again, Alpha, you're breaking up. Did you say the dots are moving toward the MISS?"

Static.

"Alpha, this is Omega Control, do you copy, over?"

Static.

"Alpha, do you read, this is Omega Control."

"WHAT THE H...IS THA..."

"Alpha, say again."

"OMEGA ONTROL, THEY'RE BREAKING INTO TH.... OMEGA, WE'RE UNDER ATTACK! THE...AKES, GIANT SNAKES!"

"Alpha, this is Omega Control. What is your situation?"

At once the microphone cracked and Omega Control heard what sounded like crunching, hissing, then gurgling and automatic weapons fire, a Russian briefly yelling profanities, and suddenly abrupt silence.

"Alpha, this is Omega Control, do you copy?... Alpha, do you copy?... Alpha, this is Omega Control, report please.... Alpha?"

* * * * * *

Katherine was dreaming again, and for the first time her vision was different. As she hung from the cliff's edge, looking out over the sea, the millions of apelike monstrosities swimming in the waters below her rose up and stood in uniform columns like soldiers preparing to march.

The great dragon came out of the waters too, metamorphosing into a strange yet desirable man wearing a ten-horned crown. He walked upon the water and sat down upon a coal black throne, facing the giant army. Speaking with the dragon's voice, he said:

"Come forth, flying serpents, you deceptive ones with your Gray legions. Come forth, for the time of my wrath is come. The humans have chosen the forbidden technology, and a body has been prepared me. I will be born the perditious son of their choosing. At their invitation I will walk the earth and enslave the Most High's creation. I will reclaim my former glory, the glory I had when I governed the Galaxy, before the time of the Fall. I will revisit the stones of fire, Mars and Nibiru, and I will conquer those who wear my mark when I am called the Beast."

Suddenly the sea divided and rolled back, revealing a subterranean world filled with fiery-eyed serpents crawling atop each other inside a hidden chaos. Katherine watched as the reptiles transmogrified into well-dressed men in black suits. The MIB crawled from the pit and took command positions in front of the giant army. Dark glasses covered their elliptical eyes, but couldn't hide what Katherine knew—the men in black were reptilian demons. Reptilian demons were men in black. What did that mean?

She awoke, and screamed. A man in a black suit stood over her.

"Now you and the other cow ssshall come with me," Apol Leon slurred with a demented grin.

17—THE
ARMAGEDDON TRAIN

"It is true that I was denied access to a facility at Wright-Patterson Air Force Base.... I can't tell you what was inside. We both know about the rumors [of a recovered saucer]. I have never seen what I would call a UFO, but I have intelligent friends who have."
U.S. Senator, U.S. Air Force General, and candidate for U.S. President, Barry Goldwater

Shaken from sleep by the ringing of the special cell phone, Joe sat on the edge of the bed and listened to Phobos as he described what had happened the night before. As a result of the Nibiruan Key's effect on the atmosphere, Operation Gadfly was moving ahead of schedule. If Joe were going in, it would have to be now. There would be no more opportunities to peruse tacticals.

Agreeing to the accelerated plans and rushing to meet Phobos in Portland, he found himself an hour later dressed in a Montero employee uniform, his hair tied back out of sight, riding through the entrance to the research facility. From the passenger seat inside the green Suburban, and with the morning sun just peeking over the mountains, the block and mortar façade looked deceptively normal, like one of a million commercial plants.

* * * * * *

What Joe couldn't see inside the building was a male nurse pushing a hospital gurney along a hall on Level Twenty. His sister Sheri, wide-eyed with fear, was strapped to it.

Moments before, in the room where she had been imprisoned, she had tried to put up a fight, but the muscular orderly and equally powerful door guard had quickly subdued her and Katherine. Also, because, unknown to her, the angel that had been casting away her fears all morning was gone now, forced from the building moments before by dozens of newly arrived "strong man" demons, Sheri's anxiety was going through the roof. She didn't understand the abrupt change of emotion, only that apprehension had suddenly fallen on her like a thousand pounds of smothering dread.

* * * * * *

As Sheri thought back over the last five minutes, an eerie, inescapable impression convinced her that she was being evaluated. Malevolent eyes somewhere in the walls, the ceiling, or maybe even the air were watching her, examining her.

She squirmed against the restraining straps as she rolled into Genetics. The nurse released the table, backed out into the hall again, and turned and hurried away. She caught his uneasiness, as if he was afraid of something, something in this room.

Her eyes slowly examined the darkness, straining to

identify the vague images filling the cubicle around her. What little light she did have was coming from bits and pieces of electronic equipment near her bed and from the imperfect seal around the entry door. She could just make out a large table of some kind, and the outline of a closet or bathroom a little ways away. A statue *or something like it* stood in one corner near several suspended attachments.

Inexplicably, the smell of sulfur began wafting through the room.

No, not sulfur, more like gas: cadaverous, decomposing, a rotting stench of some kind lacing the air.

As she considered the odor, the "statue" by the wall inexplicably *bobbed.* It looked like a cluster of balloons had been jerked sideways by a hidden, invisible clown.

Her eyes jumped to it, trying desperately to make out the image in the darkness.

Her stomach filled with nausea.

She forced herself to think, *Your mind is playing tricks on you, your mind is playing tricks on you...*

Then the form twitched...and she defined it, *them*...vacuous, horrible creatures, studying her.

The floating monstrosities acknowledged her glare, made a clicking sound, and slunk along the wall, their bodies turning but not their heads, until spider-fast they formed a semicircle around her. The vague light cast golden sheens on their bulbous-headed bodies, chalky and decrepit, as their elliptical, horrifying eyes came in contact. The light vanished into them as if into black holes: dead ocular cavities not unlike those of the minions of Dante's *Inferno.*

She wanted to scream, but couldn't.

Vivid extrasensory projections began raping into her mind, diminishing her will to resist.

Now she could see the room, indeed herself on the bed, through *their* eyes. For reasons she could not understand, the beings wanted her to perceive telepathically what she wouldn't otherwise choose to know—dreadful things about the cloning lab where...*WHERE*...*WHERE THE EMBRYO OF THE ANTICHRIST WOULD BE IMPLANTED IN THE VIRGIN THAT WOULD CARRY IT TO TERM!*

* * * * * *

Outside and above the Earth, the rip in the fabric of space continued to widen. It had grown during the night and now spanned an area sixty-six thousand miles wide and millions of miles long, the current distance from Earth to Mars.

Peering into the rift at 6:00 AM Pacific Daylight Time, NASA's most powerful telescope had turned up nothing unusual. To make maters worse, NORAD's infrared and ultraviolet detections were still undeciphered. Top-level specialists from NASA's Chandra X-ray Observatory had been called in, and had rushed to the military center to study the phenomenon.

Then at 7:35 AM, astronomers working at the Marshall Space Flight Center came up with something unusual. Using a modified high-sensitivity "hard" x-ray telescope, mysterious objects deep inside the rift had been located—hundreds of thousands of them—some bigger than football fields and others smaller than houses, moving toward Earth. The researchers couldn't explain the curiosity, only that the armada of objects would breach the rift's opening and enter Earth's atmosphere in less than an hour.

* * * * * *

Outside Portland, Oregon, hundreds of feet below ground, the Enigma pounded harder and prouder, increasing in speed and intensity as the Dark forces neared. Apol rubbed his hands together like a mad scientist. The deception was nearly complete. The Armageddon train had left the station.

* * * * * *

"We have a situation," General Layton whispered to the president, being careful not to let the secret service agent standing outside the door hear him. "It could be a problem."

The president swiveled in his stately chair and brought the tips of his index fingers to his chin as he stared at the secretary of defense. A highlighter pen lay atop the Oval Office desk next to a devotional Bible. Portions of the book of Revelation, chapters eleven and twelve, were marked.

"I'm listening," he said.

"By now I'm sure you're aware of the anomalous situation first reported by NORAD earlier this morning."

"Yes, I've been briefed on the expanse in space, the aberration."

Layton nodded. "We believe the phenomenon corresponds to the space-time vortex described in the Dropa text—the Enigma's multidimensional gateway we were hoping to achieve. As soon as we restore contact with Outpost Alpha, we plan to work with them to introduce a probe into the expanse. Of course we also need to ascertain Alpha's condition."

"But?"

"But a third situation," he began tenuously. "One that you've not been advised on, has developed since the insertion of the key. The chimera have lined up and are standing at attention."

By that Layton meant the Nephilim army had spontaneously moved into standing uniform columns at 12:01 AM. The unexpected event had occurred at each of the factory dungeons, simultaneously around the world.

"What do you mean...lined up?" the president said.

"Both cages of five thousand creatures have arranged themselves in military formation, fifty wide by one-hundred. The problem is, we didn't order them to do that, and we can't get them at ease."

Layton's cheek twitched as he stared at the president. "I guess what I'm saying is, something spooky has happened to the giants, something we are unclear about."

"Spooky, General Layton?"

"Unexpected, sir. The AngelStar system seems to have malfunctioned at the very moment we placed the key in the Reindeer."

"And...? Are you suggesting that an active connection exists between the giant army and the Reindeer's onboard system? That the Reindeer is somehow controlling the giants?"

"It's a strong possibility, Mr. President. The phenomenon occurred in tandem at each factory, at the exact moment of insertion. Currently, the chimera remain in that position, frozen like zombies. They are unresponsive to our commands."

Layton wanted to say, *It's spooky because it's as if they're awaiting orders from an unknown authority*, but he knew better.

The president sounded miffed about being out of the loop. "Why am I just now being advised of this situation?"

"We assumed it was a technical problem, sir, a..."

"Never *assume* anything, General," the president cautioned. "Especially when the technology is a product of reverse engineering, as the AngelStar microchips are."

Layton started to point out that neither the Department of Defense nor the National Security Council was mandated to brief the president on every detail of the Reindeer Project. Reverse engineering was regularly used by project leaders to re-create alien hardware and software designs. Technicians deconstructed the final products to discover how they worked, and uncertainties were to be expected under such circumstances. When he hesitated, the president said, "Have you tried shutting the AngelStar system down? The beasts wouldn't be reacting without satellite transmission, would they?"

"That was our opinion, too, sir, but we tried it and it didn't work. It's as if the microchips are being controlled by a separate, alien transmission," he said, meaning an unknown frequency source.

The president rose to his feet, circled the desk to the middle of the room, and said. "Alien? As in the Reindeer's owners?"

General Layton joined him. "That's not what I meant, sir. It's a possibility of course, but we've not come to that conclusion. Our top men are analyzing the situation as we speak. We hope to have something definitive by this morning's briefing."

"Perhaps we should just remove the Nibiruan Key and stall the project until further safeguards can be considered."

"Unfortunately, Mr. President, that's a problem too. The key won't come out."

"What do you mean, it won't come out!? It came out before...at the crash site..."

"Evidently things have changed. The ETV was either dated to lock the key at a specific time, or the crash in Sedona produced a systems failure that inadvertently released it in the first place. Either way, it's fused solid now. We have a team of specialists trying to remove it, but I'm afraid we've lost control of that situation for the moment."

"Well, until we get *that* situation *back* under control," the president fumed, "I want those beasts locked down, understand? God help us if the giants get loose without our constraints."

Layton raised his finger. "While controlling the chimera may be a problem, sir, containing them is not. As you know, we have contingencies. Every such scenario was contemplated from the outset. The Pace-Stoppers alone would be sufficient to kill the giant army if necessary."

Layton's reference was to small shape-charged plastique capsules that had been surgically attached to each Nephilim's heart. The radio-controlled miniature explosives were part of the Department of Defense's Nephilim-restraint fail-safe system. It was this very procedure that had killed the Nephilim that Buck and Tater found in the ravine. That giant had detected a problem with its AngelStar-GPS linkup and had tried to escape. When Montero technicians couldn't reestablish connection with the beast, the Pace-Stopper was signaled and exploded, rupturing the creature's vascular organ and killing it. Had the beast not fallen into a deep ravine and been covered up by Buck, the recovery team no doubt would have found it.

The president looked disdainfully at him. "Yes, that was your guarantee from the very beginning, wasn't it? The possibility of the giant army getting out of control and presenting a public endangerment was a mathematical improbability. Yet, here we are, facing something that neither the Department of Defense nor your experts at Montero saw coming."

Walking to a large aquarium near the informal sitting area, the President touched his finger to the water and watched as orange life forms swam toward him. As the goldfish gazed up, expecting food to drop down from the heavens, from the god who feeds fish twice per day, he said contemplatively, "Look at how these fish come to me, General. They cannot understand me, what I am, what motivates me. I am infinitely beyond their ability to comprehend or to control. I assume the power of a god over them, to feed or to destroy them, depending on whether they please me. While natural instinct tells them to run away, to hide from my power, their bellies bring them back day after day to feed on my gifts. I've been thinking about this all morning. Perhaps we've been acting like these goldfish."

"Excuse me, sir?"

The president bit his lip. "Did you ever stop to question where the Montero research was going, General?"

Layton was confused. The president, an avid supporter of the Reindeer project, sounded like he was having second thoughts. "I've followed my orders, sir."

"Of course, and don't misunderstand me. I've been on board from the beginning too, choosing to believe that mankind would ultimately benefit from our research and from the startling possibilities represented by the alien technology. But did you ever stop, just for a moment, and ask yourself if we were getting in bed with the Devil?"

"The Devil, sir?"

"Yes...the Devil...you know...the horned guy...the Evil One. Haven't you ever wondered if an unseen, incomprehensible power could have planted the ETV on

Earth as a Trojan horse? Something to trick the Alliance of Ten Nations into building a fishbowl for humanity?"

"I'm not following you, sir."

The president looked disappointed. "Never mind, General. It was just a thought."

Truth was, Layton understood very well the point the president had made, he just didn't want to think about it. It went along with another concept—the idea that thousands of ferocious Nephilim were standing in uniform columns at Montero waiting orders from some unseen dragon—a power who could not have acted without man's invitation...like the one made by the insertion of the Niburian Key. It sent a cold chill up his spine. Nephilim were as strong as ten men, stealthy, cunning, and immanently superior soldiers.

His thoughts drifted to the Urban and Jungle Warfare Report he'd received nine months earlier. The UJWR had described in detail the average Nephilim's unusually strong attack-kill instincts, not to mention their sheer savagery of an opponent. Only when sporting an adversary, like a dog playing with a rodent, did Nephilim let a man believe he could survive hand-to-hand combat.

The report also estimated that, without use of sophisticated weapons or contingencies such as Pace-Stoppers, more than ten million ground troops would be required to defeat the existing giant army. Whoever controlled advanced weapons *and* the Nephilim would therefore rule the New World Order.

With such power, peace could be forced on terrorists, the rule of law on anarchists, philanthropy on the greedy—and that was the whole idea. Wasn't it? To create a utopian world? The president must have thought so, at least at one time. He never would have joined the surreptitious Alliance of Ten Nations otherwise.

"Anyway, sir," General Layton said. "I did want to bring you up to speed on the developing situation and to make sure you were aware of the additional information we'll be reviewing at this morning's briefing."

"All right, General. I'll expect solid answers from your experts."

* * * * * *

As Layton excused himself and walked out, the president returned to his desk and stared down at the mysterious devotional Bible somebody had highlighted and left open on his desk during the night. For the third time in as many hours he read the troubling section from the book of Revelation:

> *And I stood upon the sand of the sea, and saw a beast rise up out of the sea, having seven heads and ten horns, and upon his horns ten crowns...*

The phrase "and upon his horns ten crowns" was circled with a line drawn to a publisher's note in the margin. The note speculated that the ten crowns represented an End-Time alliance of ten nations, which Satan would use to provide the Antichrist with an earthly seat of authority.

18—DELICIOUS
HUMAN DELICACY

*"NASA's Hubble Space Telescope has spotted what seems to be strange
planet-sized objects wandering loose in globular cluster M22."*
"Wandering Mystery Planets," NASA, 07-08-01

The smell of Douglas firs and rhododendron blossoms
laced the crisp morning air as Joe breathed a lungful of the
aroma and continued across the parking lot, up the loading
dock steps toward the designated point of entry. Phobos
was ahead of him, wearing an impressively decorated
admiral's uniform and carrying a large suitcase. Nervous,
Joe wondered how it was that a high-ranking officer, if
indeed he was one, could be involved in such a scheme.

Walking past the maintenance area fifty feet inside the
loading zone, he came to an unpretentious but wide utility
elevator where Phobos was entering a series of numbers
onto a keypad near the lift. Phobos paused as it beeped,
then turned and walked away. Joe had no idea where he was
going, only that the two of them would meet again at the
Dungeon Elevator when and if Sheri was retrieved.
According to Phobos, he was one of only a dozen
Operation Gadfly members worldwide with security

clearance high enough to get inside the areas where the Nephilim were kept, and then to the access tunnel where the three of them would hopefully escape.

As the "admiral" departed, the service elevator opened, and Joe stepped inside. He waited for the doors to close before taking off the employee shirt. Immediately the hidden load bearing vest's camouflage design was reflected against the cab's stainless steel walls. Reaching behind the battle garment, he withdrew the container with the eyeball and finger. Voice recognition was all that was necessary once he got past Montero's first floor, but to start he had to log in as employee 233—Michael Williams.

Joe wanted to ask Mr. Williams—whoever he was—to forgive him for using his body parts. Frankly, he felt like a grave robber. Who was this Michael Williams, anyway? Did he have a wife and kids? Did he live in the area? How did he die? Why? Joe knew that the answers to these questions wouldn't change what he had to do, and it wasn't the first time as a marine he'd detached himself from the distinctions of good and evil, but such things were never easy for soldiers like him.

"Please step to the ABIS for biometric identification," a computerized feminine voice said over the cab's speaker.

He squatted and placed the square container on the carpeted floor, pulled the lid up, and heard it hiss as the seal's vacuum breached. The biting smell of STF (Streck Tissue Fixative)—an alternative to the carcinogen formaldehyde—issued out of the box.

Not a job for the squeamish, he thought as he reached into the container and grabbed the eyeball with his right hand and the fleshy finger with his left. The body parts were covered with slimy, stringlike capillaries, which he blotted against his pant leg to absorb the excess fluid.

"Please step to the ABIS for biometric identification," the voice repeated.

He stood and moved to the front of the cab, pressed the tip of the detached digit to the Fingerprint Authenticator, and waited. After a moment, an aqua blue light appeared beneath it, moved silently along the fingertip, analyzed the pattern against employee data, then authorized step two.

"Print identification is confirmed," the voice said.

He lost no time cramming the dead finger inside his pant pocket, then positioned the eye, retina forward, into the Iris Scanner. He watched as another light came on and shut off a second later.

"Iris identification is not confirmed. Please remove contact and try again."

Not confirmed!? He looked at the eye. It didn't have a contact on it, but it did have some liquid debris and a minute blood vessel fragment near the front. He spat on it, cleaned it with the tip of his index finger, daubed it against the palm of his hand, said a little prayer, and placed the iris against the scanner again. This time a blue light and then a red one followed.

To his relief, the computerized voice confirmed iris identification. "Good morning, Mr. Williams. Please enter a floor-level destination," it said.

He stooped, pulled the pudgy extremity from his pocket, placed it with the squishy eyeball back inside the container, and gathered his stuff from the floor. He took the cassette player from the load-bearing vest and pointed it where he assumed a microphone was located in the ABIS. The microcassette had been set to play in the order he needed during the extraction. He squeezed the button and heard the late Michael Williams casually say, "Level Twenty."

A moment passed as the audio patterns were analyzed.

Then, with a tug of inertia, the cab jerked and began lowering into the bowls of the earth. He reached into the tactical vest and retrieved the P-22 Hand Activated Laser (PAL). The high-tech weapon felt unnatural in his hand. He longed for an AK-47, but was pleased to have an effective, nonlethal option. He turned the dial near the rear of the handle to the letter "A," then right to the letter "C," pausing to watch as the power indicator light came on.

Toggle left to stun...and right to kill, he reminded himself, glancing at the pineapple grenades and other weapons hanging on his chest.

* * * * * *

Miles above the Mt. Hood Evangelical Seminary prayer meeting, the gathering angelic host stared into the anomalous rift. Unlike NASA's astronomers, they were not at all perplexed by the expanse in space. It was the "Ahriman Gate" and they had seen it before—the doorway to Satan's abode—a supernatural chasm called *Kosmos* by ancient Hebrews and *Ahriman-abad* by other civilizations. It was the dark domain where *Ahrimanius*—or the Devil and his angels—lurked, and from which they influenced earthly governments. The last time it unlocked in this way was during the great rebellion, when God cast Lucifer from the stones of fire and destroyed the material empires of Mars and Nibiru. Thanks to modern men and their eagerness to possess forbidden technology, it was opening again. This could only mean one thing. Lucifer, now called Satan, wanted his old throne back. Unwittingly, the Alliance of Ten Nations was trying to give it to him.

"You can tell they're almost here, can't you," Justice whispered to Swift.

"Closer by the moment," Swift replied warily.

Yet the two angels would not order troop movements yet, not until instructions were received from the Captain of the Hosts. They had faced the armada before and knew it was a delicate matter.

* * * * * *

Deep beneath Montero, in his shrine to Hecate, Apol stopped interceding to the mother goddess and dipped his hand into the pool of blood beneath her bronze feet. As the emaciated woman chained to the wall watched, he withdrew a human eye from the offering bowl with tender, delicate care, and examined it. Finding it acceptable, he pulled a knife from his pant pocket and opened the middle blade. Carefully, so as not to spoil the magic, he held the organ of sight so that it looked directly at him, then carved it into nibblets. It would serve as today's communion to the deity.

As usual, the superbly crafted Swiss Army Knife performed perfectly. The sacred instrument had not left his possession since he was a boy, when on his twelfth birthday his father presented it to him, declaring him a man and baptizing him to "the goddess of three ways." Not that he understood the occult value of the oracular device at the time, that didn't come until later, when at around eighteen years of age the voice of revelation began calling to him in the middle of the night, in dreams at first, then audibly from the blackness above his bed.

Once he responded to the visitor, and the goddess had him intimately, he began trusting the things her succubus—the material substance of her spiritual self—told him, the secret, amazing truths only someone of his special nature could receive, not the least of which was that the Swiss Army Knife was more than it appeared. Although the instrument resembled its standard retail counterparts, it was, in fact, not a knife at all, but a tool of discovery, a device *she* had willed him to receive.

He recalled how, upon learning this, he had excitedly examined the portentous tool more closely than before, appreciating its cryptic design, its shiny blades for cutting, slashing, gouging, ripping apart, and unveiling, its saw for cutting through and out tendon and bone, its spoon for digging and dipping, its corkscrew for pulling away muscle, its scissors for snipping off unwanted parts and shaping the ones collected, its file for finish work.

It was indeed a marvelous invention and had provided him with immense pleasure for some time.

Then one day while sorting through parts of a neighbor's puppy he had butchered, he discovered that he had grown cold with using the non-knife to dissect live animals and to interpret their innards. He needed greater revelations. That's when he slaughtered his parents, and if it hadn't been for the goddess and her undying generosity, he might never have discovered the true path to enlightenment their deaths ultimately provided.

Although his father was a stout man and certainly not one to be underestimated or outdone in a street fight, he was not at all expecting his son to come at him from behind the door when he arrived home that day. With his thumb pressed firmly against the steel, fingers clamped tightly around the Swiss handle, Apol had brought the stabbing device down hard and fast from its wickedly high arch, just like he'd seen in the movie *Psycho* by Alfred Hitchcock, a comedy he had laughed at hysterically.

As he drove the sharp blade deep inside his father's neck

and nearly through to his esophagus, he knew the butcher knife in the kitchen would have cut deeper, maybe even clean through and out the other side if enough pressure was applied, but it didn't possess the kind of divine guidance the goddess-given one did.

Even then, he was surprised by his father's tenacity. The old man had actually reached around, grabbed him by the arm, slung him to the couch, and squealed like a pig as he flailed through the living room, clutching the back of his neck and searching for the bloody slippery handle.

Prompted by the inner urges of the quick-thinking goddess, young Apol had leaped from the divan onto him, wrapped his arms and legs around him, and held on as the two of them stumbled and tumbled to the floor. While he clawed vigorously for the handle, his father growled and tried to turn them over, but couldn't, and finally when he had dug the blade from the old man's neck, he reached around and thrust it into his right eye, drawing it down hard along his cheek bone and then sideways through his carotid artery so deeply that he nearly decapitated him. Tremors of gooseflesh had crossed his daddy's large, Popeye arms, and then he had relaxed as death's maiden warmly embraced him.

Once the old man was fully dead, Apol, a little tired, went to the kitchen and made some ice tea, adding sugar and stirring it with his bloody index finger, before sitting on the floor next to his father to examine the fresh kill. When refreshed, he had dug into "Dad" with eager anticipation, searching his cavities and canals for hidden truths, new revelations, perhaps even an alien pod harboring an infant Gray, but after several hours of such laborious exploration, he had become saddened and not a little disillusioned by finding nothing new, no discoveries any different than those he'd always found in the animals he'd dissected.

That's when his wench of a mother walked into the house and shrieked with what he thought was a phony, startled expression. Supposedly she had been shopping. He didn't believe it, not even when her silly bag of groceries hit the floor. He'd seen on television what women like her do when their husbands and sons are not around—naughty, vile, despicable creatures whose presence on this spinning globe was the highest insult to the goddess. She'd probably come home from seeing a "john" or maybe a strip club of some kind where one of those all-nude male reviews was performing. He could see it in her eyes; her diseased soul was laid bare before him. Then it dawned on him, and he wondered—why hadn't he seen this before now?

Unlike animals, which he believed had no spirit, the window to the human soul was through the eyes! His father's corpse had revealed nothing new because he had looked in the wrong places! *Or maybe because he'd damaged the eyes and thus destroyed the revelations his father once possessed!*

Jumping from the floor jackrabbit fast and grabbing his mother by the hair, he had dragged her kicking and screaming into the kitchen and mutilated her, then excitedly but gently performed the intricate work of removing her delicate eyes. The various smallware of the Swiss Army Knife made perfect sense now, larger tools would have been cumbersome for such confined areas. But if handled properly and in strict accordance with the goddess's guidance, one needed nothing more than this elegantly designed and superbly crafted portable operating utensil to dislodge an ocular "soul-gate."

How to enter that gate once you had it in order to drink in its revelations and thereby divine the goddess's will was a different matter, one that young Apol believed would require prolonged prayer and consideration.

But hardly had his parents' corpses began to stink when, by the next day, quite by accident, or maybe Hecate's providence, he had made the discovery that would change his life forever. In his father's library, in one of his many books on UFOs and Greek mythology, an unknown author, a self-anointed mystic, pointed out that in B.C. 410, while writing about the bloody rituals of the Bacchae in his famous play, *The Bacchantes,* Euripedes described how Pentheus, King of Thebes, was torn apart and eaten alive by his mother while under the guidance of Dionysus.

As it turns out, this tearing apart and cannibalizing, also called omophagia, was actually practiced by ingenious ancients who understood that by eating the flesh and drinking the blood of living creatures, the "soul" or "essence" of a victim might actually be absorbed.

According to the enlightening book, many early pagans understood this: Norwegian huntsmen, African Masai, headhunters of the East Indies, plus numerous others whose illuminated societies comprehended that by eating portions of the body while performing ceremonies dating back to the hidden goddess-mysteries, all or part of a victim's memories, strengths, and revelations could be captured by the consumer. Thus if eyes were windows to the soul, the book argued, consuming them during mystery rituals would absorb their collective revelations and strengthen one's ability to divine.

Inspired by the author's profound wisdom and armed with this new information, Apol had moved his parent's bodies to the barn where the Unitherians—the small UFO cult started by his dad—regularly met. Except for an elaborately fashioned, large bronze statue of the Greek goddess Hecate, handcrafted in Italy and financed by a wealthy stock-car driver and friend of the sect, the cult's "Temple" was actually similar to the poorly decorated backwater churches that dotted the Mississippi landscape, and maintained about the same.

Nevertheless it was in those modest surroundings, humbly before the goddess, he had become an eater of souls, consuming his mother's eyes and flooding his own with wonderful revelations. Maybe it was because she was a woman and represented a communion of flesh fashioned like the goddess. Or maybe it was just her eyes, any woman's eyes, that could produce such divine symmetry. In either case a love affair between himself, his victim's souls, and the deity began that day, a *ménage à trois* more intimate than any purveyor of pornography could imagine. And the *revelations* he received from that first communion, well, they were beyond anything he could have anticipated.

He was to become a god...who would sire a divine son, a child that would rule the world like a mythical descendent from the Mount of Olympus. This would be the dream that would remain before him for twenty years.

After burning his parents' barn with what was left of them in it, collecting the life insurance money, and selling the house and assets, he had declared the Unitherians disbanded and joined the military, where, through patient manipulation, he had climbed the ranks over the same twenty years, first as an expert sniper, then as a Special Operations officer, and finally as a Black Operations officer, ultimately leading to his stint at Wright-Patterson Air Force Base and then at Montero, where he'd been placed in charge of the above-top-secret *Project Reindeer*.

The military wasn't always aware of how he'd used his well-deserved and impressive authority for personal needs (not the least of which was the relocation of the bronze statue of Hecate from storage to her new sanctuary below Montero), especially since 1987, when his destiny was confirmed. That's when he'd met the reptilian pilot of the crashed alien ship and received the Dropa translations, including the special "for his eyes only" formula, which he used on himself. The reptilian had explained how *it* was sent from Hecate to point the way to Apol's deification. Reptiles were always used in this manner, it had said, even in the Bible, where Adam and Eve followed the serpent's advice and were well on their way to becoming gods "before you-know-who cut them off."

In his case, Apol was told, the father of serpents would succeed, genetically transforming and then using him to spawn his namesake's seed.

Now, with each passing day, his form, once purely human, nurtured the hidden transformation, the growing, clawing, painful pleasure of his new and special self.

Likewise, in his laboratory, as prophesied, the promised one had begun to gestate.

Chewing the foul communion, he kissed the statue's feet, then departed the underground shrine for the titanium cages where the Mega Nephilim were kept—the behemoths like Rahu, Bisclaveret, Chemosh, and Mantus.

It was time to let the dogs out.

* * * * * *

When the elevator stopped and the computerized voice above him said, "Level Twenty," Joe thought, *thus begins the moment of truth.*

He alerted his senses, anticipating the door's opening, and prepared for what might be on the other side. Phobos had caused him to believe the door would open to an empty hallway. A second later, with no one in sight, he was happy to find it did.

As the opening came fully apart, he closed his eyes and they twitched, as if he was experiencing rapid eye movement. The marine trick wasn't the subconscious processing of dream-state information, however. Everything he had learned over the past few days—from weapons to schematics to timing—were catalogued now in mnemonic memory groups for "at-will" retrieval.

Calling up "Memory Group One," he visualized the distance and directions to Sheri's room, dropped his intake to a controlled breathing pattern, and rushed through the doorway with stealthy liquid motion. As he stepped over the threshold, his attention was drawn to the strong odor of floor disinfectant, military issue of the familiar type he'd smelled on more than one occasion at mess hall. Besides this obvious attention to cleanliness, the glaring absence of decor took him by surprise. The elevator and even the exterior of the building had at least reflected a paltry smattering of commercial appeal—wainscoting, carpet, baseboard, and trimming. Now it was as if he'd entered an ashen-colored tunnel through which sinful interior decorators must assuredly begin their descent into Hell. The ceiling was gray, the walls were gray, even the uncovered concrete floor had been left to blandly cure. Given that the corridor was also without doors and windows, it would have been difficult to navigate the chalky passage without inevitably experiencing snow blindness if it had not been for the generous amounts of overhead lighting and the occasional wall-mounted camera.

Just as Phobos said he would, he soon arrived at a T in the hallway. Somewhere in the distance, two or three persons could be heard, speaking in a "clickity clackity" tongue-against-the-roof-of-their-mouth language that sounded more like exotic tropical birds than intelligent dialogue.

He considered the unfamiliar sound, and thought it might be extremely low frequency waves (ELFs) broadcasting along the halls. As a marine, he'd learned of mind control experiments using ELFs through which enemy targets could be subdued by distorting sensory imaging within the brain's frequency allocations, thus causing them to hear and to even "see" concocted phenomena.

Yet if ELFs *were* being openly broadcast, he told himself, the same would indiscriminately destabilize all persons on the floor except those wearing protective headgear.

Given the cumbersome nature of the frequency-absorbing helmets, and unless security personnel are already aware of my presence, it's more likely that a pair of doped-up Cockatiels have escaped the Portland Zoo and are lost inside Montero.

Either way, he had to move and move quickly, whether in reality or in a bird-populated, ELF-induced matrix.

Continuing around the corner, he reached the designated junction. The PAL's indicator light verified the system was fully operational. With his back pressed firmly against the wall, he peered around the corner. An MP was midway down the hall, at attention, his sidearm holstered, standing beside the door Joe assumed opened to Sheri's room.

Taking a deep breath, he focused then sprinted around the wall, simultaneously aiming and squeezing the high-tech weapon's toggle. By the time the MP saw what was happening, two nonlethal ultraviolet beams were flashing along the hallway. The positive and negative conduits—like brightly colored miniature lightning bolts—struck the guard in the neck. He jerked violently, surprised, then paralyzed, his arms gnarling into pathetic distortions along his shaking sides. He grimaced and fell to the floor, trembling uncontrollably, overcome by the involuntary contraction of his skeletal muscle mass. Spittle ran from the corners of his lips as he slumped sideways against the floor.

Now Joe was at the door. He stepped over the guard's body, reached into the top pocket of the load-bearing vest, retrieved the key card, swiped it through the electronic door lock, and watched as a green light appeared where a red one had been a moment before. He pushed the access open and moved halfway through the postern, careful to hold the door with one hand while pointing the PAL with the other.

"Sheri!" he whispered loudly, surveying what appeared to be an abandoned room. "Sheri!"

A camera—one like he'd seen above the entrance— aimed at him nearby. A red light blinked above the lens. He stared into it, aware that a security officer inside a control area was probably watching him and by now alerting security.

He whispered again, louder this time. "Sheri! Answer me! Are you here!?"

Suddenly he felt vulnerable, like his plan was crumbling. He wanted to run! To get out of there! Unaccustomed to such extraordinary panic, he sensed an unusual negativity pushing against the raw edges of his nerves. A ceiling mural of a goddess and six gray aliens was overhead. In as many ways as Michelangelo's Sistine Chapel could inspire, this artwork seemed to rain despair, as if an aberrant Siren from the mythical island of Anthemoessa was whispering to him, "Run away...forget about Sheri...save yourself...or kill yourself..."

Then a different response, faintly audible, came from somewhere in the room, a soft little voice that sounded like a girl.

"They...they took her away," it answered cautiously.

* * * * * *

Katherine looked at the masculine guy standing in the doorway. Who was he, bursting in here looking for Sheri? And what was that thing in his hand? A DustBuster?

* * * * * *

Joe's eyes shot to the bed. "Who's there?"

"M-me," the voice replied from beneath the anchored mattress.

He stooped and caught the big blue eyes of a frightened woman staring out from below the frame. A girl, really, an overly slender yet beautiful waif of eighteen to twenty years of age. Although she was wearing makeup and hair as intricately tiered and as stylishly done as to qualify for prom queen candidacy, a nearly transparent hospital gown was the only thing covering her dainty body.

"Who are you?" he asked, careful not to stare at her in ways that would embarrass.

"I'm Katherine, I'm Sheri's friend...they took her away."

He held the door with his foot and stretched forward to offer her his hand. "Where did they take her *to?*"

Grabbing his fingertips with one hand while closing the back of her gown with the other, she pulled herself from beneath the bed and stood up a bit too close for Joe's comfort.

"I heard the guard say she was going to Genetics...who

are *you*?"

He couldn't remember a "Genetics" room on the schematic.

"I'm Sheri's brother, and we don't have much time. Do you know anything about this place? Do you know where Genetics is?" Now he could smell her perfume.

She covered her thinly veiled chest and opened her mouth to answer, but didn't get the chance. A sharp *AINK...AINK...AINK* erupted in the hall, the alarm drowning out the two of them.

* * * * * *

When the warning went off on Level Twenty, Donald Pritchert acted nonchalant and dialed Phobos's beeper from his position near the control room. He entered the number 46, the "go" signal the admiral was waiting for.

* * * * * *

Even though Phobos couldn't hear the audible alarm from where he was, he accepted the legitimacy of the pager signal and pushed the elevator's "Open Door" button. When the panels slid apart, he stepped over the threshold into the Dungeon with the SAMM suitcase nuclear warhead in his powerful right hand. Instantly, he cringed, his senses rapped by such strong odor that he nearly lost his breakfast. The pungent smell of the Nephilim's sweat and defecation engrossed the atmosphere like waves of toxic matter.

How in the world the caretakers can stand to breathe this air is beyond me, he thought.

Starting to turn toward the target area, he paused. It

caught him as odd that the chamber was ghostly silent, different somehow, and for a moment he considered that he might be too late, that the creatures had been removed to the staging area. Then his eyes adjusted to the darkness, and he saw uniform columns of statuelike Nephilim standing mute inside their titanium cages. Other than the controlled breathing of their chests, the beings were motionless, staring straight ahead, hypnotized by something unknown.

Analyzing the situation, he concluded that he'd never seen the Nephilim so restrained. His bet was that the creatures, like so many other elements of the Reindeer project, were no longer under the military's control. In some way they too were reacting to the Enigma. He also noted a group of technicians and an officer of some rank huddled near a lamp at the far end of the arcade. They were undoubtedly discussing the development, probably looking for an explanation, something to offer somebody way up the chain of command.

* * * * * *

Several hundred feet away, beyond Phobos's view, Apol Leon and an incredible monstrosity, one of four special creatures not fitted with AngelStar chips, were walking toward the elevator. The Mega-Nephilim hoofed along the hallway with lumbering, arching strides, its massive arms swinging palm backward as it went. It looked like a blend between a gorilla and a man, its features chiseled and exaggerated with teeth dripping rancid saliva from its partially opened mouth. Its enormous eyes, maniacal and darting, constantly monitored its surroundings.

Due to its unique ability to extract the last iota of agony from a victim before its death, the creature was called

"Rahu," after the Hindu devil, "the tormenter." It grunted like a hog and sent a deep, obnoxious belly laugh echoing down the hall. It was so pleased. Not only was the Master's armada minutes away now, but Apol Leon had promised it a special treat—a tender morsel called Katherine it could ravish any way it pleased now that the "bulbous-headed ones" had approved the Sheri specimen. At 8'10" and 962 pounds, the reembodied Philistine champion and mutant cousin of Goliath could hardly wait to enjoy the delicious human delicacy.

Apol had asked only one favor of Rahu. Execute the goody-two-shoes team sent by General Layton to remove the Nibiruan Key. Slay them, and he could have the girl.

19—GOOD COP BAD COP

"The first conclusion is that [unknown] supersonic aircraft are operating over the US. Secondly, we may conclude that the USAF and other services either cannot identify them, or that they are misleading the public because the operations are secret."
"In Search of the Pentagon's Hidden Budgets," *International Defense Review*, 5-18-01

They moved secretly, quickly, methodically, driven by convictions and by the consortium's mandates. They were Operation Gadfly's assassins, and by 7:40 AM their horrible duty had begun.

In Jerusalem, a window slid sideways at the home of Dr. Abraham Wiesel, a leading Nephilim geneticist and proponent of the New World Order. Mr. Wiesel had just finished eating when a silencer-readied 9mm FN Browning Hi-Power—favorite of the British SAS—pointed through the kitchen window and fired once, accomplishing the operative's mission.

In China's capital city of Beijing, the limousine driver that transported Ouyang Fung home from the Imperial Chinese Banquet opened the door and coughed in

Ouyang's face. The Nephilim Army Commander jumped from the vehicle, infuriated by the man's action, and demanding an apology. The driver bowed over and over, asking for mercy and daubing the droplets of spittle from Ouyang's cheek with his handkerchief. Yet he knew the true nature of his offense. Within twenty-four hours the commander would be dead from a pathogen-loaded virus.

Near Portland, Oregon, Phobos stood over the body of a scientist. The man had not been scheduled to die this soon but had been in the wrong place at the wrong time and had challenged the wrong man. Even at his age, Phobos was the master of the quick, silent kill. He had cut the would-be informer off in midsentence, thrusting the heel of his powerful right palm against the researcher's nose, exploding his facial bones and hemorrhaging his brain. The blond-haired man's eyes were still open, staring up with astonishment. Next to him, in the maintenance room where Phobos had dragged his body, a light was blinking atop a one-kiloton SAMM suitcase nuclear warhead.

* * * * * *

While the consortium's assassins took out scientists and government officials in the League of Ten Nations, Father Malachi Malina, who was supposed to have flown to Washington DC to meet his family at the Basilica before fleeing the USA, had been detained at the Portland Airport. Now he was at police headquarters where two detectives working the Corsivino-Pitzer homicide were questioning him. The detectives were playing good-cop/bad-cop, with the "bad" one insisting that Malina was a person of interest in the murders.

Several times during the Q-and-A, Father Malina

detected little "tells" in the questioning, voice inflections and inferences that led him to conclude that the department was actually on a fishing expedition. They—or somebody powerful enough to give them orders—were looking for information related to Malina's Montero connection. The threat of a murder charge or complicity to such was simply an interrogation tool, a psy-ops trick to find out...what?...that he was part of an anti-UFO-alien-Nephilim-let's-invite-the-Antichrist-to-take-over-the-world group? Of course he was, but they didn't know anything beyond that, he was sure of it.

Still, Corsivino was dead, and that might mean somebody somewhere had smelled a rat. Or a fly? An Operation Gadfly?

"Get you some more coffee, Father?" Good Cop said, pointing to the Bunn-O-Matic near the candy machine. Good Cop was a solidly built, brown-eyed detective with a politician's poise.

Father Malina sat at an oblong table near the opposite end of the small dark room with a one-way mirror on his left side and Bad Cop on his right. A single lamp near the coffee machine was strategically positioned to cast the desired shadows.

"Sure, thank you," he said. The first cup of coffee was lousy but better than nothing.

Good Cop filled the styrofoam container with more of the gritty drink and returned to the table. He handed the Jesuit the twelve-ouncer and grinned sympathetically.

Bad Cop, an intimidating ex-Golden-Gloves heavyweight champion turned police investigator watched the priest as he sipped from the steaming receptacle, then continued the interrogation. "So let me get this straight," he said with a rough Brooklyn accent. "You don't know anything 'bout the murder of Dr. Corsivino or how he wound up in southeast Portland, eh?"

"I do not."

The gravelly-voiced cop took a long drag on his Winston cigarette, watched the end of it glow red, then blew the mouthful of smoke in Malina's direction. "I suppose you don't know anything 'bout this Dave Pitzer fella either, huh, or his antigovernment preoccupations?"

"I already told you, I don't."

"So we're supposed to believe that you, a close friend of the conspirator Corsivino, and a man who made it his business to challenge government agencies...even going so far as to be fired from a local government contractor I might add...knew nothing about Corsivino's trip to the...wha'd you call it?" Bad Cop said, looking at Good Cop.

"The Gray Hideaway."

"You knew nothing 'bout his recent and fateful trip to this local terrorist hideout?"

Whereas Malina knew that Corsivino was coming to Portland on the day that he died, his trip to southeast Portland and to the so-called Gray Hideaway was an unplanned digression that neither Malina nor the other members of the consortium were aware of until after the murder. Therefore he answered honestly when he responded, "I've said it once and I'll say it again, I don't know anything about this Green Hideaway or Andrew's trip to it."

Bad Cop leaned across the table, so close that Father Malina could smell the blend of coffee and nicotine on his breath. "It's called the *Gray* Hideaway...and don't get cute with me, buddy. A little cooperation could go a long way at resolving this issue."

Good Cop placed his hand on Bad Cop's shoulder,

pulled him back, and sat down beside him. "Father," he said, "if it's okay with you, let's leave this point for a moment, and let me ask you about a couple of other people. Would that be okay? Are you comfortable? Do you need to go to the bathroom or to stretch your legs first?"

Malina knew this was a game. He could play too. "I'm fine."

"Good. Now then. What, if anything, can you tell me about a professor of history named Donald Jones, a local teacher of theology who's also known as 'Indy'?"

"Don't know anything about the man," he said.

"Are you sure? Think now, because this is very important. Our investigation shows that Dr. Corsivino was in the presence of this man on the day that he died."

"Like I said, I don't know him."

"All right, that's fine. How about a local businessman named Nathan Reel? Ever heard of him? He seems to have come up missing."

"Sorry."

"What about the Ryback family—Joe, Sheri, Allie...any of those names ring a bell?"

"I've never met any of them," he said, which was technically true. Malina hoped Good Cop wouldn't press this question, for he certainly knew about Joe and Sheri's situation.

As if detecting the subtlety, Good Cop glanced quickly at Bad Cop, then back at Malina. He held his poker face and spoke softly. "I see. What about *Phobos*? Does that sound familiar? Know anything about the name *Phobos*?"

Malina smiled. "Sure, it was a Soviet probe...or actually two probes. The Phobos One, which disappeared on approach to the Phobos Moon, and Phobos Two, which was sent as a replacement probe to establish geosynchronous orbit around Mars. Its mission was to provide infrared imaging of the Martian moon. Instead, it photographed what many believe to be a fifteen-mile-long UFO above the dead rock. Curiously, it disappeared just like the first probe on March..."

"That's interesting, Father," Good Cop interrupted. "But it's not what I meant. I'm curious about a particular man, somebody whose allegiance to certain underground agencies might have led to the murder of Dr. Corsivino and Dave Pitzer. We believe he goes by the code name Phobos."

Malina answered with subtlety again, this time a double entendre. "I'm unable to identify any such person," he said, inferring one thing but meaning another. He knew Phobos had nothing to do with the murders, and he was constrained by his pledge not to give him up.

Suddenly Bad Cop leaned over and whispered something in Good Cop's ear. Perhaps he knew what Malina was doing. The two officers got up and walked to a wall at the far end of the interrogation area. They spoke in hushed tones until at one point Malina thought he heard them whispering about "holding him for further questioning." He knew they could. Ever since that awful day in New York City, when Osama bin Laden's al-Qaida network crashed two airliners into the World Trade Center's twin towers, police authority to detain anybody suspected of "terrorism" had been greatly expanded.

He glanced at his watch. Soon, the suitcase nuclear warhead would detonate beneath Montero, creating a diminutive earthquake throughout the Portland area.

Then it dawned on him. The imminent jolt might produce a distraction, a small chance to escape. If he could stall the detectives, prolong the Q-and-A and divert the subject around Phobos until the SAMM imploded, he might have a chance to run from the building during the confusion.

"Maybe I can explain something that might have contributed to Corsivino's murder," he said coolly to the detectives. "It has to do with his and my opposition to a New World Order. It has to do with what we believe is the real power operating behind the governments of this world."

Malina needed to be cautious. He wasn't sure if the detectives understood the truth about Montero. They might be legitimate homicide investigators—good men, just doing their jobs. On the other hand, they might be Montero pawns. Their questions about Phobos had made him wonder. It wouldn't surprise him if they were. Government "black operations" projects often employed local and national law enforcement personnel on a limited basis. He needed to play his cards right. Keep Good-Cop/Bad-Cop talking, stay out of the holding cell, and be ready when the earth moved.

"I'm listening," Bad Cop said, walking back to the table and sitting down. Good Cop followed and remained standing, watching Malina's facial expressions as he spoke.

* * * * * *

On the opposite side of the one-way mirror, a Man in Black was near the glass listening to the interrogation of Father Malina and waiting to see if the priest would give up the identity of Phobos. The MIB's opinion was that Malina would never squeal. Men like him were always willing to suffer imprisonment for what they believed in. He didn't need to hear any more of the interrogation to understand something else, too—the priest was stonewalling, and that probably wasn't going to change. He lit a cigarette and pulled a cell phone from his pocket, dialed it, and listened as the phone on the other end of the line rang.

* * * * * *

"Are either of you gentlemen religious?" Father Malina surprised the two cops by asking.

Bad Cop huffed sarcastically and shook his head. "Well, Father, it depends on who's asking, and what her hair color is."

Good Cop frowned at Bad Cop, then looked at the priest. "I'm Catholic, Father, although it's been a while since my last confession."

"Then you are aware of the idea of literal Evil? Of a real, personal Devil?"

"Yes, Father."

"What about the book of Revelation and the possibility of Armageddon?"

"Somewhat."

Malina didn't know if Good Cop was being honest, but said, "Well, I believe Dr. Corsivino died for his belief in such things."

"Why do you say that, Father? Was he also a Catholic?"

"No. He was Protestant, a charismatic, but his belief about certain global objectives—things he believed were being carried out by humans in league with devils—undoubtedly led to his murder."

Malina could tell Good Cop was intrigued.

"It starts with a theory, you see, an idea that Dr. Corsivino and I happen to agree with. We both believe the Kingdom of Darkness has been historically overspiritualized."

Malina was sure that, coming from a priest, this comment would sound peculiar.

Good Cop took the bait. "What do you mean...overspiritualized?"

"I mean that people tend to perceive angels and demons as lacking physical or scientific ability. Technology is often viewed as only a human trait. Yet everything we see in Scripture leads us to believe that God made all creatures instinctively capable of some level of mechanics. Whether it's spiders weaving traps, ants building colonies, or humans building factories and flying machines, God made all living things inherently creative. Does that suggest that He also made angels capable of advancing technology?"

Malina hesitated, stalling for time but pretending to want an answer.

"I don't know, Father, perhaps," Good Cop said.

"Well certainly it does. In fact, Romans 1:20 tells us that the invisible things of God are understood by the things we can see. Such Scriptures lead me to believe that Lucifer and his angels had technology at their disposal before the Genesis creation, and probably developed it to a level so far above human ingenuity as to appear 'supernatural.'"

"You mean the angels manufactured physical objects...like buildings and machines?"

"That and more, probably. Ancient books and archaeology support the notion that prehistoric Luciferian angels created cities, including extraplanetary ones, and even unconventional weapons in their quest to overthrow God. They manufactured advanced, combat flying machines, which they used in the Great War against God and His creation."

Bad Cop had been silent to this point. Now he scoffed, took another drag on his cigarette, and, as the smoke leaked from his nicotine-tainted lips, said, "What a fairy tale. All that Bible stuff was written by a bunch of tired old Jews trying to scare their enemies with claims of a mighty God, and you know it."

Malina's brow dropped. "As a matter of fact, I don't. This is a solid, universal story. Cultures from around the world documented the event I'm referring to—Sumerians, Egyptians, Greeks, and the Hebrews. Even the ancient Chinese told of a primeval war involving 'flying carts.' A sanskrit text, the Drona Parva, actually documented 'dogfights' by the angels in their flying machines."

"So a long, long time ago, in a galaxy far away, a war was fought b'tween the Klingons and the Vulcans, eh," Bad Cop sneered. "And who won this war of yours, Father? Luke Skywalker? No, let me guess. It was God! Right!?"

"As a matter of fact it was, my friend. God defeated Lucifer and his rebellious angels and cast them out of the planetary belt over which they had governed for eons, from an area the prophet Ezekiel called 'the stones of fire.' He cast them down and forbade them to use their technology again. Following that, Lucifer's implements of war were outlawed."

"So *that* was the end of Battlestar Galactica!"

"Well, it certainly put a kink in the use of Lucifer's science for a while," Malina said, refusing to let the officer unnerve him. "But the book of Revelation tells us that another war, a modern battle between Good and Evil, called Armageddon, is coming. At that battle Satan will have nothing left to lose. I believe he'll pull out all the stops and reuse the forbidden technology. That's when the Antichrist will come, and the advanced, physical war machines of Lucifer will fly again."

Bad Cop shook his head as if to pity such ignorance.

"Father," he said flatly. "Where are you going with this mumbo jumbo? Does this have anything to do with our investigation?"

"Don't you see, my son, it has everything to do with your investigation. Dr. Corsivino was killed for his belief that Satan is working in league with evil men and fallen angels to manufacture the Endgame. He believed that the earth is facing imminent war against such technology. Evidently somebody agreed, and had him killed to conceal it."

Bad Cop rose from his chair and crossed his arms over his chest. "Oh they did, did they? Well if this Antichrist is coming, and the Bible predicted it, how could Corsivino have stopped it from happening anyway? Isn't that a contradiction?"

"Not necessarily."

"Why?"

"The spirit of Antichrist has been around since the Crucifixion, always pushing to come into the world. Every generation sees his attempt at incarnation, his Caligula or Hitler. Until sufficient numbers of mankind embrace his arrival, however, God will make a way to overcome his evil plan. In each age it is our responsibility to fight the Darkness and to embrace the Light."

Bad Cop uncrossed his arms and snuffed his cigarette out. He put the stub of it in his shirt pocket and walked to the door. "And wit' that, I think I've heard about all the nonsense I can stand."

* * * * * *

Behind the police department's one-way mirror, the Man in Black pulled back from the glass, whispering into the cell phone, "Whatever the priest knows, he isn't saying.

I would go with your first impression concerning Phobos if I were you. Frankly, he's the only one I know that has sufficient security clearance and widespread knowledge of the participants. As you know, General, he's always been resistant to the Reindeer program. My bet is, he's your man."

The voice on the other end of the line said, "All right then," and hung up.

* * * * * *

Moments later the phone rang at Montero's security office. The officer on duty picked up the receiver. "Security, this is Paul."

"Paul, this is General Layton. I'm in flight to Portland and need to know if Admiral Stark is on the premises."

"Just a sec, sir," the security officer said. He punched the Admiral's name into the computer keypad. "Yes, it appears he checked in first thing this morning."

"Do you know where he's located currently?"

"I'm afraid that's an unknown, sir. He's not wearing a locator; as you know most high-ranking officers don't. I can have him paged if you like."

"I don't want him paged, Paul; I want him arrested. I'm ordering you to put him under guard and to hold him until my arrival."

There was a slight pause, then, "Arrest Admiral Stark, sir?"

"That's what I said, Paul. Do you have a problem with that?"

"No, sir, General. Does this have anything to do with the security breach we are experiencing at the moment?"

"What security breach?"

"We have an unknown on the premises. A young man on Level Twenty. The SOF team has been dispatched and should have him in custody in a minute or two. We know where he is. He won't make it far."

In a quick harsh whisper, Layton said, "Well for Pete's sake, Paul, make sure you contain that situation. Place the highest priority on this. It could be a national security issue. And find Admiral Stark!"

"Yes, sir. We'll confront the Admiral ASAP. I'll also post extra men at the gate. Call you as soon as we have him, sir? On your mobile?"

"No...that's unnecessary. I'll be there in a little while anyway. Just be sure..."

Layton paused.

"Yes, sir?"

"Be sure to put your best men on this. Don't try arresting Stark with rookies. Don't underestimate him."

"Yes, sir, General Layton."

Layton turned the cell phone off and considered what he had ordered. Arresting a decorated war hero and personal friend of the president could be political suicide.

God help us if Admiral Stark is not Phobos, he thought.

A moment later, reflecting on the situation, he reassessed that opinion. *Actually...God help us if he is.*

20—RAHU'S RAGE

"Of Course, the idea of [creating] part-human, part-animal chimeras...raises a host of ethical and safety issues.... Is a sheep with human [DNA] making up part of its brain no longer just a sheep?"
"'Humanised' Organs Can be Grown in Animals," *New Scientist*, 12-17-03

Moments before, over the incessant noise of the security alarm, Joe had shoved past the door and pulled Katherine into the hall. Now he looked at the guard who lay slouched on the floor. The man appeared to be unconscious. He stared down the corridor he'd followed earlier, then the opposite way.

"Cover your face," he shouted as he pushed Katherine to one side.

He focused on the wall between the door trim and ceiling and raised his fist, bringing it down swiftly, smashing the hall camera lens with the ball of his hand so abruptly that it made Katherine cry out, "What are you doing!"

"Closing somebody's eyes...now give me your hand."

"What?"

"The bracelet you're wearing has a locator chip in it," he said urgently. When she hesitated, he grabbed her forearm and withdrew the Ka-Bar fighting knife from the utility belt. She cringed as he slid the shiny blade between her wrist and the armband, cutting through the plastic bangle like butter. Tossing the bracelet into the room where she'd been held moments before, he pulled the door shut and saddled the knife.

"Stay with me," he ordered, and took off down the hall.

Running on fear and instinct, he realized the original plan was immaterial now. He had intended to acquire Sheri, reenter the service elevator, cut the medical bracelet from her wrist and leave it on the floor. The two of them would ride the elevator to Level Ten and, after getting off, command the elevator to resume movement to Level One. While the bracelet's beacon misled security to the southwest side of the complex, they'd move through the low security area to the northeast side of the facility. Phobos would join them there, ride a second elevator to the Dungeon, and escape through the Nephilim Training Access Tunnel to the forest outside, all in less than forty minutes.

That had been the plan, but only one thing was certain now—find and rescue Sheri, or die trying.

"Where are we going?" Katherine yelled above the alarm as they rounded a corner.

He made several more paces and stopped at the intersection where he'd gone left earlier. He looked both ways for anything that might indicate where Genetics was. He noted a long hallway leading to the maintenance elevator in one direction and a series of doors in the other. Moments ago, he'd heard strange voices or birds in this area. Now it was impossible to detect anything above the ceaseless bellow of the alarm.

"I'm looking for Genetics," he shouted back. "You're positive you don't know where it is?"

"Promise," she said, her radiant eyes soliciting his trust.

Although he had only just met her, he felt an unexpected bond with Katherine, not at all like a sister, more of a soul mate.

Besides her delicate appeal, there is subtle strength about her, he thought. *A resilience that undoubtedly sustained her in this dark and disturbing place.*

He told himself it was normal to feel this connection. They were both in the same vulnerable situation. It was something like the Florence Nightingale Effect, in reverse.

Yet he knew the truth was, in spite of the danger they were in, in spite of his singular mission to rescue Sheri, in spite of his fear of attachment and unwillingness to accept it, her beauty had caught him like a magnet.

As he stood there, considering his next move, the security alarm inexplicably shut off. The enemy was closing in. They wanted to hear his activity.

Now footsteps could be detected echoing up the adjoining stairwell. The "Down" light on the elevator was also glowing red. Different persons were coming from various directions.

Katherine was beside him, looking the opposite way when he grabbed her by the hand and spun her around so quickly that she literally flew off her feet. He maintained his grip and ran toward the corridor that led back to the room where she had been a prisoner, dragging her behind him.

As he approached the opposite end of the middle hallway, he heard a faint but distinct sound. Somebody groaning. He shoved Katherine against the wall and for a split second met her understanding eyes. He glanced at the PAL and found the energy level at eighty-two percent. Carefully, he peered around the corner. The guard was back on his feet, stumble-running toward them, his pistol drawn from its holster.

Feeling that the man hadn't seen him, he jerked back and calculated the distance between them. There was no time to wait. He took a deep breath and swept his foot into the hall with hyperagility, catching the soldier by surprise and dropping him face-first onto the floor.

The weight and inertia of the guard's body knocked Joe off keel too, and he tumbled, dropping the PAL.

Rolling over then staggering upright, the guard clutched his nose, which appeared to be broken. Blood gushed through his fingers as he started toward Joe.

Joe jumped to his feet just as the guard took a swing at him.

Easily avoiding the wildly thrown punch, Joe responded with a quick left hook that twisted the man, felling him like a timber. The back of the guard's head cracked against the concrete floor so loud that Joe thought it might have killed him. He was on the floor, frozen like a mannequin tossed from a pedestal, his narrow pupils glazed and rolling back, arms limp at his sides.

With his stomach nervous and knotted, Joe knelt beside the soldier and checked his breathing. Unconscious, maybe comatose, the man was barely alive. Joe picked up the PAL and the guard's service pistol and stepped over him, signaling Katherine to follow.

Running left, he veered from the area where the girls had been incarcerated into an unfamiliar and vacant hall, which immediately struck him as odd, maybe even poetic. The very level of Montero where Apol had insisted on the least amount of people for secrecy reasons now seemed to provide a unique opportunity to move about unnoticed. Even cameras were scarce on this level; he hadn't seen another one since the one he'd broken at the doorway.

Now as he turned the corner and came to an abrupt halt,

he discovered the real reason for the lack of cameras. Due to the accelerated plans following Phobos's urgent call that morning, he had not memorized the entire schematic and was unaware that this particular way led to a storage and records rooms area where nothing existed but a dead end. There was only one way to go: back the way he came.

Looking at Katherine, he half hoped she would offer some advice, perhaps a revelation that had just come to her from pieces of information she'd gathered about this place. She moved toward him with the natural grace of a ballet dancer, but offered only puzzled beauty. Seeing her need for him to act, he stepped to the corner and previewed the former hallway. Now he could hear somebody, presumably military police, and a brief but familiar squawking. *The bird things.*

He closed his eyes and reviewed Memory Group One. Memory Group Two. Nothing helpful. His thoughts raced as he considered what to do. Using the PAL and the MP's service revolver might disarm two, maybe three persons before somebody fired back. He also had explosives but worried about using them before he knew where Sheri was.

Then he remembered, *the Active Camouflage Shield.*

As Katherine watched inquisitively, he reached behind the load-bearing vest and jerked the thin, high-tech covering out. Unfolding the flexible shield, he motioned for her to follow him to the corner of the hall. He wrapped his free arm around her soft belly and pulled the "blanket" over the two of them. Flipping the toggle on the back of the ACS to the "on" position, he heard a diminutive chirp. Dozens of tiny cameras on the blanket's edge instantly picked up and analyzed the surrounding wall and floor textures, transmitting that data through fiber optics to the microprocessor. A second later the active matrix LCD skin projected a seamless facsimile around the two of them, matching local images and effectively rendering them invisible.

"Stay perfectly still," he whispered, drawing his right arm around her waist.

Down the hall there was movement at the T, then somebody talking about the unconscious guard.

"Sir, it's Davies. He has a pulse, but somebody's kicked the *%$&* out of him."

Joe felt Katherine's heart begin slamming in her chest. He pulled the cloak taut to her and smoothed the ACS wrinkles, whispering reassuringly into her ear, "Easy now, it'll be okay."

She clung to his stout arm.

It was, of course, a lie. Fitful images of his father's tortured body dumped like so much garbage alongside the road flashed precognitive glimpses of their future before his eyes. He breathed her perfume again, hoping for better, focusing on Sheri.

"All right...get him to the infirmary," Joe heard somebody say, probably the squad commander. "Johnson, you help,"

"Yes, sir."

"You two...go that way. Clark, you come with me."

"Yes, sir."

* * * * * *

Inside the ETV hangar, the specialist team assigned by General Layton to remove the Nibiruan Key was busy analyzing the ship's onboard system, trying to reverse what had started the night before, when Rahu, the phantasmagoric and genetically engineered monster built by Apol Leon, burst into the hangar shrieking like a banshee.

Staring at the brute with no less horror than if he had been gazing into the eyes of Satan himself, a young guard on the scaffolding yelled frantically into the alien ship, "Sarge! C'mere! Look at the size of this thing!"

He'd seen Nephilim before, but nothing as big and as frightening as this one. Its shoulders, broad as a pickup truck, shadowed beneath fierce jaws as large as an African lion's. Thick patches of orange-brown fur quivered like mats of dirty wire against its predatory salivating. Judging by its insane snarl and the clacking of its talons against the floor, the thing was on a mission.

The guard swallowed hard as the beastly eyes targeted the platform. The nightmare had spotted him. Fidgeting, he pulled his revolver from its holster and pointed it at the giant. "F-f-freeze!"

Rahu responded with a thunderous roar. The sound was territorial, like the gargled bellow of a hideously overgrown silverback gorilla.

Appearing to anticipate the firing of the pistol, Rahu bounded across the open floor before the guard could manage the trigger.

Even in his terror, the MP was amazed at the creature's supernatural speed. He raced to the edge of the scaffolding and looked out over the hangar floor. The Nephilim was gone.

Pushing the crowd aside and exiting the ETV, Sarge joined the young man at the railing. He paused, listening.

Beneath the vessel, the hull squeaked as if being scratched by dull knives.

The boyish guard trembled involuntarily.

An eerie presence...followed by rotten air drifted through the hangar.

The sound slowed. Stopped.

Bitter fetidness enveloped the platform until even the simple task of breathing became difficult.

Curious, several personnel poked their heads from the ETV.

Suddenly there was a *swisssh,* and from out of nowhere Rahu lurched from below, froze in midair, and landed on the young MP, rattling the steel structure and squashing the kid as flat as a pancake beneath his massive, ironlike heels. A gurgle leaked from the boy's collapsed head as one eye turned awkwardly toward Sarge before fading.

Standing nearly nine feet tall, Rahu loomed over Sarge, seething, wads of infected saliva dripping like thick strands of bile from his hungry fangs onto the destroyed soldier's face.

Sarge stared blankly into the monster's zenithal irises, as if he knew there was no hope. In a flash the creature grabbed him by the throat and threw him across the hangar. He slammed against a concrete wall fifty feet away, his life extinguished before his crooked heap could hit the floor.

As the curiosity seekers shrieked and ran back inside the ship, Rahu slapped his chest, wrenched the dead guard's head from beneath his feet, tossed the cranium into his mouth, and walked into the crowded vessel. A moment later the ETV vibrated with the sickening sounds of crunching bones and screaming. In the midst of the ship, the Enigma's tempo surged, fifty times stronger than before, fueled by the human suffering.

* * * * * *

The officer in pursuit of Joe stared at the end of the hallway, undoubtedly thinking his eyes were playing tricks on him. Forty feet away, a hand and six inches of arm had materialized from thin air. It hung there, as if suspended by invisible wire, holding what looked like a DustBuster. As he turned his weapon toward the anomaly, two brightly colored beams of light struck him in the face, and he fell to the floor convulsing.

A second soldier had been clearing the last hall when the squad commander dropped. Hearing it, he came around the corner and found the officer down, grunting and jerking. He drew up his weapon, turned full circle, quickly cleared the hallway, then knelt beside the commander. There was no sign of blood or weapons trauma.

"Sir," he whispered. "What's the matter?"

Seconds later powerful electricity from the PAL Joe was aiming slammed against his side, leveling him onto the carpet next to the other man.

Joe's bodiless face appeared, followed by his shoulders, Katherine's face, and finally their waists and legs. Joe dropped the ACS and moved across the hallway toward the incapacitated soldiers. He held the PAL and the service revolver forward, never once taking his sights off his targets.

* * * * * *

Katherine was standing beside Joe when without warning she said, "Sorry, guys."

Joe started to shush her—

"APOLOGY ACCEPTED," a robust voice at the other end of the hall boomed. "NOW PUT YOUR WEAPONS DOWN! DO IT NOW!"

A hulk in solid black BDUs had been stealthily positioned in the T cavity the whole time. He moved partway around the junction and assumed a standing combat position near the wall's edge. With his machine gun pressed firmly against his shoulder, he repeated the command without flinching. "DO IT NOW!"

Joe knew the soldier was serious, and that his weapon could deliver a massive amount of firepower with a single pull of the trigger. The M-249 had recently replaced the military's aging Browning Automatic rifles. This one housed 200 rounds of improved NATO 5.56 mm ammunition and could cut a man in half at this distance.

Wisely, Joe placed both guns on the floor and raised his hands in surrender. Katherine did the same.

* * * * * *

Not far away, outside Joe's view, the man with demon and animal genes in his chromosomes walked through his private laboratory to the cryopreservation area. Having been in the Dungeon when the alarm sounded and riding the elevator to Level Twenty after it shut off, he was unaware of Joe's presence.

He stood near the embryo freezer and withdrew the designated straw. The Super-Nephilim embryo had been in suspended animation since the day before—frozen at exactly 196 degrees centigrade. He placed the Devil's would-be host in the portable container and walked into the hall, distorting a Disney tune as he went.

"Oh, I whissstle while I work, do do do da da da da...I bet thisss is gonna hurt, la la la la la la la..."

21—FACE-TO-FACE WITH EVIL

"With this new knowledge comes new power, the ability to shape our fundamental form—and, one day, to better it. Within our lifetime, scientists say, we will see the advent of genetically enhanced human beings...."
"Supertots and Frankenkids," *Village Voice*, 04-25-03

Around the corner and down the hall from the service elevator, Joe and Katherine marched ahead of the Special Operations Forces soldier with their hands clasped on top of their heads. The warrior towered behind them like an oversized villain of an Arnold Schwarzenegger film. His exaggerated pectorals formed near-perfect rectangles against his black cotton shirt, while neatly pressed BDUs squeezed firmly around the remainder of his explicitly honed physique. The man could have been a poster boy for the Special Operation Forces, and from the way he maintained his finger on the M-249's trigger, Joe had the feeling he was proud of his steroid-enhanced anatomy and was itching for a chance to use it.

Nevertheless something else was bothering Joe more than the hulk in BDUs. A peculiar aura, like liquid death, was rolling toward them. He smelled it in the ozone, felt it on his skin; even the light in the hallway seemed muted with toxicity.

Moments before, he'd tried to shake it off, to tell himself it was just his imagination, that the very nature of these surroundings nurtured paranoia. Then he saw fear in Katherine's eyes, and heard something approaching...a faint, familiar tune, one he'd listened to a long time ago in a child's video. Something was wrong with the melody. Instead of eliciting the innocent joy the songwriter had intended, the vocals were diffusing a terrifying essence that infected the timbre and contaminated the idyllic verse.

Now as he considered it, something like a man came around the corner at the end of the corridor and started his way. The dark figure was *hissing* a song from *Snow White and the Seven Dwarfs*, swinging a container like a child carrying an Easter egg basket.

At first Joe wasn't sure if it was a man at all. The character seemed to have large, insectoid eyes, and for a brief moment he thought he saw a forked tongue dart from its scabby lips.

Then the body slowed and stared at him through ebony-tinted sunglasses.

A man, not a bug-eyed creature, stood before him, although his skin was indeed unusual, diseased and mottled like the desiccated hide of a discarded snakeskin.

Joe found himself transfixed by the figure as it resumed movement. An unexplainable sense of corruption, of doom, was all around.

"Yesss, I whistle while I work..."

The closer it came, the more troubling the song, less like a man than an animal dirge. Prickles of gooseflesh blossomed on Joe's neck as suddenly he recognized the voice. *That voice!* It was unmistakably the one he'd heard on the answering machine a few days ago...Apol Leon offering "a substantial finder's fee" for his fathers image. He'd remembered the name not only because Phobos and Dr. Corsivino referred to it, but also because it sounded like Apollyon—the King of the Bottomless Pit.

He glared at the man, his eyes moving slowly over him, sensing a dark melancholy.

Ceasing to sing, Apol stared at Joe and said dryly, "Well, well...who do we have here?"

Joe felt the same otherworldly tinge he had experienced when hearing the voice on his home recorder. The repugnance of the vibrato, the unearthly intonation of the vocal chords, it was as if a wraith in an abandoned graveyard was struggling to express itself. Joe half expected creepy crawlers to come tumbling out of his mouth.

"M-Mr. Leon!" the hulk stuttered, suddenly sounding much less confident than moments before. "S-Sir...we had a security breach! But I've apprehended the perpetrator!"

"Oh?" Apol sneered. "How fassscinating! I suppose you'd like an applause, yes?"

"Huh...well...I..."

"An internal memo to your superior requesting an invessstigation into the intruder's method of entry, and the prefatory and subsequent efficiency of your post during the break-in is more likely."

Hulkster dropped the defense and looked at the floor while, almost slithering, Apol moved forward and placed his forehead so close to Joe's that for a split second it appeared he was going to bite him.

A peculiar mark above Apol's brow caught Joe's attention. It looked vaguely like numbers. Bestial rage lurked somewhere beyond it, malevolence so complete as to be as lethal as cyanide. The acrimony melted the gallant expression from Joe's face as he tried not to think about what this jackal might be planning for his adopted sister.

"You're afraid of me, aren't you, boy," Apol chafed. "That's good."

The way he said "boy" caused Joe to bite his tongue. He *was* afraid, and of more than the man. He didn't know what. Something suppressed, like a two-edged sword cutting against the leathery canvas of his subconscious, trying to surface the answer. For reasons he couldn't understand, he wanted to thrust his rigid knuckles through Apol's throat and jerk *something* out of him. He knew better than to try under the circumstances.

* * * * * *

Apol sensed that the young man was an enemy of some sort, a threat to his plans, and hated him for it. He'd given himself to the goddess as a child and had worked too hard to have things messed up by a long-haired leatherneck. As nauseating as it had been, he'd played the part of American patriot for more than twenty years, keeping the government's secrets and pretending to follow their decisions. Now the Army of Darkness was at the gate. The archdemon Quetzalcoatl and the lesser "deities" of mythology had reestablished dominion over Mars. The rulers of wickedness had joined the demoness Hecate in Kosmos. The Nephilim army was entranced, awaiting his command, and the Master's body was ready to be implanted. Nobody would interrupt the Endgame now.

He glared menacingly at the young man and attempted to read his thoughts, an ability he'd acquired only recently, a result of his metamorphosis. The youth's mind was blocked.

Obviously a Christian. Sheri's brother, Joe, no doubt, trying to rescue her. That would explain why Katherine was with him. Evidently he'd gone after Sheri and found Katherine instead. *How chivalrous. How brave. How vain.*

He felt the thing inside him stir, and his eyes fell on Katherine's exquisite body. She was, of course, a fantasy of his. He'd often dreamed of clamping his strong hands around her soft, slender throat, and releasing her of the burden of living. He'd imagined the lovely bulge that would inflate her bloodshot eyes as she fought to survive, his fingers closing around her neck with convulsive delight. Several virgins before her had offered up such ecstasy, dying appropriately only after entertaining him with their pathetic and therefore delectable rage. Watching a woman's lithe limbs struggle until her anger gave way to tears, and finally to terror at the shock of imminent death, was second only to the pleasures of consuming her succulent eyes.

It was unfortunate he couldn't kill Katherine in this way. She was, after all, an unusually gifted dreamer. Undoubtedly she would have provided him with an abundance of revelations. Nevertheless, a promise was a promise. She was Rahu's indulgence to look forward to.

Drawing his leathery fingers through her silky, long blonde hair, he mocked her with the bestial singing voice. "Fairwell and ado to you, fair Spanish lady, fairwell and ado to you, lady of Ssspain..."

Katherine grabbed his hand and wailed, "I'm not Spanish and don't touch me!"

In a flash the hulk swung the butt end of the machine gun against the right side of her head and knocked her to the floor.

Joe spun to retaliate but the Hulkster kicked him in the chest with such force that he flailed backward onto the concrete aisle beside her. The quick-moving soldier jumped forward and aimed the M-249 at his forehead, feigning to pull the trigger.

Apol cheered, "My, my, this is all just ssso exciting!"

Stepping over and gazing down at the two of them, he added malignantly, "I simply love these kind of games! Don't you? I just wish I had time to enjoy them right now. Too bad I don't, and you want to know why?"

He patted the top of the embryo container and said matter-of-factly, "I've got a date with a sassssy redhead named Sheri...that's why."

Joe's face flushed red with anger, his hands curled into fists.

"Shoot the girl if he tries anything," Apol ordered the soldier.

Tightening his grip on the M-249, Hulkster pointed at Katherine.

Her hands rose instinctively.

Joe started to move in front of her, then froze.

Apol grinned. "Good boy. Now take them to the Dungeon and place them in Rahu's cage," he commanded Hulk.

The SOF warrior hesitated, then motioned with his weapon for the two of them to stand.

Apol caught the uncertainty. Perhaps the big soldier was questioning the appropriateness of the order. After all, Security had rooms for potential detainees. The hulkster might be feeling there were procedures to follow, protocols to adhere to.

"Don't worry, my inept friend," he said. "I'll take full ressponsibility for the prisoners. You don't need to worry about Rahu, either. He isn't home right now. He's on buisness for me. So hurry along and I'll join you in the

Dungeon momentarily. First, I have to deliver this genetic bouquet to my new love."

Then with visions of impending tyranny beyond what the others could imagine, Apol turned and walked off down the hall, embryo container in hand, his destination the secret corridor where Genetics was.

"Do do do da da da da, la la la la...."

22—TICKING TIME BOMB

"We often forget how much unites all the members of humanity. I occasionally think how quickly our differences worldwide would vanish if we were facing an alien threat from outside this world."
Former President Ronald Reagan, in a speech to the UN,
09-21-87

During the moments that passed since the hallway encounter with Apol Leon, Joe had become sorely troubled by the idea that they were going to be locked in Rahu's cage. *That creature could return, and we can't be there if it does.*

If the being's physical characteristics compared to the skeletal remains he'd found in the ravine, the Nephilim or Bigfoot or whatever it was would be impossible to defeat without sophisticated firepower, and he didn't have his vest or weapons anymore, thanks to Hulkster, who was carrying them.

Now as they approached the elevator to the Dungeon, he looked beyond Katherine and noticed the "Up" light above the entry doors glowing. Hulkster didn't seem to care about it, punching the button repeatedly, no doubt agitated by the humiliation he'd received from Apol Leon. He spat on the floor, keeping the M-249 fixed on them, and moved back a few feet.

Joe glanced at the formidable opponent and considered making his move. He vacated the plan a second later, deciding it would be smarter to wait until they were inside the cab where the closed-in quarters might inhibit the big man's movements.

I'll need every advantage I can get over this superior foe. Plus there's Katherine's safety to think about now, too.

Once inside, I'll surprise him, beat him to the floor and recover my vest and weapons.

Then I'll move out and find Apol Leon. I'll kill that insidious fiend if he doesn't surrender Sheri immediately!

Or perhaps I could hold him as prisoner and demand a hostage exchange? Is that possible? Probably not.

At least my hands are unbound. That makes surprise feasible.

Just then the elevator pinged, and something inside it moved.

A graphic image of mutants swarming through the cab's doors and tearing them apart flashed through Joe's mind. He recalled the dreadfully enlarged skull, the baseball-size eyes rotting in the ravine.

The gates hummed and swished opened.

There was a blue flash and a muffled *pop*.

He ducked instinctively.

Katherine screamed.

Groaning behind them, Hulkster fell backward in the middle of the aisle, blood trickling from a small hole in the center of his forehead.

Diluted gray smoke was still coming from the barrel of the silencer-equipped Walther P-38 as Phobos stepped out of the cab. He was drenched with perspiration and fixed Joe with a slightly wild look. "I figured something went wrong—we're running out of time. We need to get out of here—quick!"

* * * * * *

Sheri watched as Apol Leon walked into the Genetics room and handed a container to the biggest of the Grays. He spoke to the chalky creature in quick, excited sentences that sounded more like clicks and squeaks to her than language. *Bird-speak*, she considered nervously.

The Gray took the container and placed it on the table in front of them, then floated sideways and pulled a hose from a ceiling attachment. The creature's back was to her, shielding what it was doing. She preferred this angle to the frontal view anyway. Every time the thing looked at her, its opaque insectoid eyes glazed over and she'd see herself through *it*.

Please, God, don't let it look at me, not again.

Now Apol was watching each move the entity made. When finally he appeared satisfied, he turned to Sheri's bedside and studied her.

She was as naked as the day she was born. Humiliated and embarrassed, she started to look away, then suddenly found herself glaring defiantly instead at the man in black. She didn't know where the strength came from, only that somehow the daughter of Lieutenant Colonel Clarence Ryback—a decorated war hero—would not go passively into the night. The thick leather bands that strapped her to the gurney could keep her from desperate heroics, but she would honor her father's memory before dying if by no other means than spiritual and emotional resistance.

* * * * * *

Placing his hand on the polished bed rail, Apol drank in Sheri's apprehension. While death and sex were the primary consequences of power, he was not interested in having her physically. Unlike other acquisitions he'd collected in the past, she was not here for that. Her pale blue eyes, not measurably distinct in color or shape than others he'd consumed, seemed to look straight through him, to glow in a way that was as distant and as unfamiliar to him as the well of the cosmos. If he were merely a cannibal, he would have found them quite succulent, a tempting cuisine.

Truth was, he was more than a cannibal, he was an eater of souls, a devourer of divinations. Because of his incredible success both in the military and the spiritual world, because he had been selected as the predacious father of the Beast, because he was patient with the need to assimilate her revelations, the quality of her eyes offered more than the opportunity to taste her terror or to corrupt her unpolluted innocence. She was key to infiltrating the enemy's intelligence in order to later manipulate and control them through psychological warfare. Once absorbed, he'd know what she knew about her conservative religion. That was certainly more vital than sex or a couple of fine hors d'oeuvres.

Of course her first role would be to serve as incubator, a richly amusing two-month period in which her insides would be invaded and ruined. While the actual purpose of this was the gestation of the special zygote, some retribution could also be made against young women in general—the ones that got away, the devious, conceited, competitive creatures that taunted him during his youth.

More than once while in military training, female cadets

had brushed against him during drill, mocking him with their contemptuous eyes, intentionally spreading their pheromones in order to disturb his concentration. He'd wanted desperately to injure them, to torture and make them pay. He'd dreamed of flamboyantly destroying their bodies, then collecting their eyes for display in a sacred museum where he and other deities could enjoy private devotions. He'd even gone so far as to design what the dedicatory plaques would look like upon which the history of each contributor would be engraved—the identity, hair color, height, and circumstances by which each offender was acquired. Were he lucky enough to collect tears from their lacrimal sacs, these would be embedded in tiny glass containers memorializing their final miseries. Although no portions of the body other than eyes were necessary for divination, it would be interesting and entirely appropriate to include mortal remains where instruments of vision were collected as trophies—hides, eyelids, lips, and shellacked cheeks propped about and prominently exhibited in artsy, inventive ways.

Regrettably, the strict regimen at the academy had never allowed time for the development of the concept. Though, over the years when he could, he had treated himself to small, collectable parts anyway, momentos he could store in safe places, to look at when uninspired. Now, as his triumph was about to be sealed, he'd revisit the idea of the ocular museum. He doubted he'd actually have time for it, but it never hurt to dream.

He leaned over, cupped Sheri's face in his hands, drew his warty tongue slowly above her left eye, then whispered through his decaying breath, "I've got a little errand to tend too, Hon, but I'll be right back, I promissse. Be brave for me while our big Gray friend over there implants a little gift in you while I'm gone. Okay?"

* * * * * *

A memory flashed through the back of Joe's mind. "This one means the most to me," he recalled his dad saying that happy spring morning so long ago.

It was his twelfth birthday, and he had been opening presents for several minutes, eagerly anticipating the Daisy BB gun from the Western Auto variety store on Main Street, when his dad walked into the room holding a small box. "I saved this for your twelfth birthday," he had said, smiling. "Next year you'll be a teenager, and I want you to keep your priorities straight."

Joe remembered how eagerly he had ripped into the package. He couldn't imagine a gift his usually stoic father would be excited about. *Maybe it's a case of ammo for my new gun,* he had thought. Yet inside the box he'd found something quite different—his father's Marine Corps Good Conduct Medal.

At first, the gift was puzzling. Then his dad explained that while every honor he had received during his thirty years of service was important—the Silver Star and Purple Heart awarded following the battles of Taejon and Inchon in Korea, and others—the humbler Good Conduct Medal was his favorite.

"See, Son," he had said. "Every battle I participated in and each medal and ribbon I received are very, very important to me. Though the truth is, I was ordered to each of those campaigns. I didn't have a choice of whether or not to go. The Good Conduct Medal is different. It's awarded on a selective basis to enlisted members of the Marine Corps for good behavior and faithful service even when one is not following orders."

Still perplexed, Joe heard the old man simplify it for him. "It means I did the right thing when nobody was making me."

Then he understood. His dad wanted him to have a symbol of the things he cherished most in life—virtue, honor, morality, integrity. And even though the glorious air rifle was eventually given to him that day, he'd grown over the years to appreciate the more important gift—the heirloom that reminded him that doing the right thing is always important.

That was his intention now.

"Not without Sheri," he said, looking at Phobos. "I'm not leaving without her."

Phobos pointed at Katherine. "I thought she was Sheri."

Looking mesmerized by the dead SOF soldier sprawled in a pool of blood in the middle of the floor, Katherine was holding her hand over her mouth.

"She's a comrade," Joe said as he picked up the vest Hulkster had taken from him. He pulled the load-bearing apparel around his chest and buckled it tight, grabbed the M-249 with one hand and the PAL with the other, adding, "Katherine, meet Phobos. Phobos, meet Katherine. Now you two get out of here. I'll find Sheri and join you if I can."

Phobos shook his head. "No time. In a little while the escape route won't even exist and you'd never make it out the front door alive."

"What do you mean, the escape route won't exist?"

"Take my word for it, it's now or never."

Phobos looked at Joe as if he knew he would be stubborn. He glanced at his watch, appeared to be making a quick mental calculation, then said, "Do you know where Sheri is?"

"Genetics," Joe said, looking at Katherine for confirmation.

Phobos glared down the hall. "She's in genetics!?"

"According to Katherine."

"That maniac devil is really trying to do it, isn't he..."

"What?"

Stepping over the soldier's body, careful not to slip in the expanding sea of blood, Phobos gazed down the corridor. A sharp edge came over his eyes, as if he were staring down a dismal breezeway to Hell. After a moment he whispered, "Never mind, just follow me."

Joe glanced over his shoulder to make sure Katherine heard him, then pursued Phobos along the corridor, around three corners to the threshold of an unimpressive, unmarked metal door.

Phobos slid an identification card through a slot in the wall and watched as an alloy drawer opened beside it. He placed his hand on the apparatus and whispered to Joe, "Safety off?"

"I'm ready," Joe answered, then thumbed the safety on the machine gun to be sure.

A moment later Phobos pulled his hand from the biometric device. Following a metallic *click*, he pushed the door open and peeked inside. The hallway was empty.

"It's not far," he whispered, quick-stepping through the opening. He placed his back against the wall and held the precision made 9mm automatic in front of him with both hands. Katherine followed, then Joe, who assumed a similar defensive position against the opposite wall. Joe was familiar with the posture—standard military procedure when clearing a corridor—stay quiet and sweep the openings, returning your back to the wall so that only three sides need protection and nobody gets behind you.

Moving gingerly along the fifty-yard route, they soon arrived at a set of doors marked "GENETICS." Phobos held his finger to his lips to emphasize stealth, then began checking the clip on his weapon.

Suddenly there was wailing coming from inside the room, like shrieks from possessed pterodactyls vibrating through the walls. *The birds!*

In a flash, Phobos kicked the door so hard that it flew open. Inside, Joe saw six gray *things* descending on a young woman strapped to a gurney. Was it Sheri!?

"The blood of Jesus be against you!" Phobos shouted, and the lights to the building went out.

* * * * * *

Glowing with brilliancy so white as to be imperceptible to human eyes, the beautiful, silver-skinned herald flew across the eastern horizon toward the awaiting angel assembly.

Justice looked thoughtfully at the approaching messenger. Even he could appreciate the glorious contrail of hyperdimensional particles flowing out from behind the being, down into the camp.

Swift watched too, as did the myriad of other warriors, as the luminous presence drifted from the fourth dimension into the third, alighting atop the cloud. The herald's wings ceased rushing and folded gently to his sides. Then he walked forward and held out a golden scroll. Justice, the host's commander, took the parchment and unrolled it. He paused for a second, then shouted, "IT'S TIME!"

At Mt. Hood Evangelical Seminary, the prayer group sensed the mystical event. While the ominous clouds outside had grown larger and blacker by the hour, a sudden presence of light and peace flooded the modest chapel, compelling the Bible students to depths of intercession and praise unlike anything they'd known before.

None of them could explain what each of them had felt. It was as if the small crowd was abruptly visited, strengthened, and joined to an unseen yet tangible upheaval. They were inexplicably endowed with what to say, how to say it, and when.

Simultaneously across Portland, startled Christians leapt from furniture, from behind desks at work, from cars they had quickly pulled to the roadside, as visions of glorious beings passing over the earth flashed before their minds.

Then without warning, people everywhere began to plead for the blood of Jesus to cover them.

Off the Columbia River, at the north end of a small alcove, a single candle flickered inside the tiny bedroom of a nearly forgotten cabin. Too tired to continue reading, the old man placed his Bible over his racing heart and clutched the tattered anointing cloth his wife Ruby had sewn. At his feet, Tater sniffed the air, hackles raised, snarling.

23—REMOTE VIEWING

"The ultimate danger of [biological] technology comes from its power to change the nature of human beings by the application of genetic engineering to human embryos." Freeman Dyson, Physicist for Princeton Institute, *Cosmiverse*, 09-10-01

Donald Pritchert counted to five and threw the main breaker back on. A second longer and the research facility's emergency backup generator would have started, resulting in a dispatch of security and maintenance crews. His hope was that both departments would perceive the event as a temporary utility failure. Phobos would know better. The blinking lights were a predetermined signal. He had just enough time to safely depart any level of Montero and to exit the Nephilim Training Access Tunnel to the forest outside.

Donald released the breaker arm and returned to the maintenance corridor, then to the site of the nuclear warhead. It was hidden behind a row of furnaces, next to the body of a dead scientist laying facedown on the floor. The SAMM's digital clock read 43:41 minutes to detonation.

* * * * * *

Desperation more than courage pulled Joe like potent gravity into the darkness. Even as the lights came on and his eyes adjusted to the details, the trace glow of the vanishing phantoms—like psychic shadows searching for ways to rush through spectral dimensions—lingered before him. The pungent smell of decaying flesh gripped the air as he turned the M-249 along the walls, fingering the trigger, fearful that the jittering in his belly might give way to unrestrained machine gun spray. Finally, satisfied that the *things* were gone, he lowered the weapon and moved toward Sheri.

An astringent taste filled his mouth as he found her isolated stare.

"Sheri," he said softly, downplaying his own fear, knowing restraint and not alarm was what she needed most. "It's okay...don't cry now...I'm here to take you home."

He carefully pulled the gag from her mouth. Her distant and unfamiliar expression conveyed what he already knew—they were up against something far more sinister than he had prepared for. Even now, malevolent beings could be watching them through shadows, angles in the walls, the very thought of which caused gooseflesh to crawl on his skin. He felt a superstitious terror he'd known only as a child, a nervous dread crouching deep inside him like a cornered, frightened boy, waiting for a single opportunity to throw off its pretensive guard and run. Yet circumstances mandated he remain calm, be a marine, protect Sheri for as long as was necessary, then he could abandon his wits; heck, maybe even go crazy and kill somebody, like Apol Leon, for instance.

He pulled the Ka-Bar fighting knife from its holster and looked at the floor so as not to embarrass Sheri, then began cutting the thick leather bands padlocking her to the table. Katherine was already there, covering her with a hospital gown she'd found on the end of the bed. Smiling sympathetically, she brushed Sheri's hair from her face and whispered calmly, "We're here now, everything's going to be okay."

Apparently in shock, Sheri began whimpering, "W-what...were...those...things..."

"It was *them*," Phobos said from across the room. "And by now they're alerting the others."

Joe glanced at him. "Them? What do you mean?"

"Powerful, alien devils. They come from another dimension—from what some in the consortium call 'the darkness'—to deceive and enslave mankind."

* * * * * *

As Sheri gazed silently upward, Phobos shifted his attention back to the corner of the room. The grays had dematerialized there like ectoplasm through a fantastic-spinning void. He wasn't sure what he would have done even if he had caught the fiends, but the simple act of their fleeing had invigorated his nerve. He clutched the crucifix in his pocket and reminded himself to be careful; overconfidence against such beings could be fatal, even if he did understand spiritual warfare as taught by Father Malina.

Continuing a silent prayer for the name of Jesus to cover them, he glanced around the lab. Sheri was his primary concern now. Her awkward position in the stirrups and the contents of the room told him everything he needed to know. The Grays had intended to impregnate her with Apol's experiment.

He made a mental inventory of the various high-tech gear. Near an oversized microscope, a mechanical arm held a rubber hose connected to a pump, a system he believed was used for injecting DNA into eggs. In the middle of the table a monitor for observation sat next to a tray of operating utensils. The polished tools looked undisturbed, but the object next to them didn't. Eight inches tall and approximately twenty inches in diameter, the portable embryo container's lid was open. Fatalism rushed his imagination at the sight of it. If the beast had been transferred here and implanted in the girl, she would have to undergo emergency abortion, hysterectomy, or even be destroyed.

His hands were shaking for the first time today as he held his breath and looked into the receptacle. Midway down, in a straw with proper identification, was the embryo.

Thank you, God, *thank you.*

There was no doubting whose body the zygote was meant to be. The specimen's key, written in Apol's own handwriting, was actually coded 666, the number of the Beast. He replaced the lid and breathed a conspicuous sigh of relief, then turned to the others.

"Okay people, the blinking lights were a signal to me. We've got to get out of here...now."

* * * * * *

As Apol stepped from the elevator into the ETV hangar, not much was left of the men General Layton had sent to dislodge the Nibiruan Key. A lone survivor inside the alien craft was screaming. Blood-curdling, imploring screams. It sounded like he was being ripped apart, chewed up, devoured piece by piece.

Apol rushed to the craft to catch a glimpse of the entertainment, but was too late. By the time he left the scaffolding and entered the vessel, froth was dripping like sludge from Rahu's wiry beard, but there was no sign of the man. The giant was on his haunches beneath the blue-red glow of the Enigma, his blood-soaked appearance looking particularly depraved in the poor visibility. Fragments of several other corpses lay beneath his feet, and bits of hair and flesh were scattered nearby.

And something else...

For the first time in over eight hours, the Enigma, next to him, was silent. Other than Rahu's heavy breathing, the ambience inside the Extra Terrestrial Vehicle had taken on the characteristics of a motionless tableau, like the single frame of a gory B-rated movie.

Apol knew the only reason the thumping ovoid would be absent from the Enigma in this way was if the Ahriman Gate had opened. The Army of Darkness was at the portal. Satan's invasion was imminent.

"Follow me to the Dungeon," he slurred gaily as he combed Rahu's bloody mane with his desiccated fingertips. "It's time for that little treat I promisssed you. I'll bet Katherine's juicy with fear by now."

* * * * * *

"That's exactly right," Katherine said, turning from Sheri and agreeing with Phobos. "They're coming from the shadows to enslave and rule over us; I've seen it in my dreams. They have a king over them. He's the Dragon that rises up from the sea."

Joe, still cutting the thick leather bands from Sheri's legs, found Katherine's comments particularly disturbing, as though from somewhere deep inside, he knew the beautiful young woman was onto something.

"Phobos," he asked, "where did you learn to use the name of Jesus against those gray creatures?"

"Father Malachi Malina taught us," Phobo said, studying how far Joe was on the straps. "And by the way, there's no point in continuing the secrecy. My name is John Stark."

Joe paused, then, "That would be 'Admiral Stark' according to the uniform," he said.

"You're right."

"So...*Admiral Stark*, who's *us*?"

"What?"

"You said Father Malina taught *us* to use the name of Jesus against the beings. Who's *us*?"

"The consortium. The members of Operation Gadfly."

"Does it work every time, the name of Jesus, I mean?"

"As far as I know, it's a matter of faith in Christ. True believers don't have to put up with aliens. They're actually demons, you know."

* * * * * *

Stark allowed Joe to consider what he had said, then, knowing where they would be later, added, "But the Nephilim downstairs are a different problem. We created them. We're not certain how they'll react."

Sheri blinked rapidly, then whimpered, "Y-you ...mean ...I didn't have...to put up...with those things...in...my head...?"

Stark approached her. The beings might have explored her psyche for intel. Quietly he asked, "Did the Grays penetrate your thoughts?"

She looked confused and uncertain. Then, without

improving her deliberation, replied, "It...it was more like...they injected their own."

"You mean it seemed as if you were looking through somebody else's eyes?"

"Y-yes...yes...I could see the room around me...as though...as though...I were one of them."

"It's called remote viewing. They couldn't penetrate your thoughts, so they showed you theirs. It's a mind game they play. They get you to consider their meditations first, in hope you'll open up later and invite them back in. So, in answer to your question, no, you didn't have to put up with that."

Her eyes became distant again as she started to drift away. "I...I...wish I had...known...I wish..."

Stark knew from Father Malina that the best thing for postabduction therapy is to keep a person grounded in God, faith, and family. Placing his large hand on hers, he reassured her, "Don't worry, they'll never bother you again, I'll see to that. In the meantime, if the memories trouble you...."

He pulled the crucifix from his pocket and placed it in her hand, folding her fingers gently over it as her eyes returned to his, seeking hope.

"Y-yes?"

"Rebuke them in Jesus' name, and they'll have no choice but to flee."

"But...but...why did...." Her voice broke again.

"Why did God allow you to be brought here in the first place?"

She nodded, her cheeks flushing red, her eyes lowering demurely, flooding with tears of shame.

Katherine grabbed her by the arm. "He brought you here so I could be rescued!"

"Not only that," Stark said, holding up the embryo container. "If you hadn't come to this lab, neither would I have, and I wouldn't have found this."

"W-what is it?" she stammered.

"Only the consortium's number one target. This thing could have represented the end of everything good in this world, but now we have it, to hold as hostage if necessary. Because you were here, Sheri, mankind might get a second chance."

She searched his face, as if looking for sincerity.

"I guess God just likes using virgins to destroy the Devil's plans," Stark added with a wink. He could hardly believe the embryo had been delievered to them this way.

* * * * * *

Stark's comment struck Joe as odd. He knew it was a veiled reference to the mother of Jesus and not only to Sheri's situation, but this was a side of the admiral he'd never seen before, albeit a welcome side, however Catholic. The rugged military persona was softer now, even fatherly. It was helping Sheri, which made his next question particularly difficult.

"What did you mean when you said the Nephilim downstairs could be a bigger problem, Stark? Won't spiritual warfare work against them too?"

Just then the last strap Joe was cutting broke through. Stark patted Sheri's hand, then motioned for Joe to step away from the girls. The two huddled a few feet away. He whispered, "I don't know. They're not entirely demonic like the Grays are. They're transgenic—a mixture of human, animal and alien. We may have to fight them on the physical level, like ancient Israel did."

Joe thought about that. "How many of them are there?"

"Approximately one hundred thousand worldwide. Ten thousand at each facility."

This was the first time Joe had heard how large the giant army was. It startled him. "The consortium can engage a number that big?"

"Not if they get outside the facilities we can't. The Nephilim have to be destroyed where they are. That's my primary mission today, and the reason we need to get moving."

"So you plan to destroy this facility? You have the power to do that?"

"It's already started. From the flickering of the lights, I'd say we have forty minutes to leave. After that, we're in big trouble."

"I understand," Joe said grimly, and turned toward the girls.

Katherine was helping Sheri off the bed into the gown. She tied the cords on the back of the garment, being sure to overlap the flaps as far as they would go, then stepped around to face her.

When Stark saw what Katherine was doing, he pulled his coat off and gave it to her, which she placed around Sheri before wrapping the single bedsheet around herself.

Glancing at his weapons vest, Joe realized he had nothing to offer the girls. There didn't appear to be any sources of covering elsewhere in the room, either, typical of what he'd learned of Apol thus far. His subjects were animals without the least need of human comforts.

24—PANDEMONIUM'S ENGINE

"Scientists say they will attempt to create a new form of life in the laboratory.... If the plan works, the...manmade [thing] will begin feeding and dividing to create [something] unlike any known to exist..."
"Scientists to Try New Life," *Fox News*, 11-22-02

Where hope lingers not.

A probing force pressed tightly against the dark side of the Ahriman Gate as demons, large and small, gargoylian and beautiful, drew swords and held them aloft. Strange, ancient machines, designed for supernatural warfare, floated behind the wicked troops inside the timeless cavity. With unified depravity unknown to men, the abysmal life forms inched the dreadful mechanisms forward. Their determination was as deep and as immutable as the well that had spawned them.

Gazing back with equal resolution was a different wall, one of righteousness—Justice, Swift, and the hosts of Heaven. The angels would not move. They could not. Not until the act of righteousness was done. They believed it would happen. Joe would do the right thing when the time came. They had to believe he would.

* * * * * *

Sheri leaned against the elevator's stainless steel wall, closed her deep blue eyes and hoped the subtle vibrations of the systems hum and vague quivering of the descending floor would subdue some of her fears. She was breathing harder than usual, still clutching the crucifix John Stark gave her in the Genetics room. Although miraculously she was already forgetting some of the terrifying details of the Grays, she worried that the sulfuric scent that still lingered on her skin from the laboratory was calling to them, as if a diabolical symmetry existed between the lab, the Grays, and the forces of Hell.

She adjusted her position against the elevator panel and stared at her three companions. Katherine was behind Joe, holding the back of his belt. Perhaps she planned to use him as a shield in case of serious trouble. Or maybe this was her way of keeping up if he ran. Whatever the reason, Sheri knew her clutch was about more than safety. Several times already she'd caught her staring at him in ways girls do only when they're attracted to a man. Katherine even blushed once when she thought Sheri saw her, another telltale sign.

Closer to the door was the mysterious man named John Stark. Composed, strong, decisive. The way he carried himself reminded her of her late father. His set jaw, his square shoulders, his graying hair cut short around his serious expression. He seemed at once to be passive yet determined, as if he could survey any situation and immediately take command.

And then there was Joe, standing there like Rambo with his machine gun held firmly forward. Inside this elevator, hundreds of feet below ground, surrounded by minions of hostility and death, she was glad now more than ever to have such an overprotective marine brother.

Suddenly the elevator made a clanking noise and thudded to a halt.

She felt the black dregs of fear erupting inside her.

A recording blared sharply through the intercom, "Warning! Now entering restricted area!"

Her gaze darkened. She dread what lay ahead, her imagination telling her that creatures of the abyss, lurking outside the cab, were ready to jump through the opening to tear them apart.

The synthetic voice repeated, "Warning! Now entering restricted area!"

She focused on Joe and saw him tighten his grip on the machine gun.

Somewhere, concealed levers squeaked, and the elevator's doors slid apart.

Through the opening came banshee whines from indiscernible shadows, goblin groans fluttering upward in torment, amber glowing reflections of flaming sulfur molding like eyes glittering from nether regions, as the devilish black mouth of the subterranean gorge brought her face-to-face with the transgenic new millennium.

* * * * * *

The fetid smells of rotting flesh and sewage wafted into the elevator with such force that Joe's ability to breathe was temporarily halted. He winced and wanted to turn away. Katherine gasped behind him, "Oh...my goodness...nasty."

Plunging a finger to his lips, Stark held his breath and motioned for the others to quickly and silently follow him into the man-made hell.

They stepped through the threshold into the bitter Dungeon, beneath foggy shades of bluish green-gray that cast eerie specters across the jagged sixty-foot ceiling.

A disturbing ambience crawled on Joe's skin, as scabrous and plutonic as any scene he'd seen in a Stephen King novel.

Except for concrete floors and fabricated steel structures, the entire chamber looked ancient, as if Titans, thrown from the burning cores of Tartarus after fighting Zeus to a draw, had hewed the cavernous opening with the hundred-handed monsters in their quest to escape the underworld.

The main corridor, wide as a two-lane highway, felt claustrophobic nevertheless.

To the left was an operating theater. Beyond that an enclosure with barred windows housing sophisticated-looking equipment. In the other direction a series of cell-like cages cut succinctly inside the cavern's wall. These extended southerly for approximately one hundred feet. Beyond them, a high-pitched carillon rang out, as though somebody was hammering something in harmony with a deeper monotonous throb.

Automated activity. Pandemonium's engine.

Stark nudged Joe, tapped his finger beneath his right eye, and pointed, directing Joe's attention to the middle of the room. As Stark's hand glided silently through the air, emphasizing one end of the courtyard to the other, Joe barely saw through the somber haze of the expanse to what he was pointing at—rows of sliding doors attached to long lines of gigantic metal cages extending floor to ceiling. Brightly colored signs marked two rows in yellow on black—Quadrant One and Quadrant Two. The pens appeared to be constructed of immense cylindrical bars, like zoo stalls for larger animals. On either side of the streets, at approximately six feet from the floor, feeding troughs spanned the length of the exteriors.

As Joe struggled to discern what looked like tall statues standing up inside the massive enclosures, something to his right moved and emitted an eerie, guttural growl.

Twenty yards away, clutching immense titanium bars, an incomprehensible behemoth squatted inside its dusky cell. The thing studied Joe from the darkness, its amber eyes burning as hot as a werewolf's on the night of the full moon. In spite of the dismal, muggy air, Joe had no difficulty discerning the lathering hatred of the monster's facial demeanor. Its fangs were as hideous as long steel spikes, curled dangerously inward beneath a macabre and gaping snarl.

He shuddered. For the second time in only the last ten minutes, Joe felt they were in immediate and incalculable danger. The boogeyman was real...and it lived beneath Montero.

The beast let out a second threat, full-throated this time, so unnatural and loud that the corridor seemed to vibrate beneath its intense and menacing squall. It sounded like something between a gorilla, a human, and a pig.

An icy gasp leaked from Sheri's trembling lips as she placed a hand over her mouth and took a step away.

Joe moved in front of her and raised the M-249.

The thing stood up. It had to be at least ten feet tall.

A moment of intense silence passed as the ruddy creature's chest swelled in assessment of the foursome. It raised its muzzle and tested the air. The admiral's scent was probably familiar to it, but not Joe's or the girls'. It flexed and shook, as if feeling the exhilarating rage of animal appetite whetting its ancient palate, then stared at Joe again.

* * * * * *

In spite of Stark's familiarity with the creatures, he knew no power they possessed could stop the hell of the Mega-Nephilim if they got outside their containment. Signaling the others to follow, he made brief eye contact with the caged monster, then turned and headed north, toward the rendezvous point where Donald Pritchert was supposed to be waiting.

As he led the gang away, the level of fear he'd just felt surprised him. He could only imagine how spooked the three young people behind him must be. He studied the abrupt change in his self-control for the moment, until fifty yards on, with shadows spreading like ink from the murky overhead crag, his thoughts returned to the larger meaning of their mission.

Now a set of train tracks formed a casual turn onto the street they were following. Stepping over the rails, he watched as Joe jogged up beside him. Katherine, having released Joe's belt a few seconds before, was holding Sheri's hand now, pulling her to keep up.

* * * * * *

In the distance, the big monster howled again, differently this time, as if calling to others. The creature's reverberation played tricks on Joe. In every darkened corner, black-cloaked beings sprang from the ceiling and scurried over the floor after them. When he looked forward, imaginary hands clawed from the shadows, grasping at their legs to catch and hold their squirming bodies until their killers could arrive. He had never been afraid of the dark or paranoid of the unknown, but this was the first time he'd caught a glimpse of Hell, so it was natural when he nearly squeezed the machine gun's trigger against the outline of a man standing wraithlike near a bend in the road ahead.

"That's Pritchert," Stark cautioned as Joe swung the weapon to fire. "He's our ticket out of here. He has the access code we need to get outside."

Squinting, Joe whispered between breaths, "Pritchert? Donald Pritchert?"

"You know Donald?"

"He's the guy I was supposed to meet upstairs a couple weeks ago. I was to give him the image, the stone head my father found."

"The Nibiruan Key?"

"From the home of the Annunaki, according to Corsivino."

"Yes, well, that's the title given to it by Montero's researchers. It turned out to be the key to the ETV, anyway."

This time it was Stark who glanced back at the Nephilim depot. The beast was quiet now. Stark appeared to be studying the area between the caged monsters and them, then continued. "Besides turning that blasted spaceship on, it seems to have actually enabled the Enigma to obtain a space-time vortex. At least that's what the executive brass believes. As for me, I think it's opened the gates of Hell."

Joe remembered Corsivino discussing a dimension-machine that existed between four columns inside the ETV. He'd called it the "Enigma" and said it was able to manufacture a multidimensional gateway to Heaven or Hell. Joe wanted to ask Stark about it, but knew this was not the time or place. There would be plenty of opportunity to discuss such things once they got outside, if they got outside.

Ahead, Pritchert pranced like a bladder-bloated child in the middle of the tracks. He was holding an item about the size of a Palm Pilot, although Joe doubted that's what it was. He motioned excitedly for the group to hurry, then turned and disappeared around a blind spot in the tracks. The group raced forward, anxious to catch him and to put as much space between themselves and the Nephilim as possible.

As they arrived at the bend in the road, they found Pritchert standing next to the access tunnel entry. He was about Joe's size, darker hair, slimmer features, attired in nice clothes—sweater, tie, dress pants, and loafers—holding the Palm device against an illuminated panel. He was plugging it in when he glanced up, half smiled at the others, then continued what he was doing.

Joe could see the path they were following made a wide arch at this juncture and joined a second set of tracks at an uneven Y in the road ahead. One set of rails entered a cavernous area occupied by parked boxcars while the other continued into the access tunnel beneath a mammoth set of gates. He thought these looked like the Wicked Witch of the East's legs stretched out below Dorothy's house in the Land of Oz.

Now he could hear Pritchert begging, "C'mon baby...please," and watched as the casually attired man typed anxiously on the handheld device. Above Pritchert, an unambiguous advisory, partially covered in spiderwebs, warned in three languages: NO UNAUTHORIZED PERSONNEL BEYOND THIS POINT!

Suddenly a gear snapped at both ends of the gateway and the massive assembly unlocked.

"Yes!" Pritchert said, swishing his free hand through the

air like a high-school enthusiast. He unplugged the equipment and gazed uneasily at Stark.

"Problem with the code?" Stark whispered judiciously, studying Pritchert's perspiring face. "Looked like you were having trouble."

The hand-sized contraption Pritchert was holding could override biometric locks. It belonged to Montero Security and was used in cases of malfunction. Operation Gadfly had "borrowed" the device for the day.

"Uhm...not really," he said.

"Then everything's in order?"

"Yes, sir."

"Good."

Walking forward, Stark pushed the gate open far enough for the group to squeeze through. "Let's move," he said.

Joe placed his arm around Sheri and motioned for Katherine to join her between the men. Pritchert squeezed in next to the girls, and Joe felt him trembling. Under the circumstances, he wouldn't interpret the man's terror as weakness.

* * * * * *

Five floors above, in the ETV hangar, the service elevator dipped beneath the massive weight of the grotesque creature. The being contemplated its exceptional existence, and what it would be like to command an entire legion of singularly obedient but biologically inferior Nephilim—the police force of the new global community.

The thing was not accustomed to such grandiose meditations. Usually its thoughts were...cybernetic...a mirror of those imposed on it by the stalwart entity masquerading as Apol Leon. Yet of late, Rahu's introspection had possessed a higher destiny, an incomprehensible promise from Beyond...of orgiastic pleasures and limitless cruelty. He felt the raging desire coming closer, calling him. The attraction was both ethereal and biological—an inflamed harmony of spirit and passion, of creed and lust, and he was aroused by it.

He watched the archdemon beside him—and caught the impatience on Apol's demeanor as he pushed the button that would take them to the Dungeon....

And to the start of the New World Order.

25—APOLLYON

"Scientists said Sunday they expect to discover so-called space warps—
hidden extra dimensions of existence other than space and time...."
"Scientists May Find Space Warp," UPI, 02-18-02

Having stepped through the gigantic steel gates into the access tunnel, then carefully to one side of the railway, Stark paused, troubled by the appearance of the horizontal shaft extending before him. Though the corridor had been fashioned to match the outer hall, darkness as thick and as black as nurtured coal ebbed around him. This was unexpected.

Turning, he glanced at the ceiling. A maintenance bulb hung sideways on a conduit fastened to a cracked and tar-coated timber. The crooked light dangling from it painted the gang's silhouette against the floor and up one wall as fish-eyed and angry, like uninvited ghouls standing bent and impatient for the group to move along. Halfway between it and the darkness, a tiny waterfall dripped lazily from a new crack in the wall. A murky pool formed beneath it on the uneven floor, from which a cluster of rocks emerged in a long crooked line, like the bony finger of a lost adventurer beckoning them forward into the cursed unknown.

"I believe there's a penlight in your vest, Joe. May I have it, please?" Stark said. He watched as Joe unsnapped the appropriate pocket, withdrew an object slightly smaller than a cigar, and handed it to him. Stark twisted the flashlight and, when nothing happened, tapped it against his palm. Inspecting it, he found it had been crushed.

Joe moved closer to examine the damage. "That must've happened when the Hulkster fell down," he said, clearing his throat.

Stark gave the penlight back to him. "The Hulkster?"

"You know, the big soldier you killed."

Though Stark knew Joe didn't mean anything by the blunt response, the comment stung like a firebrand. The fact that he had killed an American soldier was already heavy on his mind.

Clearly unaware of the offense, Joe added, "I have light sticks we can use. Five of them."

"All right...but you'd better pray those are broken bulbs ahead, not a cave-in blocking our path."

A chill moved through Stark even as he uttered the sober words. This could be the end of the line. He had often taught cadets that if ever they needed shelter, they should seek natural formations. "You don't have to worry about them collapsing," he had said. "Cave-ins occur where men have blasted through the rock."

Now, if the impending void were due to a cave-in, if the joists had broken recently and dropped the unnatural ceiling, the tunnel no longer represented a path to freedom, but an abysmal, tomblike trap.

"What about the other set of tracks we passed a ways back," Joe asked. "The ones with boxcars on them? Is that a way out?"

The alternative tunnel had been designed to transport

the giants to their appropriate staging areas when the time was right. It eventually exited the mountain and joined the Columbia River Railway at I-84.

"It could have been, but not now," Stark said.

"Why's that?"

"It's a much longer tunnel—several miles longer—and we're out of time to consider it."

Pritchert checked his watch and agreed. "We have little more than thirty minutes to implosion, sir. There's no way we can go back—unless you think returning topside and out the front gate is feasible."

Joe looked Stark in the eyes. "Implosion?"

Accepting a light stick from him, Stark cracked it and said bluntly, "Don't ask, and as far as going topside now, not a chance."

* * * * * *

As Stark started down the tunnel to investigate the darkness, Joe followed into the haze. The unusual haunting he had felt moments before was worsening with each step. The lack of light alone was so absolute it felt contemptuous, like the abandoned tunnels he'd explored with Garth Pumphrey a few years ago along the old Lewis and Clark trail. Those had been boggy and caliginous too, filled with unknown secretions and crystalline formations that had crusted within the deserted rocks over the last half century, though he knew the frontiersmen that built those tunnels had never encountered anything like the mutations these walls had seen. Indeed, to be surrounded by so many meters of Montero's infernal stone was equivalent to falling down the proverbial wormhole on the boulevard to Hell, a fine location for gremlins and other tricksters, but not a place for people to be stuck.

Twenty yards further, the phosphorescent rod Stark was carrying glowed neon green against a solid rock wall. At his feet, Joe could see light fixtures crumbled in a messy heap, wiry and torn apart at the mounts. The tunnel had indeed collapsed.

Kneeling, Katherine ran her petite hands along the edge of the debris. The farther she reached into the darkness, the deeper the earth must have been, for it was as if the loam slanted upward and away from her until it no doubt reached the top of the ceiling. A pyramidal blockade.

"Now what?" she whispered, looking despondently at Joe. Her eyes were as deep as they were puppy-dog sad.

"Hang on a second," he said. He leaned into the void and, before the group knew what he was doing, started up the vertical mound. He heard Stark behind him warn, "Be careful, soldier, you could get buried doing that."

"I know, I know."

As if there were options.

* * * * * *

After Joe disappeared into the darkness, Stark could hear him straining, grunting, pushing something out of the way.

He gazed overhead.

Couldn't see anything.

Imagined the worst.

Death had been a risk all along, and Stark had accepted it, for himself and the others. The ethics of what they were doing had been rehearsed and the options weighed over and over, leading to the same conclusion each time— Operation Gadfly was the right thing to do. This was war, and war was hell. It had to be this way for the sake of the greater good.

Suddenly from somewhere above, Stark heard Joe say, "Hey!" He sounded excited.

"Yes?"

"There's a crawl space up here! I can see light on the other side!"

Oh God. Thank you, Jesus.

Stark shouted, "Strike another rod. Wave it at us so we can find our way to you."

Then, for reasons he couldn't comprehend, the embryo container *jerked* in his right hand. He froze, waiting to see if the movement had been in his mind.

* * * * * *

An eighth-mile away, with monster in tow, Apol emerged from the elevator and walked into the Dungeon. Immediately he sensed something calling to him, and stopped. Rahu flared his nostrils at a lingering residue of uninvited guests. In a cage nearby, its hackles raised against its quivering skin, Mantus, the Mega-Nephilim only slightly smaller than Rahu, made a keening sound, sending information to Apol about unscheduled visits to the Dungeon by Donald Pritchert and John Stark. Strangers were with them, the thing conveyed, and they had gone toward the access tunnel. They were carrying a round container.

Although encumbered by the temporary shrine of its fleshy costume, the foul and ancient spirit beneath Apol's skin suddenly heaved its malformed head upward with a shriek so plaintive and inhuman that Apol's eyes, usually alive with fire, rolled back into pale cataractic discs. The scrape of the inner rogue convulsed agonizingly through his throat and burst into a thunderous wail that echoed down the Dungeon's passageways.

* * * * * *

The group of five whirled around. A screeching sound, unlike anything they'd heard before, unearthly and deranged, filled the corridor behind them.

Joe struggled backward and stared down the tunnel.

From the shadows, as though expecting something monstrous to fly at them through the gateway, Sheri winced. "W-what was *t-that!?*"

Stark's usually vibrant demeaner, illuminated by the gentle radiance of the light stick, went flat. Rubbing his hand across his mouth, he whispered nervously, *"Him."*

"H-him?...H-him!? *W-who?*"

Stark pulled a necklace from beneath his shirt and took it off, kissed it, outlined the sign of the cross over his heart, and wrapped the rosary around the embryo tank's handle. He hoped it would bind the spirit that had shaken the container, if indeed one had. He thought about removing the embryo and destroying it, but somewhere in the back of his mind he knew it could be needed as a hostage for their freedom. He would destroy it when the time was right.

For now he stared at the others, his face sunken and gaunt.

"Apollyon," he breathed apprehensively. "He's here."

26—MAMMOTH HOOVES

"We find ourselves faced by powers which are far stronger than we had hitherto assumed, and whose base is at present unknown to us. More I cannot say at present."
Dr. Werner Von Braun, First Director of the Marshall Space Flight Center, *News Europa*, Jan. 1959

Terrified by his unusual comment, Pritchert stared at Admiral Stark. He'd known the man for at least a decade, and had never seen him afraid of anything or anyone at any time. Usually two steps up the rung from most military officers in terms of personal control, Stark was the last person on earth one would expect to succumb to paranoid or delusional outbursts. Yet his claim that an ancient demon had arrived inside Montero was simply more than Pritchert could accept. Searching Stark's face for hope, Pritchert stammered, "Y-you mean Apol Leon, r-right?"

Although he tried to sound composed, the words came out of him in an impotent, nervous squeal. Deep in his mind he could hear Apol's voice whispering, *"Look at how well we've adapted to your environment."* He shifted his attention to the gates behind them. Moments ago they had been like portals to freedom; now they seemed as cryptic as enclosures to an outrageous mausoleum.

Glancing warily at the Admiral, shaking visibly, he raised his voice and murmured again, "Y-y-you said *Apollyon* is h-here! John! You mean Apol Leon! Right! John!?...John!?...Mr. L-leon! Right!?"

* * * * * *

Stark focused on the girls. He couldn't allow Pritchert's rising hysteria to unnerve the two of them. He pointed toward the darkened area where Joe had disappeared, and whispered to them as calmly as he could, "Run."

As if unsure what he meant, Katherine blinked and said, "What?"

Stark stepped toward her to repeat the command, the beat of his heart responding to what he knew was about to happen. Pushing both ladies toward the hidden mound of earth, he implored them, "I said run!"

The sound of his voice, although controlled, must have terrified Katherine and Sheri as they screamed and charged into the rubble, thrashing and clawing up the avalanche.

"Find Joe and don't look back!" he called after them as they fled. When they were gone from view, he turned and grabbed Pritchert by the shirt. He pulled the "overrider" from his hands, shoved it behind his own belt, and jerked him face-to-face. "Snap out of it, soldier," he said roughly. "You hear me? You're frightening the girls."

Pritchert gazed at him, strangely disconnected, his lips quivering like a child's when they know they're about to cry, but no words came out of him.

Seeing that his anxiety was paralyzing him, Stark slapped him across the face, hit him so hard that he fell to the floor, then grabbed and lifted him from the muddy ground. "I said snap out of it, Donald, we've got to move," he growled.

Slumping as the Admiral let go, Pritchert looked as if he'd lost his best friend and was in shock at the thought of it all. He sniveled with a mesmeric stare, and stumbled toward the embankment. "O-okay...okay."

Now a clattering sound in the distance caught Stark's attention. He knew what it was; he'd seen the training videos and how the Mega-Nephilim whip themselves into a feeding frenzy before they begin their final assault. It was more horrifying than impressive. The creatures had been designed to do one thing very well—kill, period. Heeding his own advice, he clasped tightly on to the embryo container and rushed into the void.

* * * * * *

Pritchert's response to the bansheelike wail had scared Katherine half to death. As she struggled to make it up the mound, she could feel the Dragon of her dreams all around her, moving phantasmagorically through the darkness, brushing against her skin, swishing its claws at her face. She cried desperately to Sheri, "Sheri! Hold up! Wait!"

* * * * * *

Sheri heard Katherine screaming behind her and, with no thought for herself, turned and headed her way, surprised that under the circumstances her instinct to offer assistance was as strong as it was. Normally, she would not have been shocked by the reaction. But for the last twenty-four hours her need for self-preservation had weighed heavily on her mind. She had never been controlled so maliciously, had never been denied physical liberty, had never been manipulated and induced to obey a total stranger, like she had the past two days. The experience had convinced her that, from now on, she needed to protect herself and her own personal interests at any and all costs.

Yet now that it really mattered, the dissociative inclination had been without real strength; no self-indulgent, self-centered debate about the ethics of survival, simply the innate reaction to a frantic cry for help. The desire to rescue Katherine had actually cleared her troubled mind. Apol could kill her body, she told herself, but he couldn't touch her soul.

* * * * * *

Stark was on his way to help Katherine when suddenly Sheri came out of the darkness. Illuminated by the phosphorescent rod he was carrying, she looked like an emerald angel swooping down from God above. He watched as she grabbed Katherine by the hand and said, "Don't be afraid. Follow me, and I'll show you the way." The way Katherine's face abruptly lit up, Stark could tell the scene had meant something unusual to her.

* * * * * *

A second baleful sound, malignant and terrible, escaped the human costume of Apol Leon, as Rahu's equals, Bisclaveret, Chemosh, and Mantus, reeking of methane, crawled from their cages and stood abreast the rougher beast.

The demon in Apol glowered at the four of them in a low, boiling voice. "You'll bring me the embryo," it said.

"Sssee to it that it's not harmed. And capture that cow, Sheri. I can ssstill use her."

The dreadful hunters leaned forward, their steely eyes shooting back and forth inside their pebbled sockets, heads cocked, ears pricked like warhorses, waiting for the command.

Now Apol glared at Rahu. "And you'd better not fail me like that night at the river, when you let the boy essscape. I want him dead like his father. I want him eviscerated!"

With a violent jerk, Apol curled his head back, forcing his concealed and hideously forked tongue to unfurl like a mottled leather strap. A short, delightful pain shot through his throat as the lengthy muscle fell from its grotesque gullet onto his chest with a putrid, sloshy *flop*. He shook his transgenic bones, stretching his mouth in pleasant agony as the bloody organ swung in front of him like a tumorous pendulum. A phlegmy gurgle more reminiscent of dragons than of men disgorged a sulfurous stream of arterial blood over his lips as black as oil and as rotten as clots of stinking sewage. It ate away his thyroid cartilage, larynx, and esophagus on its way through his ruined throat to his cancerous alien mouth. He was changing rapidly now, and so was the thing inside him.

* * * * * *

In the access tunnel, near the top of the mound, Stark paused as Katherine slipped through the crawl space to Joe and Sheri on the other side. The shaft, formed by the tunnel's ceiling and a muddy collage of rocks and sludge, was barely sufficient for a large man to fit through. He considered the damp, seeping walls that shaped the vaulted passage. The roof could come down on them at any moment.

Joe pulled Katherine from the other side of the hole and said, "Okay, Admiral. You're next."

Without hesitating, Stark threw his cap off and pushed into the soggy hollow, his arms out in front of him, the embryo container in one hand while he dug at the floor with the other. The passageway was only eight or nine feet long, but narrow and restrictive. If Joe hadn't taken hold of his wrists and pulled him through like he did, he doubted he could have made it out the other side. Once his shoulders penetrated the craw, he erected himself and stood up on a berm beside Joe.

"Thanks, soldier," he said. "Is that everybody?"

"All but Pritchert."

Kneeling down and staring through the crevice, Joe said in a loud whisper, "Donald?"

Nothing but his echo returned.

Pausing, he looked at the Admiral as if to ask something, then started into the passageway after Pritchert. Stark caught him by the seat of the pants and pulled him back out. "Wait," he said delicately. "Let me handle this."

Stark placed his head into the burrow and with a fatherly voice said, "Donald...come on now, son..."

When nothing happened, he repeated a little louder, "Donald? Can you hear me?"

* * * * * *

On the other side of the shaft, near the bottom of the debris pile, frozen in terror, Pritchert's face was bleak with fear, the whites of his eyes barely discernable against the dreary cavernous gloom. He'd heard the Admiral, but dared not answer. Fifty yards away, at the tunnel's entrance, five horrendous creatures—one resembling Apol Leon—were looking his direction.

* * * * * *

Joe had the feeling something besides Pritchert was beyond the crawl space now. He focused, straining to detect...what? He did not know.

Then he heard it...a sound—so horrible, so inescapable, like mammoth hooves galloping toward them. His face went pale as the otherworldly presence slammed against the opposite side of the mound.

Donald Pritchert began screaming: tortured, blood-curdling screams, as Joe spun to the girls and shouted frantically, *"RUN! RUN! RUN!"*

Right beside him, Stark jerked his head from the crawl space and braced himself against the ledge. He reached for Joe's vest, as if trying to grab a grenade, but something wet and hard flew through the passageway and struck him with such force that it knocked him head over heels down the bluff onto the railed landing. He dropped the embryo container on the way to the bottom.

Since the utility lights were working on this side of the shaft, Joe saw what happened. He headed for Stark, scooping up the embryo container as he descended toward the floor.

On the ground next to the Admiral was the object that hit him—Donald's left leg from the kneecap to the heel. It was covered with globular drool.

Now monstrous hands were tearing at the undersized crawl space, bone-chilling sounds blaring from the voracious predators as they clawed to move the rock.

Joe pulled John Stark to his feet and looked for the girls.

Sheri and Katherine were running down the corridor, their ragged, filthy gowns fluttering ghostlike around them. He withdrew a pineapple grenade from the load-bearing vest and pulled the pin. Acknowledging the admiral, he tossed the explosive device toward the opening.

Just then, a large, talon-tipped fist punched through the hole.

Joe's thoughts spun. If he hadn't seen the gigantic fingers with his own eyes, he wouldn't have believed them possible. The digits were much larger than those of the dead beast he'd seen in the ravine, as thick as baseball bats, covered with warty, razorlike protrusions. At the tip of each finger, armorlike claws, pointed and flexing, curled in and out toward the palm.

He spun and raced toward the girls.

Stark ran.

Sheri ran.

Katherine ran.

And then the grenade exploded, and they couldn't run anymore.

27—TERRIFYING REPTILIAN

"An experiment that has led to the deliberate creation of a human chimera—named after the Greek monster that was part lion, part serpent and part goat—was presented to the European Society for Human Embryology in Madrid on Wednesday...."
"Test Tube Monster Condemned by Scientists,"
The Telegraph, 03-07-03

Quetzalcoatl's army slithered from beneath the surface of Mars, along the War Planet's canals into the ancient City Center. Imprisoned since the great conflict with Michael the archangel, the spirits were anxious for freedom and hungry for human blood.

Millions of miles beneath them, the demons at the edge of Kosmos were likewise growing impatient. Along the mouth of the Ahriman Gate, they pried, challenged, searched for weaknesses in the angelic barrier, while behind them, saucer-shaped objects with hieroglyphic markings along their rims formed a massive armada, pushing against Earth's atmosphere to get to the human race.

Yet for now the heavenly host held them—galvanized by

the intercessory group at Mt. Hood Evangelical Seminary and by the other "suddenly burdened" prayer warriors on their knees around the globe.

* * * * * *

In the access tunnel, John Stark lay dazed on the floor. The grenade had dislodged a large rock from the ceiling that had grazed his left temple in the fall. For the moment he thought he was at the academy at West Point where a choir of cadets was singing: *From the Halls of Montezuma, To the shores of Tripoli; We fight our country's battles, In the air, on land, and sea; First to fight for right and freedom, And to keep our honor clean; We are proud to claim the title of United States Marine.*

"Admiral...John...you okay?"

A cloudy figure...over him...a strong hand rubbing his wrist...a familiarity of voice...transforming now...a face he recognized...kneeling down...

"You okay?" Joe repeated, wiggling his arm. The girls were there too, looking at him anxiously.

He blinked...remembering where he was...the gravity of the moment...his head felt like it was splitting apart...then he heard himself mumbling as he rose gingerly onto one elbow, "Y-yeah...yeah...I think so."

Carefully, Joe clasped his hand and gradually pulled him up. "You've got a nasty bump, but it doesn't appear to be bleeding."

Standing tentatively, swaying woozily, he saw that tons of stone and earth had filled the access tunnel behind them. The pineapple grenade had been more than enough to bring a huge portion of the ceiling down. Inches away, the boulder that hit him could easily have taken his life. He steadied himself against it and said, "Let me sit on this for a second. How long was I out for?"

"A couple minutes," Joe said. "The grenade did the trick though. It's been quiet...I think the creatures are dead..."

Sitting, Stark whispered soberly, "Don't count on it."

"What's that?"

He drew in a deep breath and repeated sluggishly, "I said don't count on it. Pritchert was wrong...I did mean Apollyon."

* * * * * *

On the opposite side of the cave-in, next to the ape-demon-snake-men, Apol knew what he had to do. Mantus, Bisclaveret, and Chemosh would go back to the depot and kill the remaining technicians. While they prepared the regular Nephilim for the Master's appearing, he and Rahu would recover the embryo. It would take Rahu no more than ten minutes to dig through the rubble, catch Sheri's helpers, and hold them. Apol would thoroughly enjoy watching Sheri's eyes as she witnessed her male companions butchered. Then, feature by feature, Katherine would excite him the most. Yes, he had promised her to Rahu, but his mind was changed. Authority had its benefits, and the sweet terror of the Swiss Army knife's delicate ocular extraction would start even before the blood in her carotid arteries could dam against her garroted throat to relieve her of the misery. The communion that followed and the dismemberment of her body would be particularly amusing, even practical, now that Sheri needed additional convincing to submit to implantation. Perhaps something of the scraps could be left for Rahu.

* * * * * *

A chill radiated from the embryo container's handle upward through Joe's right arm as he pondered the ramifications of Stark's "Apollyon" comment. He looked at the admiral and said, "Then we'd better get moving, hadn't we?"

Stark nodded with a grunt and struggled upright. As his legs steadied, the four of them began moving as swiftly as deliberation would allow. Following the tracks through the earth, they soon descended into a dank area defined by what might have been coal veins cutting deep inside the rock in angled tectonic lines. As the patterns passed, Joe saw Stark studying the geological designs, as though he was trying to figure something out. Before long Stark sighed and said, "You may as well know, the giants aren't the worst of our problems."

When neither Joe nor the girls responded, Stark raised his voice a little. "Some time ago my team became aware of a top secret experiment called 'New Messiah.' Frankly, it should have been called 'False Messiah' or 'Project Antichrist' since at the core it represented a fantastic plan by Apol Leon to produce a Super Nephilim—a genetically altered replicant of his DNA—the Apollyon incarnate."

Joe closed the gap between them. Perhaps Stark was feeling that if only he talked, it would help the group stay focused and keep moving. Or maybe the admiral needed to get things out in the open and off of his chest. Either way, Joe wondered why he was telling them this now. Was it a need-to-know issue, or was he simply trying to motivate them?

"The demon?" Joe said incredulously.

"Afraid so. The sole survivor of the Sedona crash—a

terrifying reptilian in constant contact with Apol—provided the genetic formula for the creature. The reptilian later died at Wright-Patterson Air Force Base, where its remains were used in the first phase of the experiment."

"An experiment to incarnate a demon?"

"I understand how incredible it sounds. The reptilian's DNA was somehow transgenically combined with Apol's genome to create a single malevolent strand, a cellular catalyst to a metamorphosis in which Apol would become host to the Apollyon. In phase two of the procedure, the morphed DNA would be used to provide raw genetic material for the embryo of the Man of Sin—the prophesied one, who would enter the world in the last days, to lead the New World Order."

Pushing back at least a dozen other questions, Joe said, "Even if such science was successful, surely Apol knows not *all* nations would agree to follow him or this creature son of his."

"He may be a tyrant, but Apol's not unwise. He's contrived an 'alien invasion' that will create a global crisis brought on by mass panic and fear of the unknown. Any day now, the UFO presence will arrive and demand a representative from the world's leaders. That's when Apol will emerge as the alien's ambassadorial choice. The Men in Black will also use their Majestic-12 influence to ensure the compliance succeeds. The nations will follow him all right, because he'll terrify them into it while paving the way for his hadean son."

"Who, or what, is the Majestic-12?"

"A top secret research group inside the National Security Council. The MJ-12, as they also are known, were established by President Truman right after the Roswell UFO incident. Today they are part of the 'Disclosure

'Trigger,' if I can put it that way, those who will decide when the alien presence on Earth can be revealed to the world."

Suddenly something clicked deep inside Joe's memory, and he said, "And the Men in Black?"

"MIBs are paramilitary agents who work specifically to eliminate predisclosure evidence of aliens on Earth by using terrorism, fear, and intimidation as a psychological weapon against UFO witnesses. In a nutshell, they're synthetic slaves of the Majestic-12, who serve Apol's draconian plan."

Joe felt his throat go dry. He immediately remembered a line from his dad's secret letter. *"But beware the Men in Black. You'll know them if you see them, especially their leader. He's an old snake."* The implication of that line finally made sense. His dad was onto them. Somehow he knew Apol was possessed by an "old" snake, a very old, prehistoric one, in league with the MIB.

Sheri raced forward, careful not to lose her balance on the uneven floor, and said, "But what about the Constitution? Wouldn't that protect us from this...this...hostile takeover?" She had clearly intuited enough of what Stark was saying to get the picture.

"Given an invasion by extraterrestrials? Sorry. FEMA will suspend the Constitution and martial law will be imposed."

"Who?"

"The Federal Emergency Management Agency."

"Can they just *do* that?"

"You better believe it, and it's the perfect setup when you think about it, the making of a global police state in which Apol becomes a god, and his son becomes president of Planet Earth."

Joe raised the special container with a heavy sigh. "So, if Apollyon is somehow embodied in Apol, we could actually be carrying the embryo of the *Antichrist* here?"

"That's correct. According to the Bible, the Antichrist will be 'the son of perdition,' the male progeny of the Greek *apoleia*, or Apollyon. The implication couldn't be clearer—the Man of Sin will be the physical offspring of the destroyer demon, a transgenic of the highest order."

"Then why don't we just *destroy* this thing?"

"We may need it as a hostage."

Katherine had been silent until then. Now, out of the blue, she said slowly, "But that's what got Pritchert."

Joe glanced over his shoulder at her. "What?"

"Pritchert. I keep hearing him screaming. It's so awful, how they got him."

Through the cavern's faint lighting, Joe could see tears welling up in her eyes. "I know, me too," he said.

Stark picked up the pace. "He was a good man."

"You and he were friends, weren't you?" Sheri said.

"Professional acquaintances, really. But we'd gotten together for social drinks a time or two."

"Did he have a wife?"

"Yes."

"Kids?"

"One boy, I think."

"Who will tell them about their husband and father?"

"I will, I suppose."

Sheri jogged a couple steps to keep up. "Did his wife know his death was a possibility?"

"Today?"

"Yes."

"Hardly."

"Why not?"

"Because."

"Because why?"

"Like all our wives, she had no clue what he was doing."

Silence returned as each of them reflected on those words. Except for the scuffling of their feet against the floor and the swishing of their clothes against their limbs, they continued now without a sound, the girls between the men, clutching hands, Stark in the lead, Joe watching their backs with the M-249.

As they went, the walls and ceiling of the tunnel became progressively rougher, until finally Joe could see bats squirming in darker areas above where muddy heaps of guano stacked deep upon the floor. The foul odor, present elsewhere in the cave, rose and subsided as they passed each pile, but the air here was breezier and so less stale than the other side of the cave-in had been. Even so, the faint scent of sulfur, like weak echoes of Prometheus's theft of fire from the gods, combined with the guano to create a wretched stench that in some places was nearly impossible to breathe.

Seconds turned to minutes as they counted the overhead bulbs, passing between them to shadow, then under them to light, the passageway becoming an endless maze of guano piles to avoid, like a travel game they could play called "dodge the dooky." It seemed a peculiar environment to Joe, something he'd never considered before, a hidden world where ancient lava veins formed housing settlements for daddy longlegs, crickets, moths, bats, and other nocturnal creatures whose sole purpose in life seemed to be to feed and then to crap.

At least they were moving, he told himself, and away from the Nephilim. That was the important thing.

A second later, as if to challenge his hope that some distance might be put between them and the giants, a crawling sensation moved over him as a dull thumping started in the walls. It felt to Joe as if a mining company somewhere had turned on drilling equipment of such size and strength that its mighty vibrations were being transferred along miles of volcanic basalt. Soon the sound changed to digging and finally tapered off. Upstairs, when he'd first entered the Dungeon, he'd heard a metallic clanking of some kind there, too. Perhaps this vibration was associated with that. The vast facility was, after all, largely automated. Yet as he walked another block, a different scenario entered his mind. What if the sound indicated something *alive* in the walls or beneath the floor? For all he knew, the creatures he'd stopped earlier with the grenade had survived the blast and were burrowing toward them even now, like giant moles or mutated rodentia, about to burst through the rock at any moment to catch and rip them apart.

Now the vibrations resumed and magnified. From the feel of the echo, whatever it was had grown closer in less than a minute.

Another thump. Stronger this time. The floor of the tunnel shook.

A trip wire tied to a grenade might be a good idea at this time.

He listened again, the sound rising, then falling, like the breath of the mountain flexing beside him, until at last it seemed to reach through the walls and brush up against the hair of his legs. He forced himself against everything else to pretend whatever it was, was benign.

Minutes later, nearly one hour after entering the research facility, a catwalk appeared above them as they began a sharp right turn. It was brightly painted, or perhaps luminescent, as if treated with fluorescents. Joe was not able to determine the method of its gleaming until at last, a yellow light like the gentle radiance of fireflies, beamed down the pathway, reflecting on the steel.

Taking a cue from Stark, he paused and stared at the anomaly directly ahead. Pale saffron seemed to encircle what looked like characterized letters shimmering against a solid black wall. As he discerned it, an illuminated sign embedded in the rock came into view: WARNING! YARD PERSONNEL EXIT ONLY!

Given the events of the past forty-eight hours, Joe was surprised at how quickly the reader board caused hope to surge within him. Here in this black and craggy hellhole, the effect of his faith in God was still strong. Mom and Dad had always said the Lord goes before you, and he was starting to believe it was true.

Although they were obviously approaching another dead end, a diminutive trace of ivory-yellow light was clearly outlining a spectacular doorway beneath the amber glowing sign.

As with him, Stark also seemed invigorated by the exit and grabbed the overrider from beneath his belt. Clutching it firmly, he took off running toward the door.

Seconds later, eyes wide with anticipation, breathing half as much from excitement as they were from hurrying, the group reached the end of the tunnel. On one side of the barrier several ports were illuminated by ocean blue dots inside a shiny metal plank. Stark lifted the palm-sized instrument into the light and plugged it into the mechanism. He began typing a series of numbers onto the keypad.

In the static silence that followed, the rhythmic pounding Joe had heard earlier moved along the floor and joined a vague digging elsewhere, like a mouse clawing in the wall—a big, dangerous, mutant, demonic mouse, grunting, breathing, burrowing hard to reach them.

Stark inspected the readout as Katherine timidly stammered something about the need to hurry up.

"We're almost there," he reassured her, sounding as if in fact he believed they were running out of time.

Joe turned and knelt on one knee. He pressed the machine gun tightly against his shoulder and aimed it at the area they had just come through. The M-249 had an effective range of five hundred meters. If anything came through the tunnel after them, it would meet two hundred rounds of explosive ammunition. Even so, he felt like Davy Crockett guarding the lives of Alamo soldiers against Santa Anna's vastly superior Mexican army. Crockett had used his .40 caliber flintlock, Bowie his famous knife, and Travis his bravery, but the men burned anyway in a funeral pyre at three o'clock in the afternoon, March 6, 1836.

Now he heard the exit doors open behind him and suddenly brilliant sunlight shot down the passage like a spotlight from a stage. Where a second before the maintenance bulbs and the faint glow of the exit sign had vaguely lit the cavernous hall, momentous illumination abruptly filled the area all around him.

Curiously, the vibration that had been so prevalent within the walls and floor moments before seemed to move up his legs now *and echo inside his head!* He could clearly hear a voice burning in his mind...

"*I need...I need...the embryo...I need...*"

* * * * * *

Stark wrapped his huge hands around the nape of both girls' necks and pushed them through the doorway. Following them outside, he turned and stared back beyond Joe. Though he couldn't be sure, he thought the grenade pile was holding. He hadn't heard or seen anything since the explosion that had brought so much of the ceiling down.

Yet as his eyes adjusted to the brightness, he caught sight of something huge, a shadow maybe, large and moving stealthily along the carvern's wall, lumbering near the area where they had first seen the scaffolding.

He held his breath, looked harder, squinted.

The darkness slowed, became defined, the enormous silhouette of a beast creeping forward near the sharp turn in the tracks.

Standing very still, Stark whispered to Joe, who seemed to be frozen. When he didn't respond, Stark thought, *He must not have heard me, but can't he see the shadow?*

A second passed. Then a claw as large as a plow blade slipped slowly around the corner. Above it, a face, wicked and menacing, peered down the corridor, pulled back, slipped away. A moment later, water sloshed beyond the bend in the road. Joe still wasn't moving. On a whim, Stark silently prayed, *Lord, don't let Joe's eyes be blinded by the enemy; don't let their psychic trickeries work on him.*

* * * * * *

Just like that, Joe heard a sound, saw a shadow, and stood up. An instant later a gorilla-like roar blared down the shaft with acoustics so immediate and thunderous that he jerked backward, lost his balance, and stumbled to the floor.

A phenomenal creature sprang around the corner toward him, faster than could be imagined, water spraying off its pads as it propelled itself twenty yards through the air in a single bound.

Joe flew to his feet in a panic, vaulted through the opening beside Stark, and rolled onto one side to aim and fire the machine gun.

The beast was snarling vicious, hungry, sloppy, guttural sounds of anger as it closed the gap between them.

For a split second Joe made eye contact with the fast approaching *thing*, gulping at the intensity and ferociousness of the creature.

Standing next to him, Stark jerked the connector out of the overrider and let the titanium door slam shut. He grabbed the Walther P-38 from its holster and shouted, "Cover your eyes!"

Two shots rang out in quick succession as projectiles from his weapon found their mark against the entry panel. Flame poured from the locking device as smoke drifted from the silencer.

Joe watched the door. He could hear the giant, breathing heavily, as it approached the other side.

* * * * * *

A mile down the mountain on the Columbia River's shoreline, Buck watched as Tater jumped from his favorite blanket onto the aging boat's deck.

"What's th' matter boy?" he said. "Yeh hear somethin'? Huh?"

The dog was alert, ears straight up, eyes fixed on the forest. His breathing stopped and his tail dropped, then his jowls drew above his fangs and quivered as a deep growl rumbled evenly in his throat.

"I think he heard a gunshot," Allie said to Buck. "I think I heard it too, up the mountain somewhere."

With his tousled hair fluttering gently in the breeze, the old man swiveled in his chair and with a voice as gristled as a saw blade drawn on timber, said, "Gunshot, eh? Don't reckon I'd read too much into that, missy. Lots a' hunters 'round here use these woods, uh-huh."

The truth was, Buck didn't want to frighten her. He knew Tater was riveted by something else, something unusual. The dog was accustomed to hunters and gunfire. Tarnation, he'd practically grown up on the stuff. Something *different* had alarmed the dog.

28—STANDOFF

"There are worse things than death, I suspected. And I was beginning to get the distinct impression that one of them had taken an interest in me."
Whitley Strieber, *Communion* (William Morrow, NY: Beech Tree Books, 1987)

Standing on the ledge outside the access tunnel, Joe surveyed the lush forestlands blanketing the mountainside ridge and found them curiously compelling. Naturally twisted firs stretched eagerly above the green crest into the moist Pacific air, while here and there stands of big-leaf maple, Oregon ash and cottonwoods crowded together within the picturesque canopy. Black basalt, jutting randomly from the crag, formed countless natural lookouts on which native Indian tribes stood for hundreds of years watching the bountiful Columbia feed into the Pacific Ocean. The river's musk was drifting up from the gorge, but the richer fragrance was of wildflowers, as if the Almighty had strewn a fresh bouquet to purify the forest of the Nephilim stench that had so recently spoiled its florid sanctuary. In stark contrast to the unrefined beauty, a metal sign on the exitway behind Joe read—U.S. MILITARY INSTALLATION: NO TRESPASSING BEYOND THIS POINT. Below that in slightly smaller print was additional indication that, although the malodor of the creatures was dissipated outside, the foul and ancient things were never really far away. IT IS UNLAWFUL TO ENTER THIS AREA WITHOUT PERMISSION OF THE INSTALLATION COMMANDER. LETHAL ENFORCEMENT IS AUTHORIZED.

Every instinct Joe had rushed with urgency. He clearly remembered the night he'd scarcely made it through these woods to the river while an unmistakable malevolence pursued him every step of the way. Now a similar chill was passing through his veins when suddenly, *BAMM BAMM BAMM!* A terrific thud jarred the cracked platform he was standing on, rattling the ominous sign above him and nearly knocking him off his feet.

* * * * * *

Nine hundred and sixty-two pounds of Mega-Nephilim—named after the Hindu devil of torments, Rahu—punched the titanium door again. Its uncontrollable rage sent its immense fists colliding with the closure in excess of one hundred miles per hour.

* * * * * *

Joe caught his footing and swung the M-249 over his shoulder. He clasped the girls by the hand and pulled them off the landing toward the woods even before he had time to contemplate the trees and what might be waiting inside them.

Heading the opposite direction toward a deer trail, Stark waved at them and yelled frantically, "No no no! This way! This way!"

BAMM BAMM!

Joe zigzagged along the forest's perimeter, stumbling around a short rock arch before following the admiral into the woods. Soon he found himself in a canopy of limbs that on other days would have made for a nice picnic area. The ground was softer than in the tunnel, covered with pine needles and colorful leaves that formed a mushy trail beneath the branchy overhang. Fortunately a web of fallen interlaced limbs kept the woodland floor from shifting too far beneath their feet as they rushed over the soggy covering.

"It can't break the door down, can it!?" Katherine gasped as she ran.

Stark was slightly ahead of the others when he shouted, "Not that door, it can't. It's titanium...several inches thick!"

* * * * * *

BAMM-CLANK!

The frame around the closure budged a little. What none of the officials at Montero knew was that the subcontractors had taken shortcuts on costs and that the jams were insufficiently lagged into the rock. Rahu grabbed the door by the bar and jerked it back and forth as milky white foam flew from his rabid, thrashing mouth. His testosterone was at ten thousand, driving him to the breaking point.

CLANK-CLANK! CLANK-CLANK!

When the door held, Rahu jumped back angrily and rushed it again, his immense shoulder colliding with the barrier like a runaway locomotive. Two j-bolts snapped in the jamb.

* * * * * *

Outside, through a clearing, Joe spotted a logging road. The Columbia River and the Washington side of the gorge were also visible from here. He considered the distance to the path, then continued, carefully placing each step on the safest places of the trail. On one side of the avenue was a mountain face while on the other side a wild and occasionally steep precipice carved dangerously close to their feet. Before long the course widened, leveling off onto a plateau against the logging route. He raced across the tract onto the lane, then started downhill, pulling the girls aggressively to keep up with Stark, who seemed to be back to his energetic old self.

Joe wondered how long it would take to get to the river. If Allie had followed the plan, Buck would be on the beach by now. As he looked across the fir-clogged embankment paralleling the road, the Columbia River sparkled like a rhinestone neckband above the tree line, but the Oregon beach was not visible to him yet.

Suddenly a *crash-bang-clang* up the hill brought the group to an immediate halt.

Sheri, limping from what could have been a stone bruise, shouted, "Shh!...listen!"

Katherine, scanning the bluff, whispered uneasily, "I-I don't hear anything. Not n-now."

"Exactly," Sheri breathed gravely, clutching a ruby lock of her hair. "No birds. No frogs. Nothing!"

A preternatural hush had fallen over the woods. Insects and other critters, which moments before had filled the background with nebulous buzzing, were silent following the racket, as if nature's volume knob had been inexplicably turned off.

Joe slid the M-249 into position and carefully traced the trees with the tip of the barrel.

A moment passed...then a rumbling...muffled at first...then limbs cracking...stones dislodging...small trees shattering off at the stump...something big plowing down the mountainside toward them...

* * * * * *

Admiral Stark understood the gravity of this situation more than the others did. He'd seen the beasts in action, both on video and in a controlled environment. Once during a live demonstration, he'd actually witnessed a fully-grown lion being ripped apart like tender-fried chicken. The Nephilim hadn't broken a sweat.

He also knew a command decision was necessary, and that it was up to him to do it.

In a flash he was at the edge of the road near a particularly steep portion of the cliffside. A plan was unfolding as he moved.

* * * * * *

Joe tugged Sheri while she held Katherine, and they joined Stark at the ridge.

Heavy footsteps were approaching through the woods.

"What are you doing?" Joe whispered to Stark, looking out over the precipice. His boot dislodged a small handful of stones that rolled over the cliff in a jittery downhill race.

Stark held the embryo container above the embankment as if threatening to drop it. "It's called a standoff."

Placing the girls on the ground between them, Joe assumed a classic combat position. He understood Stark's plan, but compared to what was coming, he felt like a toy soldier, a Kmart G.I. Joe.

"You still have the laser?" Stark asked softly.

"Yes, but it's nearly depleted."

"Then I'd stick with the machine gun."

"My thoughts exactly."

Something huge crunched to a stop in the thicket nearby. Joe sucked in a deep breath and held it. The watcher in the woods was somewhere beyond the tree line, panting like a racehorse after a strenuous run. He carefully scanned with the weapon's scope looking for it. He wouldn't fire until he was certain he could hit a vital organ. He needed to kill the beast, not wound it; that would be a mistake. He'd aim for the heart and lungs, or maybe the guts if he had no other choice. He remembered what his dad told him years ago about grizzly's having a thick skull. "A bullet can ricochet off their head and fail to bring them down," he'd warned. "When hunting bear, always aim for the heart and lungs."

Of course the thing in the brush was no ordinary animal. It was something much worse. It brought a wrongness to the forest, a throbbing, terrifying, trembling aberrance that burned against the edge of his nerves. The animals must have sensed it too, raccoons, owls, elk scared to silence by something pushing at them from deep inside the earth, a relentless disorder on the fabric of reality, an imminent doomsday driving up from the evergreen boughs and down from the air above them, pushing, pushing—

Swooosh!

Douglas firs up the mountain thrashed, and something dawned on Joe. The nonbear was stationary because it was waiting for someone. *Something?*

"Crrria ank! Ni bada ayanth!" the dark creature across

the road abruptly shrieked. It was the same bird-speak he'd heard on Level Twenty, so creepy it stopped his breath in his throat.

Further away, something responded with a strangely imperial voice. "Sssgratha! Sssri poct! Caw saalish! Ank cotta sssatania!"

Sheri stood, her face flush with fear, her eyes sparkling with unspent tears. "J-Joe," she said, trembling.

"Shh," he said. "Listen..."

Then they heard it. Slithering toward them.

"Here he comes," Stark whispered. "Get ready...."

Undulating, a dismal figure uttering a concatomy of unknown jargon emerged from the woods forty feet away, serpentlike, swaying, the archdemon behind the Apol mask more visible now than before, the malignant details and sickening minutiae of its malformed structure pressing larvaelike against the underside of Apol's fleshy membrane.

* * * * * *

As secretary of defense in 1987, Major General William H. Layton had been rushed to Wright-Patterson Air Force Base the first night the alien bodies and the ETV, later code-named "Reindeer," were brought in for study. That's where he'd first met Special Agent Apol Leon, whom he'd later appointed project director of the research arm at Montero. He'd never regretted that decision. Although eccentric, Leon had proven to be proficient at interpreting the Dropa discs and at keeping the various aspects of the all-black project on target.

That was, until last night, when gremlins got into the machinery and the AngelStar system malfunctioned, reducing the giant army to automatons under alien control.

Moments later, all contact with the Mars colony had been lost, and the Air Force's Satellite Control Facility had recorded unclassifiable blips within the anomalous rift. To make matters worse, at 8:05 this morning, Admiral John Stark had been identified as Phobos—the leader of the mole mercenary group, Operation Gadfly.

Now as he rode the elevator to the Dungeon, General Layton couldn't help but smile as he reflected on the potentially explosive situation. He understood what a magnitude-one catastrophe in the Reindeer Project could do to his professional life. Yet he believed this day would ultimately be remembered with mirth. Years from now, he told himself, he'd sip beer with his colleagues and laugh about that crazy time when everything went wrong, when he'd been forced to visit Montero to straighten things out. The future would vindicate the Reindeer Project and exalt him as a last-minute savior, a defining personality within an esteemed career.

Yet, the odd thing about the future is, you never really know what it holds. It could hold laughter, or terror, absolute terror, like the kind he'd found just inside the Dungeon...where Chemosh and the others had been waiting...to eat him.

* * * * * *

The girls screamed in horror at the sight of Apol Leon. Pine needles and limb debris hung from his ruffled hair, and wriggling maggots oozed from deep lacerations on his mottled skin as he slither-walked to the middle of the logging road and screeched what sounded like an anguished warning to the nonbear. On either side of him, his malformed fingers snapped open and closed as if clawing at invisible pests. Behind his ripped and rotting tissues, glimpses of moving bone gave him the appearance of an exoskeleton, an outdated Terminator struggling for one more opportunity to kill. He froze, glaring through his empty black eyes at Stark dangling the embryo above the ledge. In heavy modulation more dragonlike than human, as if each gurgling syllable began deep in his belly and passed through boiling magma on its way to his mouth, he groaned, "Give me the zygote...and I'll let you live. Rrrefuse me...and I promissse...you'll die on this lonely road."

Stark was evidently so startled by Apol's rapid decomposition, the tangled mass of ragged skin, worms entwined around inner alien mass, black and oily, writhing—no—*mutating* inside him, that he didn't wait for the rest of the speech.

"Listen up, Apol, or whoever the heck you are," he grunted. "I'm one millisecond from tossing this container with its cargo back into the Hell it came from. Once my friends are safely on the other side of the river, then and only then will we discuss the embryo. Got it?"

Joe shot a glance at Stark. What was he doing?

Apol made a rumbling sound and looked into the woods. A portion of the thing clutching his clavicles slithered out of his stomach, crusty and wart covered like a lizard's hide, then frenziedly withdrew behind a reeking flap of skin, as if scorched by the clean mountain air or in hiding from the Believers in God. Shifting wind blew an all-pervasive stench from the appendage that distended through the open air like vile water rolling off a rotting corpse on the beach. The rancid odor of decaying flesh carried an undertone that felt quaverous against the skin of Joe's arms.

* * * * * *

Seeing the mobility of the callused thing hiding inside Apol, Stark said, "Disagree with my terms, and you and your dog Spot will suffer Heaven's fury!"

Stark had no idea what "Heaven's fury" meant; it simply felt like the appropriate thing to say. If the comment served to confuse the creatures, to bluff them into thinking he had an ace in the hole, it might buy the kids the time they needed to make it to the river. He was sure the only reason the giant in the woods hadn't attacked already was fear of harming the embryo. The squawking demonese spoken earlier between the two beings had no doubt included orders to protect the incipient mutation.

* * * * * *

Apol's eyes flared elliptically and his teeth clinched in rage. He had once been opposed by another military officer—Lieutenant Colonel Clarence Ryback—and had wasted him as easily as he would John Stark. The moment the Master's embryo was secure, he'd summon the flying horde to do it.

* * * * * *

With the memory of his father's death still fresh in his mind and the knowledge that John Stark knew more about the mountain path than he did, Joe tethered what he believed was the only hope the others had for survival. He summoned his father's face from memory, the thinning black hair and the hazel green eyes he had inherited, and wondered if he would ever see his mom and the girls again.

Then, surprised at his grit, he turned and boldly demanded that Stark give him the container.

When the admiral didn't move, he gripped the M-249 with one hand and reached around with the other.

"The embryo, John. Give it to me. Now."

* * * * * *

"Sorry, Joe, no can do," Stark said flatly. He assumed Joe intended to replace him as hostage. He appreciated the heroism, but couldn't allow it. It was one thing to bravely resign oneself to the possibility of sacrifice, and another altogether to negotiate a stand against the Devil.

Joe narrowed his eyes and replied firmly, "I'm afraid I really must insist."

"Use your head, son."

"I am," Joe growled.

"Then you know we don't have time for this."

"Right, time *is* of the essence, so give me the damnable thing, now!"

"Can't do it, *Joe*."

"Sure you can, *John*."

In the middle of the road, Apol looked amused.

Stark kept his eyes on Apol as he whispered to Joe, "Your sister and Katherine need you now."

"At the moment, they'd be safer with you."

"How do you figure?"

"You're the only one who knows the quickest route to the river."

Stark blinked as it dawned on him that Joe was right. As the most informed among them, he was the logical person to lead the girls to safety. He also realized Joe was correct about time being of the essence. Given the SAMM's imminent implosion, there was no grace remaining to debate the issue, and apparently no other alternative. With time running out, he moved as robotically as a tank barrel as he brought the container slowly around toward Joe.

Sheri grabbed Joe's shirt and tugged frantically from behind him. "Whoa, wait, Joe...you can't!"

* * * * * *

Katherine's mouth fell open as Joe clasped the embryo container and looked at her and Sheri. Was the biggest hero she'd ever seen going to die!? Would he sacrifice himself for them!?

* * * * * *

Joe smiled at Katherine, then met Sheri's frightened, deep blue gaze. "Don't worry," he said. "I'll be with you in a minute, I promise."

But he knew it wasn't the truth.

29—AS AN ANGEL OF LIGHT

"Greater love hath no man than this, that a man lay down his life for
his friends."
John 15:13

Along the forest's edge the Douglas firs swayed gently, nudged by a slight Pacific breeze meandering along the wooded canyon outward toward the sea. Under the easy wave of the low-hanging limbs, droplets of morning dew fell from the branch tips onto a shimmering polder of groveling ferns that, beneath the early morning sun, appeared to be kneeling in humble obeisance to the dog.

Tater leaped from the boat deck and landed gracefully on the river's edge. As his legs sank into the wet sand, murky fields of water seeped up in tiny brown pools around his paws. He could hear somebody or something coming down the concealed gravel way. He and Buck had discovered the logging road some years ago, back before climbing became too difficult for the old man. On a few occasions since, he had explored the abandoned route, but not lately, not since the hairy-smelly things started coming there.

From behind him, Buck studied his canine behavior, his fretting and intermittent tail wagging, probably thinking it was a good sign, something friendly coming their way.

* * * * * *

After watching Stark snatch Sheri up screaming for her brother and Katherine following them down the gravel road out of sight, Apol turned to Joe and with spittle flying, seethed, "Now give me the container, quickly, and I'll let the others live!"

Joe's palms were sweating. He knew the monster in the underbrush would kill all of them the moment he handed the embryo to the snake man. He had to buy some time, give the admiral a chance to get the girls to safety.

With one eye on Apol and the other on the woods, he shook the M-249, then swung the container above the ledge, indicating his willingness to drop it.

The threatening gesture brought a menacing growl from the thing inside the trees, primordial and pointed, a warning to Joe—drop the embryo, and die.

Joe half expected the strange being to fly at him anyway, but when he returned his attention to the road, Apol was looking at the woods in the way a pet owner might whose authoritative glance can hold a well-trained dog as well as any chain.

Chortling now with low, piggish laughter, Apol returned his attention to Joe. Drumming his fingers against his palm, he said sarcastically, "Ahh, yesss, well, there's plenty of testosterone to kill all of us today, isn't there. Yet what would we benefit from dying? Hmm?"

A moment of silence passed, as if the demon inside Apol was considering a new approach to getting the embryo, perhaps a ploy learned from the Dark One himself.

Having no idea what the monstrosity was planning and

feeling something was about to happen, Joe warned nervously, "Y-you'd better stay right where you are."

Apol grumbled, his eyes becoming as black as smoldering holes, twitching strangely, as if listening to somebody unseen. After a few contemplative seconds he raised his spiky arm and said, "Ahh, perhapsss there is a way to resolve our dilemma after all."

Joe's heart raced as the former man's mottled hand slowly raised and unfolded. His warty fingers began drifting along the horizon in a broad deliberate circle, as if he was drawing a grandiose zero in the sky. Joe thought the action might be contrived, a distraction to keep his attention off the forest and away from the movements of the huge beast. Yet by the time the claw of Apol's right tentacle reached the end of the outline, something inexplicable was occuring. A pressure expanded around him, and for reasons he could not anticipate, the space in front of him *sizzled,* and with a *snap,* the ring of air Apol had traced inexplicably burst into flames.

Like the best of David Copperfield's illusions, the intangible loop quickly spread outward into unusual flaming steps. For the life of him, the fire looked to Joe as if it was made up of millions of tiny witches marching in circular chorus with puppies and black lambs roasting in oblation to Apol.

With his heart pounding like a hammer, Joe wondered if what he was seeing was actually there, or if his imagination was running away with him. The stress of the day could have distorted his ability to discern the difference between reality and illusion. He feared he might be losing his grip.

Then the ground beneath his feet undulated, as if he were standing on the back of a giant snake that insisted he pay attention, and he heard audible voices, strange and chanting near the edge of the strange circle, breaking through the cyclone of fire.

"All these things will he give thee," they were saying, *"if thou wilt fall down and worship him..."*

A chill shot through him as he jumped sideways and nearly dropped the embryo. The boldness he had felt moments before vanished as a phantasmagoric darkness, thick and absolute, began spreading over the gravel road from the place where Apol stood. The adjacent greenery, previously as stable as reality itself, seemed to dematerialize right before his eyes, first pulling toward, then disintegrating into the growing revolving fire. Near his feet, the grass began vibrating and whistling as the wind shifted around the green and yellow blades to get to the flame.

Even the M-249 seemed attracted to the anomaly. The ozone, hot against the stock and magazine, escalated sensations of fire like molten steel against his burning palm and fingers. Resisting the urge to throw it down, he swallowed hard and held the scorching gun as steadily as he could, forcing himself to remain alert as the whirling pulsar slowly encased Apol.

Now as the flames grew thicker and raging, a terrible form, like crude oil bubbling up from the ground, ascended from below it and metamorphosed into a shape inside the veil, black and vaporous, fearfully hypnotic, staring at Joe from within the stormy facade.

As if a part of him knew that by simply looking at the dark essence he could be in mortal danger, he started to turn away.

Yet a second later he found himself strangely fascinated by the form.

He wondered what would happen if he fired his weapon at the entity. Would it react, or would it shatter like a sorcerer's mirror used for black magic and sleight of hand?

Contemplating the option, he watched as the thing in front of Apol—whatever it was, wherever it came from, whatever it intended to do—abruptly stepped through the pillar toward him.

At once its appearance changed, feminine now, glistening with vibrant streams of silver and blue and gold, the most beautiful presence Joe had ever seen.

The gun cooled.

Lifting its radiant arms, the being opened its mouth and announced in a voice as seductive as soft velvet, "Greetings, Joe. You've won. You're a hero."

He took a deep breath, let it out slowly, and with as much control as he could muster, said, "I swear I'll drop the embryo if you come any closer."

The traveler froze like a marionette suspended on wires. Were unseen hands, obscured beyond the cloud, controlling it?

The resplendent creature, so alluring, so enchanting, explained pleasantly, "But I've been called to negotiate a trade, Joe. Tell me what you desire. Anything you want can be had in exchange for the container."

The being's eyes were at once as comforting as a grandmother's and as sensual as an inviting lover's. It's skin glistened with inlaid jewels beneath the sunlight; burnished armor molded its chest as if it had been poured into place; the sturdy arms, well defined and muscular, supported its feathery appendages with graceful control; below its breast, plumed mail covered its large and powerful loins like those of an angel of light. From the look on its face, the presence invited a compromise. There was familiarity in its expression too, an acquaintance Joe seemed to know from somewhere in time, like the memory-glow of weaker moments when he'd given in to temptation.

He stared back without speaking, astonished at what was happening, until from between the being's wings a scroll slowly unrolled beneath the pinions, and scenes of a future, *his future*, prepared to play out on the silvery parchment.

How did he know this?

"Would you have wealth?" the floating creature pressed warmly.

Joe studied the puzzling monitor as *he himself* appeared on it as clear and as believable as if he were viewing a home video. He was beside a pool at a manor house somewhere: a Mexican villa perhaps, or maybe in Spain. The depiction was obviously a destiny, one possible future where he could lounge with wealthy friends and laugh his days away. A Faustian proposal.

For a split second the screen flashed and he thought he discerned something else, a vague, hidden presence, alive and churning, seeking an entry, then the image was of him dining with celebrities at the luxurious Hotel Bel-Air. Next he was in Rome, vacationing with supermodels, buying a $228,000-dollar Aston Martin Vanquish.

Flashing, churning, questing.

Inching forward...

"Or...do you prefer power?" the radiant presence continued.

The cinematic conveyance of the alternative personal fate—his potential existence bathed in kingly riches in which nobility would regard him, media would adore him, and the coveted things in life would be at his beck and call—suddenly took a different tone. Now he was brokering business deals and capitalizing on industry's leading trends: outwitting competitors, outsmarting lawmakers, overcoming enemies, crushing strangers beneath the copious gains of a new and powerful affluence.

Pressing, seeking.

"Women would adore you! Desire you!"

Members of the opposite sex, voluptuous, provocative, beautiful, flooded the spectral screen, some naked, others hardly covered, all amazingly curvaceous, wanting him.

"Simply ask!" the creature tempted. "You can have the world!"

Closer...

Each time the screen flashed, powerful, subliminal messages invaded his subconscious mind, searching for a hold, intoxicating him, systematically entrancing him with the seductive visual enhancement.

"You *are* only a man, right?" the being asked persuasively. "Don't you need these kind of things?"

A weary part of him unexpectedly agreed.

Increasing in rapidity and allure, the dramatization filled the magical future-screen with electrifying depictions. Now he became extraordinary in knowledge, divine in understanding, able to comprehend the benefits of both good and evil, and with power to manipulate it all.

Feelings of supernaturalism filled him as he beheld the adoration of mystics. He would become a mighty clairvoyant, the creature declared, a telekinetic god. The world would become his footstool.

"For it is written!" the glorious being misquoted the New Testament. "Anything you want will be given you...that your joy may be full!"

Mesmerized by the powerful conjuration, thoughts melting into and through him, he found himself whispering, "That's right out of the Bible...God wants me to be happy...to have the things I want..."

Then, abruptly, he paused, stopped by something deeper,

a still small voice that countered: *But what of others? Family...and the rest of the world? How will they fare in Apol's apocalypse?*

Flinching as a kaleidoscope of kindred images erupted at his core, he saw his mom, the girls, Katherine, Garth, other friends he had known, each looking abandoned...then...then...the vision was back...so compelling ...so mesmerizing...everything he had ever been tempted by.

Wealth, power, pleasure.

"Yes! Yes!" the beautiful angel encouraged. "Think about yourself! Your wants! Your needs! You can have them all! The things that make you happy!"

"BUT A MARINE NEVER SEEKS SAFETY WHEN OTHERS ARE AT STAKE!" a distant voice shouted.

Gunnery Sergeant Hubert Franklin?

Further away, weak and quavering with emotion, his mother's voice admonished, "Doing the right thing even when it's not convenient is the mark of a man of God."

Reaching forward...

"But every one that asketh receiveth!" the artificial angel resounded. "You've got to think about that too!"

Suddenly a twig snapped, and he came to himself. No longer spellbound, he saw the dazzling wraith, very close now, reaching forward. The vision had been a telepathic distraction, a ploy to grab the embryo.

With a flash of instinct, he rattled the container and drew his weapon up, focusing a nervous glare on the being, as if awakening from a nightmare.

"I...I can't...I won't do that," he stammered.

Dizzied by what the puppetmaster had tried and at how quickly he'd been overcome, he added firmly, "Not to my family...and certainly not to the world."

At once the shape and rhythm of the mutagenic façade

sizzled like fireworks into a million outward-flying particles. The viscous, serpentine presence was in its place again, wearing Apol as before, no wings now, nor feminine appeal, squirming with anger.

"THE WORLD!" it hissed furiously.

Blossoms of blood broke through Apol's forehead, trickled down, mingled with rotten pus below his dangling severed lips.

"THE WORLD! WHAT DID THE WORLD EVER DO FOR YOU? WOULD YOU DIE FOR A PEOPLE WHO WOULDN'T BOTHER TO GIVE YOU THE TIME OF DAY!?"

Joe swallowed hard. The end was coming. He could feel it. An attack on him was imminent. He couldn't run, couldn't hide, and wouldn't trade his safety for the welfare of his family, not that any deal with this nemesis would be honored anyway. He gazed unblinkingly forward and prayed silently for strength.

On the river, a popping sound precipitated a signal flare shuttling through the sky. Buck had spotted the girls and had marked the boat's location. The trio would get away.

Joe considered the circumstances. He knew what he had to do. He dared not linger. A moment of indecision could bring a second onslaught of telepathic blows from which he might not survive.

He also knew that the insidious New Messiah project would never cease until it had enslaved the human race. He recalled what the admiral had said about the embryo back at the Genetics room: "This thing could have represented the end of everything good in this world, but now we have it, to hold as hostage if necessary. Because you were here, Sheri, mankind might get a second chance."

It was his turn now. The moment of truth had come.

Thirty feet away, Apol caught the determined expression and stretched his hands toward him with a strange and bitter anguish that resonated balefully along the steep canyon walls: "No...NOOO-O-O!"

Joe fixed his eyes on Apol and flipped the embryo container open. Dropping it over the cliff, he began discharging the M-249 in an even spray along the road and into the thicket where the monster was. The gun's recoil pulsed back and forth mellifluently. *Chuga-chuga-chuga-chuga.*

Time froze as the container drifted downward and crashed into an outcropping of rocks that sent it hurtling end over end like a punted football. It burst apart, dislodged the embryo straw, and rained into the Columbia River with a splash. A second later, the drag pulled the transgenic fetus underwater, damning the dispossessed god to a frigid netherworld.

* * * * * *

High above Earth's atmosphere, angels observed Joe's selfless act.

"IT IS DONE!" Justice shouted, his voice echoing hard and strong along the opening in space.

On the opposite side of the Ahriman Gate, the evil that was there refused to acknowledge the embryo's destruction. Madness as deep and as frenzied as hungry piranha erupted as violence so intense and insane rolled across the demon ranks. The fallen hordes began slashing in angry circles, their swords cutting through the air and then finally upon each other. Against their mischievous, apocalyptic play, the rift began closing around them, drawing together like a cosmic curtain call.

Without saying a word, Swift withdrew a large chain and

unfolded his powerful wings. In a sudden burst of pure energy, he spiraled untethered through the vastness of space toward the planet Mars, leaving behind a glittery vapor trail. He had an appointment with Quetzalcoatl, and shackles to bind him with.

* * * * * *

Joe paused, released the M-249's trigger, and stared at the demon in the cadaverous costume. Shot numerous times, the damned thing remained upright. No cries of pain, no shudder of dying, it simply coiled inside Apol's rotting body, winding through the gaps, examining his throat, fingering the bloody slit where the machine gun had ripped through his esophagus.

Then it stopped and peered out at Joe.

"Chitowa nok!" it screeched.

Something filled the corner of Joe's eye.

The monster from the underbrush.

30—A GIANT PROBLEM

"Thou shalt not be afraid for the terror by night...nor for the
pestilence that walketh in darkness.... Because thou hast made the
Lord...even the most High, thy habitation."
Psalm 91:5–9

"RELEASE THE DARK GUARDIAN!" Justice commanded.

In front of him, a sparkling messenger departed in a flash to deliver the call that would prompt the chosen one.

Moments later, the black creature on Earth, less than three feet high, obeyed the angel's order. It slipped silently through the forest, camouflaged by the trees, following the chilly stream to cloak its beastly smell. Its instincts, animated beyond human, sensed the unnatural mischief that required its small but deadly response.

* * * * * *

Like Polyphemus the Cyclops grabbing Ulysses's shipmates in order to gobble them up, the indomitable giant from the thicket moved with mythical speed.

Joe knew it was coming the instant he heard the enormous stride crashing through the woods and breathed the pungent odor he'd smelled inside the Dungeon. He hardly had time to reengage the M-249's trigger before the unworldly thing was upon him. With the chugging sounds of the machine gun echoing across the canyon, the vicious chimera appeared, filled with rage and mutant strength, its bear-trap jaws opening wide a mouthful of bitter, horrible air.

Stunned and running on instinct, Joe shoved the barrel—hot as blazes with static fire—against the monster's flabby girth. He pressed the trigger down hard and emptied the last thirty-six rounds of NATO munitions into its scaly abdomen. A particle splash of beast-flesh and viscera shot across his face and arms as bile dropped from the being's ruptured stomach onto the ground with a gushy, intestinal *flop*.

A second later, the gun exhausted of ammo, he watched in amazement as the monster, shot dozens of times by the powerful, upgraded shells, sagged, but did not fall. The repetitive blows of the M-249 seemed to have only infuriated the dreadful beast as it snatched the precision-made weapon and hurled it over the cliff.

Grabbing him by the throat, the fiend lifted him from the ground and pulled him eye to eye. Snort-blasting a rancid sludge through its pebbled nostrils onto his tiny reddening face, the brute's talons tightened around his neck, the sharp spikes driving into the soft bones near the base of his skull, choking him so completely that he fainted away at once.

As quiet as death and as ineffective as a rag doll, he awoke moments later to find that the *thing* was cradling him as tenderly as a child. He coughed into the 962-pound nanny's face, grimaced and tried to scream, but couldn't. The monster had squeezed his windpipe so firmly that, for the moment, it wasn't working properly.

But the utility vest was still on him.

He reached for a grenade.

In an instant, the monster's talon-tipped finger drew through the garment with rapid, surgical precision, tearing it off and throwing it a thousand feet into the woods.

Rahu grinned smugly, then raised and tilted him toward Apollyon.

In the middle of the road, portions of his face on the ground now, Apol was shambling his way, tiny streaks of red and yellow flame leaking past his gritted teeth. His angry, vermilion eyes were directly focused on Joe.

Not many human parts of Apol were left. He had rotted from the inside out, as something worse had acquisitioned him. *It* seemed to be on fire, a *thing* movement that told Joe everything he didn't want to know. Something terrible was about to happen to him for dropping the embryo container.

He closed his eyes and quietly whispered, "Mom."

Salty streams of sweat and tears began gushing down his amber cheeks. *Sheri and Katherine are going to be all right. That's the important thing now.*

Yet his tongue curled to the roof of his mouth as what remained of Apol touched his bludgeoned body, the feeling radiating through him like the pestilence of pain and death.

"Caw nos! Krockita-kah!" the near-corpse screeched.

Twitching at the command, Rahu rattled him, then relaxed his powerful grip and swatted him to the ground. Joe struck the road hard, splashing in Rahu's bile. The rotting substance burned acidly against his skin as he gasped for a breath of air. When the giant didn't follow the infliction with another serious blow, he struggled to his knees and ran his hand along his leg. He found the Ka-Bar fighting knife and reached to unsnap the pouch.

As if on cue, Rahu dropped his foot, slamming him

against the stony ground hard enough to torture but not enough to kill him.

He gasped and grabbed his side. A rib might have been cracked or broken. He quickly probed the sensitive area and found no abnormalities. His breathing was troubled nevertheless; the creature had knocked the wind out of him. He moaned and reached for the knife again, trying hard to stand.

With rounding motion like that of a serpent uncoiling itself, Apol's hand swung about and clasped the top of his trembling head. The disfigured, dappled hand somehow paralyzed him, as if injecting disabling venom directly into his scalp.

* * * * * *

Through the stream, up the hill, rapidly closing in. Breathing, breathing, must stop the mischief.

* * * * * *

Joe's mind flooded with extraordinary panic. From the bony fingers squeezing his skull, somehow he knew telepathically that, little by little, bit by bit, Apol, or whatever this thing was, meant to eat him, guts and all. He would capture Joe's essence and swallow him whole: his hair, scalp, ears, and then his cheeks and lips, tongue, and nasal passage, chewing and slurping and consuming him while he watched.

Yet, as the blood seeped from the talon punctures in his neck, Joe heard himself instinctively resist the psychic assault. "So, j-just when d-did you sell your s-soul to the Devil?" he mocked.

Apol jerked his head up so he could see the horror coming. His fiendish expression, no longer mortal, conveyed through vertical slits a fearful and malicious message: dinnertime.

"You'd probably think it was when I murdered your father for refusing to divulge the whereaboutsss of the Nibiruan Key," he breathed from somewhere beyond his mouth. "But you'd be wrong. I invited the demon to take me as a youth, and now, he shall have you, too."

Apol's words pierced him to the core. Although he'd dreamed of the day when he'd avenge his father's death, he'd never envisioned the monster with which his dad had been dealing. His father never had a chance, any more than he did now, regardless of how valiant he was.

Grotesque and enraged, Apol's mouth opened wider, a nightmarish cavity lined with jagged molars and angled razor fangs, drooling with unnatural protoplasm. A hellish stench, thick and putrid, dropped out of the gorge as the shredded throat flexed and a crusty tongue, cyst-covered and forked, flopped over Joe's face. The demon salivated in anticipation of the sanguine flavor, its oily gullet expanding to encase his entire head.

Joe wanted to scream, to cry out for help, but couldn't. His wearied eyes flooded with hysteria as his neck stretched beneath the rancid, wormy shadow.

* * * * * *

Standing next to Apol and observing the helpless young man, Rahu burst into uncontrollable belly laughter at the thought of what was coming. His tittering rumbled from his ruptured abdomen and gurgled out through his mouth and snout in a sloppy, bubbly fest. Grabbing his mangled paunch, he squeezed the blood from the bullet holes, throwing back his head and quivering with ecstasy for the moment. He would laugh until he cried, he thought, Joe's terror was so satisfying.

Yet as he drank in the palpable fear, a glimpse of something caught in the corner of his eye, running toward them—flying through the air. By the time he contained himself and realized what it was, a black dog had locked its powerful canines around the snake man's throat and yanked him over the bluff.

* * * * * *

Suddenly collapsing onto the edge of the uneven gravel road, Joe caught himself before falling over the cliff. *What was that black thing!? Buck's dog!? Tater!?*

He sucked in a lungful of fresh mountain air and listened to the toppling snake man screaming....

"FRIE-KAGA! *FRIE-KAGA!*"

The former human sounded terrified, like a child plunging to its death: frantic, utterly desperate for someone to help.

* * * * * *

Rahu bounded to the cliffside and squatted on the ledge beside Joe. He placed his claws near the bank for stability and watched as Apollyon somersaulted to the beach hundreds of feet below.

The large dog was tearing at Apol's throat, thrashing its head wildly, growling as it drifted along the sheer canyon wall.

A moment later the duo struck the ground with

tremendous impact.

WHHHAM!!!

To Rahu, it looked like the Labrador trampolined off Apollyon, who actually landed upside down, softening the dog's fall. The canine bounced sideways and fell on its side against the river's murky edge.

The dog immediately jumped up, hobbled a few feet, then crumbled to its belly, whimpering. Rahu thought the Labrador's legs must have been fractured or that its internal organs were traumatized.

Nearby on the beach, Apol slowly opened his parabolic eyes and moaned. He raised one arm sluggishly toward Rahu, then dropped it. His chest heaved as he muttered something in demonese to the mother goddess.

Rahu didn't understand. Perhaps the body Apollyon possessed—the transgenically modified Apol Leon—was too rotten to repair. Possible, but not likely, at least not yet. The mutation inside him had matured only twenty-four hours ago.

Seeing Joe crawling away now, he stood and turned his way. If he disemboweled the boy, he might be able to strengthen the injured creator with his intestinal supplements. After all, even the incarnated metabolism of the Destroyer needed a little nourishment now and then.

Joe was in the middle of the road in a combat posture, a knife in his hand.

Rahu stepped toward him, thinking how much he looked like a trained chipmunk beneath his own massive shadow.

He smiled. This wouldn't take long. Not long at all.

Then he sensed something wrong in the ozone. His psychic connection to the other Nephilim was also rapidly changing.

On the beach, a distinctly *human* voice erupted from Apol

Leon, screaming, imploring Joe for help.
Like a soul just discovering the true wages of sin!?
Rahu sniffed the air, and found it curious.

31—WHEN
MOUNTAINS MOAN

"In 1996, the late Alexander Lebed, Russia's former chief of national security, asserted that Russia may have 'lost' up to 100 one-kiloton 'suitcase-sized' bombs...."
"Russia's Scattered Tactical Arms a Temptation for Terrorists," *Boston Globe,* 06-18-02

In a hidden, out-of-the-way place inside Montero's research facility, in a briefcase measuring just twenty-four by sixteen by eight inches thick, a tiny red light flashed on the fail-safe countdown detonator.

The marauding monsters didn't have time to register the accompanying sound as a blinding fire equal to one hundred suns shot at the speed of light from the SAMM's hypocenter.

In the blink of an eye, temperatures inside the lower complex reached ten million degrees Fahrenheit. The once-powerful beings, together with everything around them, were reduced in a flash to raw atomic material.

At six hundred fifty feet the steel boxcars designed to transport the Nephilim melted. At fourteen hundred feet, rubber objects as well as plastic signs and wooden furniture exploded into flames.

Within the same millisecond, a wall of immense pressure created by winds of six hundred seventy miles per hour expanded the nuclear fire outward from the hypocenter into a compressed spherical cavity. The Dungeon's ceiling lifted above the amazing pounds-per-square-inch of pressure, then collapsed in a deafening roar that filled the subterranean chamber with molten rock and radiation.

A short-period borehole seismometer nearly a mile from ground zero began registering the seismic waves, while further away, at the Pacific Northwest Network, it was quickly determined that the wavefield had been 95 percent dilational (explosive-like) and 5 percent deviatoric (earthquake-like), leading to the conclusion that a one-kiloton nuclear explosion had occurred deep underground.

Over the next twenty-four hours similar findings would be made in nine other countries around the world as Operation Gadfly's SAMMs detonated simultaneously, obliterating the giant army.

* * * * * *

Joe felt it at the same time Rahu must have.

First came the human cry from Apol.

Then the earth jerked violently and pressures shot through his eardrums and out of his eyes.

The mountain moaned deeply, as if in great pain.

Then a vacuous tremor moved along the range, thunderously crackling, rushing along the ground, wrenching and fracturing the indigenous soil.

Momentarily perplexed, Joe stuck his hands out to steady himself as huge loams of earth and plant life began slipping forward nearby, slowly at first, then faster, until suddenly a *whoosh* brought the ground where Apol stood earlier lurching onto the road and flowing over the bluff in a deafening, path-cutting cascade.

LANDSLIDE!

Joe leaped sideways and away from the surge, struggling to stay upright as the street in front of him pitched and splintered under the adjacent dynamic load.

A growling-tearing sound drew his attention downward. He felt the direction of the motion and caught sight of a fractured crack tracing ghostlike his way, then another one appearing just beneath his legs. Joining, they formed an oblique tear, rolling with a wavelike pattern that began rapidly peeling the earth apart like a giant yawning mouth.

He fought to get away from it.

His arms flailed, teetered, grasped at anything he could reach in order to catch his balance and to avoid the snarling abyss.

He captured a solid area with one foot, dug his heel in hard, jumped at the slope in front of him, caught an anchored, mangled root, and used it to pull himself tight against the rim. He froze to the vibrating barrier as the incomprehensible river of rocks and dirt began rumbling like a freight train thirty feet away.

Now there was a closer sensation, and the road in front of him *snapped*.

Instantly a magnificent portion of the ground just inches away dropped from the street to the river in a thunderous, dusty flume.

CA-RAAASH!!!

The relentless tearing moved closer, hammering and rending the earth, billowing up from the slide into his face, blasting his skin and filling his nose and mouth with bits of gravel and chunks of hard debris.

He squinted and held his breath. His eyes watered as he prayed to survive. Lost for several seconds in the whipping rain of chips, pebbles, and limbs, he felt the tree root vibrating aggressively in his hand and worried that it was about to pull apart.

His thoughts raced. *What in the world did Stark do!? Plant a nuclear bomb!?*

Moments passed as winds created by the slide brought a heavier cloud of silt and debris raining down upon him. He began coughing and couldn't stop. He pressed his face to the hillside, aware that it was the feeblest attempt to filter the particles but also knowing that too many minutes of the coarse dust would suffocate his life away.

Then there was a creak, and a pop, like train cars banging together, and a halting sound tugged at the rolling soils. Here and there moving boulders caught new places to abide while surfing sands struggled for just one more inch of progress before slowing to a grumbling halt.

Except for the *ping* of small rocks bouncing here and there and the larger echo of trees falling in the distance, silence returned as quickly as it had gone.

He stood against the newly formed and potentially unstable mantle, hoping a breeze would appear and blow the dust away.

As the worst of the tremors subsided, he scanned through the settling dust cloud, gagging and spitting out mud, but saw no sign of the monster.

Maybe the slide had taken the beast when it had torn the road away.

Despite his fear of falling and the questionable stability of the ledge, he was happy to pretend the avalanche had killed the hideous thing.

32—BACKTRACKING

"Weeping may endure for a night, but joy cometh in the morning."
Psalm 30:5

Joe waited until the canyon was quiet and the air had cleared a little; then he surveyed the hillside above him from the corner of his eye. It was too steep to climb, plus he could lose his balance and fall. He decided to move laterally along the ledge to find a way back to the unbroken portion of the road. He clamped on to the tree root he had unearthed earlier and carefully took a step. Studying the narrow two-foot shelf he was on, he inspected the slope for additional roots and spotted others of different sizes. Holding the tubers firmly, he gingerly scaled the mantle. Before long he discovered fresh air seeping from the thicket when the flora was pulled apart. It refreshed him.

After a few minutes he arrived at the slide's bank and dug his way to the top. He plotted the path he would take across it to the road on the other side, then hugged the unstable loam and moved as safely as he could.

When he reached the logging road again, he hopped from the mound onto it, noting for the first time that the sun was peeking over the trees. Its warmth was soft and invigorating. It gave him strength. His faith was returning too. He recited Psalm 23 from memory, matching the words and sentences to his breathing cycle as he hustled down the road.

Yet the thought hadn't escaped him that he'd dropped his knife somewhere, and he didn't know the correct route to the river.

* * * * * *

On the water, the gang had heard the machine gun fire and watched in horror as the partially obstructed cliff broke from the mountainside and crashed thunderously to the beach. There had been an earsplitting sound just before a huge wave from the impact smashed against the eighteen-foot fishing vessel's hull, nearly tipping it over. Stark was running on his way to help Joe when it happened. Now he stood frozen at the edge of the dust cloud and looked back at the others offshore.

"Everybody okay?" he shouted to the boat.

Buck was picking up hooks and bobbers from a fallen tackle box. He poked his head above the cab. "Look's like nothin's broke here. B'lieve we're okay, uh-huh."

"All right then, everybody stay put. I'm going after Joe."

"Hold up! Wait a minute!"

It was Sheri. She looked desperate.

Throwing one leg over the vessel's edge, she yelled, "I'm coming with you!"

Stark turned to the river again. Now his voice was adamant. "Sheri, did you hear what I said?"

"Yeah. I heard you."

"Then wait for me here."

"But he's my brother."

This girl could be a pain in the butt. She had fought him

all the way down the mountain, refusing to accept the need to leave her sibling behind.

"So you want to get Joe killed?" he asked impatiently.

"No...of course not...but..." she said, her voice thickening.

"Well he might if you don't stay put. You're only going to complicate things by following me."

"But I can help!"

"Yes, you *can*, by sitting down and being quiet."

Her eyes widened in disbelief. "What!? And if I refuse!?"

"Then I'll make you."

"You and what army!?"

"Walther's."

"Excuse me?"

He pulled the Walther P-38 from its holster.

"You wouldn't dare!" she screamed angrily.

"Right in the leg, if I must."

She glared at him.

He glared back.

A hand gripped her shoulder. It was Allie. She surprised her by saying, "I think he's right, Sheri. I'm worried about Joe too, but maybe you should stay in the boat."

Sheri, who typically would have challenged her big sister until the sun settled in the west, raised one eyebrow above a teary eye. Following a moment of silence and only after glancing at her watch with exaggerated suspicion, she said to Stark, "All right, you have ten minutes. If you're not back by then, I'm going after Joe."

Stark lowered the gun. The last thing he wanted was a tag-along, and he was learning something about Sheri—you had to be firm; she could be hardheaded.

He faced the woods again. This time the heavy dust from the avalanche was clearing from the fall area. What he saw wasn't good. The winding trail back to the logging road was buried beneath tons of debris. The only way to reach Joe's last known location now would be straight through the forest and up the mountainside. He flipped the Walther's safety off, surveyed the timbers for the best opening, and ran into the trees.

* * * * * *

Wind from the gorge rippled gently along the roadside scrub as Joe searched for a place to descend. He had no weapon, no shirt, and no clear sense of direction. The only thing he knew was that he needed to get away from this place, down off this mountain, to the boat on the river.

He pulled the low-hanging limbs apart and pushed into the thicket. Blackberry vines cut against him, sending sharp thorns through his pant legs into his wavering skin. He forced himself to ignore the pain as he thrashed through the underbrush.

Reaching a rolling meadow, he thought he heard something following, listened, then dismissed it as his own echo.

Crossing the grassy field, he entered the woods again, stopping long enough to pick up a thick tree limb to use as a club, just in case.

* * * * * *

Stark moved stealthily through the stand, up the hill, over mossy obstacles toward the trail above. He held the P-38 in front of him and carefully measured his moves. Stop, look, listen, move. Stop, look, listen, move.

Eventually the hillside steepened and he had to holster the gun. He zigzagged, dragging and launching himself up the precipitous crumbling route. He yanked and struggled and lifted his weight, grunting and scaling the arduous hill, until at the pace he was moving, the inevitable didn't take long. Soon he was physically spent. He paused against a berm, dropped his forehead against his arm, rested a minute, then moved on. Joe had traded his safety for his; he owed the young man—and his father—his best.

Staying close to the shelf, contorting up and over the crag, he labored until his heart pounded so hard that he thought it would explode. Sweat poured from his forehead as he strained, breathing raspy, chugging the cool mountain air with increasingly painful gulps. He felt like a track runner in a Bill Cosby routine he'd seen some years ago, a sketch with a jogger that ran until temporary rigor mortis set in and froze his muscular movements. At any moment his body would seize like the comedian's character and his cardiovascular system would cease to function. He would die of a heart attack right here on this mountain, he was sure of it.

Yet he had to keep moving.

He prayed for strength and pushed even harder.

Then for reasons he couldn't understand, his pace returned. A second wind came to him so quick and so strong that he was amazed by it. Although he hadn't discerned the healing touch of Justice the angel, who was back on Earth after having sealed the Ahriman Gate, Stark took the hill with newfound power, scaling outcroppings, moving around fallen trees, climbing straight through to the target area. In a few minutes he was there. He jerked himself onto the old logging road and pulled the P-38 from its holster. He scanned the area for bodies. The site was unsettling: Joe, Apol, and Spot the monster were gone, together with a substantial portion of the road.

He inspected the massive slide area and feared for the worst. Then he found something familiar on the ground.

* * * * * *

Joe's pulse quickened as he heard it again. There was also an inaudible sense that something was following him, matching him step for step, staying just out of visual range.

He waded through the brambles, treading softly on the foliage and studying the trees to the right of him.

Earlier, when Apol's monster had first entered the woods, the buzzing of insects and the chirping of birds had dropped to an instant hush. He hadn't thought about it since, but now it dawned on him. Once again, he couldn't hear any wildlife, no birds, no chipmunks, nothing other than what he'd detected moments ago when he'd been sure somebody was following.

He took a few steps and this time, on the path he'd just come down, it happened for sure—a rustling in the brush not far away. Something was there.

He squinted through the overgrowth. A shadow crept over a low-lying branch, then pulled back.

Something hissed.

He pulled the club into both hands.

It hissed again, not like a snake, more like wheezing, as if somebody was calling to him through laryngitis or a cancer-ridden throat.

He stood perfectly still, listening. Fear slashed at his nerves as sharp as razor blades. Studying the trees uphill, he thought he saw the shadow return, then noticed something embarrassing. A slight breeze was moving a tall tree that cast its shadow on the brush. It moved over the branches, then pulled back, moved over the branches, and pulled back. As far as the whispering he'd heard, he told himself it could have been the wind whisping around the scrubby limbs.

Hah! What an idiot greenhorn. Letting your imagination run away like that.

The woods were safe.

Quiet.

Normal.

He resumed movement along the trail. Using the club he was carrying to knock down blackberry vines and other scrub as they got in his way, he had gone less than a hundred yards when a twig snapped behind him.

He paused, saw nothing, and when he'd almost decided it was his reactive imagination again, a glimpse of something jumping behind a thicket caught his attention. He squinted, straining to hear, and thought he detected the vaporous voice again. The sound repeated, and this time he was sure of it. The ghostly presence whispered his name. *Joe.*

The river.

He had to get to the river.

He could think of nothing else as he rushed desperately forward.

He dared not look back.

The icy chill of horror was closing on him.

* * * * * *

"We've waited long enough," Sheri said out of the blue. "We should have formed a search party by now!"

She'd been sitting on the back of the boat, twirling a curl of her hair, staring at the woods, combing the beach with her eyes.

"I think it's time we stop messing around."

Allie, imbuing her words with a lecturing tone, said, "Admiral Stark ordered us to stay put."

"Well, he's not my boss, you know. Besides, It's my fault Joe's out there."

* * * * * *

Suddenly the light went on in Allie's head. Sheri was feeling responsible for Joe. Softly, she tried to comfort her.

"Oh, Sheri, that's not true."

When she realized how unconvincing she sounded, she glanced at Buck for support, adding, "It's nobody's fault...but those freaks in that cave."

Buck dropped his spit over the side of the boat. He'd been watching the beach, undoubtedly thinking Tater should have been back by now. "That's fer sure, missy. None of this'd be happen'n if those fellows hadn't tried t' play God, yeh know. So don't be blamin' yerself fer what bad men do."

"Besides," Allie continued, "I'm sure Joe will show up any second now."

* * * * * *

Glancing at Katherine to see if she agreed with Allie and Buck, Sheri found her new friend wide-eyed, frightened, looking beyond them to the woods.

"Uhm...I think I saw something," Katherine said uneasily. "Something moving in the trees. There! There it is again!"

Sheri turned, just as a form came running out of the timbers, a dirty mess, waving something shiny in his hand.

"This is all I could find," Stark called as he came close.

He was holding Joe's fighting knife and breathing heavily. "Everything else seems to be gone."

"Gone!?" Sheri said. "What do you mean *gone*!? You didn't see any trace of Joe at all!?"

"Sorry...but..."

Sheri jumped to her feet, cupped her hands at her mouth and began screaming over the bow, "JOE! JOE! IT'S ME, SHERI! CAN YOU HEAR ME!? ANSWER ME!"

* * * * * *

Stark wondered how he would tell Sheri if Joe had been swept from the ledge and buried in the slide. He waded through the current and climbed onto the deck of the boat as Katherine and Allie joined her. He made his way past them to the old man.

"What say we fire this thing up and make a run upriver, Buck? We can search the beach faster that way, don't you think?"

Stark knew this would mean moving away from the target area. If Joe was somewhere beyond the slide, he'd gotten lost for sure.

"Sounds like a plan t' me, uh-huh," Buck said.

The decision made, Stark pulled the anchor in as Buck started the outboard. The old man backed the tri-hull gently from the beach and rammed the two-stroke Johnson forward full throttle. The front of the boat lifted as gravity gave in to horsepower. Moving upstream, the girls waved from the side, calling out Joe's name repeatedly.

* * * * * *

Joe came at last to the forest's edge and ran onto the

beach in a panic. He continued straight over the sand into the river, sloshing out waist deep before turning to see what was chasing him. The water was so cold it took his breath away. Muddy ooze swirled into his insulated boots, forming a squishy filler that flowed between his toes.

He clung to the club and waited for the snake man or whatever the heck was there to charge from the woods after him. Groping with his feet to find level ground beneath the sun-dappled water, he watched the trees and listened. Every inch of his body was filthy, hurting, tired, running on nearly depleted adrenaline. He had to force himself to breathe.

Seconds passed.

When nothing happened, he clutched the club and stared down the river both ways. To his east was a craft like the one Buck owned speeding away from him. The people in it appeared to be jumping or dancing. To his west was the massive rockslide. He could see something beside it; it looked familiar...*slithering his way?*

Trying to ignore the fatigue burning in his muscles, he waded downstream a few yards, then returned to the beach. He stopped and studied the distant object. Against all common sense, he gripped the heavy club and staggered toward the figure on his wobbly rubber legs.

* * * * * *

Buck had never pushed the tri-hull so hard. He didn't know the old boat could go so fast. As the underbody bounced on the water, fresh waves moved across the Columbia in a diminishing v-shaped spiral.

"We'll turn 'round at Rooster Rock," he shouted to Stark over the engine. "Then we'll make yer slow pass 'long the south shore!"

"How far to Rooster Rock?" Stark yelled, steadying himself against the quivering plastic windshield. His salt-and-pepper crew cut was twitching wildly in the wind.

"Jest there," Buck pointed.

An enormous rock bearing the faint resemblance of a rooster jutted up and out of the gorge. The monstrous plug had been shot into the water by an ancient volcano hundreds of years before.

* * * * * *

Stark gave Buck a thumbs-up and turned to transfer the message to the girls. He saw something on the beach behind them, grabbed Buck's arm, and thumbed rearward like a hitchhiker.

"Hey Buck! Something's back there!"

"Hold on," Buck stuttered as he pulled on the throttle. He made a quick sharp turn with the wheel, then hit the accelerator again.

As the boat drove against the water and came around, the gang, holding on to the rim, focused on the shape. It was hunched over...or maybe being pulled down...struggling with something.

A quarter-mile away.

The vessel lurched as the outboard clattered noisily. The boat moved faster now, with the river, toward the animate object, Buck pushing the throttle arm firmly forward with his trembling hand.

The chilly wind against Stark's face made the form difficult to discern. He checked the handgun's clip. Several rounds remained. He made the sign of the cross over his heart.

As the boat skipped on the whitecaps, Buck seemed to be

aiming directly at the outline on the beach. "Can yeh tell what it is?" he shouted.

Stark's voice returned through the misty kaleidoscopic spraying off the fiberglass hull. "Not sure yet."

Fifteen hundred feet.

The shape stood.

Its back was to them.

Its midsection looked distorted, baroque, like a python swallowing some large prey.

Four hundred feet.

With the surge of the river pushing hard against the deck, Buck reversed the throttle and let the Glastron level out. A temporary swell lifted, then gently feathered the boat back down.

The thing on the beach was defined now: a shirtless man, holding something, his back black and blue.

Sheri stared intently at the muscular physique and long brown hair, then shouted, "J-JOE!? JOE!? IS THAT YOU!? OVER HERE!"

Turning toward them, beaten, bloody, cradling Tater's limp body, he was too exhausted to answer.

Buck rammed the boat forward as if intentionally beaching the craft. Joe was barely standing. Tater was slumped over his arms, dead still.

* * * * * *

As the crew jumped to land, Buck somehow got to Joe first, even with his limp. He was encouraging him, telling him everything was going to be all right, as he took Tater into his arms to relieve him of the weight. The dog was barely breathing.

While the others grabbed to support Joe, Buck stepped

away, complaining to the unconscious Labrador as he carried him to the surf.

"Hey, boy, why'd yeh run off like that fer, huh? Yeh scared poor old Buck half t' death! Got yerself all torn t' tarnation too, didn't yeh. Well. It'll be okay. I'll fix yeh up some curin' viddles as soon as we get home. Yew'll be hoppin' like a texas jackalope b'fore mornin' comes, uh-huh."

* * * * * *

Sheri could see blood trickling onto Joe's shoulders from puncture wounds in his neck. His hands and arms appeared beaten and bruised too, drained of life like the rest of him. With a tight loving hug, she pulled his arm over her shoulder and let the admiral take the other side. They walked him through the water and loaded him onto the boat, where moments later he seemed hardly aware when Sheri laid his head in her lap and let him drift into the trusted bliss of a dead and welcome faint.

* * * * * *

Katherine didn't know if there was a proper way to thank God for Joe's safety, but she felt appreciation in her heart as she stared at her brave marine. That, and something else, something she had tried to brush off, but was starting to believe in. Love at first sight.

* * * * * *

Taking a seat aboard the craft, Stark studied the forest until a shadow caught his eye. Something was moving silently behind a grove of tall firs, a talon-tipped finger, maybe. It slid quickly around a tree with an unintelligible sound.

A moment passed as his eyes went to Joe. He was nuzzled against Sheri's soft arm on the rough deck of the boat. Stark glanced above them at Allie, Katherine, then Buck, who was trying to hold the dog as he moved to the wheel. He looked at the trees again. They swarmed with shadows. Suddenly the outboard roared and began struggling to pull free from the sand. The vessel slid left, then right, before finally pulling away and heading toward the Washington shore, the frigid waters going from dirty brown to gray and finally to deep blue as they crossed over the ancient river.

Watching the forest wane, Stark pushed strange feelings aside that monsters were preparing to rush them from the grove. Paranoia was playing tricks on him, he told himself. Nothing would come of the phantasms. Rahu was dead, buried alive in the landslide, along with Apol.

Yet, what if...

What if the beasts had survived? Rahu was efficient beyond measure, and Apol was a wise old snake. They could have made it, even be under the boat, in the river, swimming to meet them on the other side of the gorge. *"De profundis,"* Malina had warned him during Operation Gadfly planning: *out of the depths.*

From the diminishing corners of the woods, he imagined Dragon eyes following them like the lair of the beast from which serpentine forms slither across sand into glittery channels. He stared across the basin and polished the P-38's trigger with the tip of his finger.

"Mother of God, protect us from evil," he whispered.

The sound of a dull explosion came from the top of the mountain.

Smoke drifted skyward above Montero.

Still higher, the heavens looked odd, as if receding into a soft reddish glow.

He could see flames licking into the clouds, dying embers leaping up from Hell's busted lantern.

Sirens blared in the distance.

Hope was breaking free of chaos.

Against all unanswered questions, Montero was burning.

33—EIGHT WEEKS LATER

"New forms of being might be able to stake out an interstellar future. They could view us as kin, carrying some essence of our ideas, a memory of Shakespeare secure in their vast webs of intelligence. [But] Transhumanists are asking whether we'll embrace these kinds of life as necessary extensions of ourselves or shun them as monstrosities."
"Cyborg Liberation Front," *Village Voice*, 07-30-03

Eight weeks later, September 26.

Driving to Granny's farm for a highly anticipated and overdue family barbecue, Joe contemplated the last eight weeks for at least the thousandth time. He had not been surprised when government spin doctors made the media rounds following the explosion at Montero, blaming terrorists for the attacks on the United States and the other League of Ten Nations members. Nor was it a shock to him when investigators on the scene agreed with the officials, citing Montero's military research as cause for targeting by extremists. As stock markets around the world focused on the economic ramifications of the nuclear attacks, the president of the United States appeared on national television, pledging to "relentlessly pursue these enemies of freedom to the far corners of the earth."

Concerning the Ahriman anomaly, not many in the public even knew it occurred. Mysterious men in black uniforms reportedly visited those private firms that had recorded the rift, "counseling" them for their memories of the event and helping them reinterpret it. Suddenly concerned with protecting the United States from future acts of terrorism, the patriotic business owners had been more than happy to donate their files and equipment to the MIB.

Raiders News Update, refreshed daily by new and equally conspiracy-minded owners, reported that agencies including NASA were being similarly instructed to delete evidence of the phenomenon from repositories and computers. Although the space authorities were not happy with the orders, more important issues evidently required their immediate attention. Satellites in orbit around Mars had confirmed their worst fears—Outpost Alpha was gone.

For Joe, the day after the explosion had been the most intense. Armed with a warrant, FBI agents searched his home and interrogated him for two hours at the hospital where he was treated for a fractured rib and several smaller injuries. It was obvious the bureau was more interested in locating Admiral John Stark—aka "Phobos"—than they were with arresting him. The fact that Portland police hadn't simultaneously arrived to shackle him and his desperado sister on the trumped-up charges of robbing Montero indicated that law enforcement was also under orders to leave them alone.

Yet if federal investigators were hoping he would lead them to John Stark and Operation Gadfly, it'd be a long wait. From the moment he'd awoken at the hospital with the girls and Katherine at his side, Stark had been missing. According to Sheri, he'd disappeared soon after riding with them to the emergency room. She had no idea where he went, and Joe was glad about that. If the government's pursuit of the bad boy admiral kept him and Sheri from being arrested and prosecuted—if it meant the FBI would back off in hopes that over time Stark would try to contact them—it was a welcome paradox. He knew Stark wasn't that stupid, and meanwhile Sheri and he would be left alone to work things out, to mend physically, psychologically, and spiritually.

He had personally found the most theologically difficult issue to be Sheri herself, and why she'd been allowed to go through this. To keep from getting angry, he'd taken consolation in Stark's words that the human race was receiving another chance due to her ordeal. Of course there was Katherine's salvation and the question of where she would be if Sheri's kidnapping hadn't forced him to enter Montero when he did. He suspected meeting her was as much a part of his destiny as destroying Apol Leon had been. The event hadn't seemed to affect her in the way it had the others, at least not that he could see, and consequently she brought a sense of normality he needed and desired.

Besides all that, he found her irresistibly attractive. The way she walked, the sound of her voice, her dimples and ditsiness—everything about her was cute to him. The fear of attachment he'd nurtured so long was slowly crumbling beneath an unexpected passion for companionship. His father's murder avenged, his sisters and mother comforted, romance was free to blossom.

The strongest evidence of this new affection so far had been last week. He'd taken her on a date to the Oregon coast to celebrate her eighteenth birthday and to play in the sand with Tater and *his* new girlfriend—make that *dogfriend*—Granny's golden retriever, Princess. It took some real persuading to get the old man to concede that a picnic at the beach might be good for the dog's recovery, but in the end it had been terrific, filled with energetic silliness, canine antics, and innocent flirting with Katherine. Her company had been immensely pleasurable to him. He'd actually smiled for the first time in a long while, laughed, talked for hours, and shared so many things.

Though not yet everything.

It wasn't that he wanted to keep secrets from Katherine. He simply didn't know how to describe what he'd found on the riverbank near Tater that terrible day two months ago. Looking back, he could hardly believe it himself—Apol's fleshy membrane all ripped apart like that, the way the ground under the corpse was pushed up and charred, as if fiery demons had crawled from the earth and ripped the snake man's soul from within him.

Then there was the strange serpentine trail leading from the scorched carcass through the sand into the woods, as if Apol had gone to oblivion while something separate slithered from his remains into the trees. Reacting without thinking, he had kicked the human shell into the river that day, cursing the slimy hide to Hell.

Later he'd wondered if he'd destroyed important evidence. The skin's DNA might have been valuable in tracking the alien-thing down. Although so far, investigators had discovered nothing out of the ordinary, and frankly, he was tired of thinking about it.

Maybe a creature *had* crawled from Apol's skin. If so, had it died in the woods with Rahu, its leftovers eaten by wildlife? For as many times in as many hours he'd told himself that was true. The monsters were gone, consumed by critters or washed down the Columbia into the sea, scavenged by the very fish Buck had resumed angling.

Now there was a thought! Buck eating a sturgeon...that had eaten the dead monsters...that had tried to eat him!

Whatever the case, all had been quiet since, and this would be the best day yet. He'd spend it doing what had become his favorite hobby—being with Katherine.

He grinned at the thought of her...*and those lips!* They provided the private kisses by which all others would be judged. It energized him even now as he arrived at Granny's farm.

Leaping from the Colt, he saw Katherine standing with Allie, Sheri, Donna, Dr. Jones, and his wife, Joyce, by the porch. The six of them were watching Mom and Granny, who it appeared, were being held captive by Buck as he gave lessons on how to make proper barbecued vittles. Off to one side, Carl and Garth were pitching horseshoes.

Everything, he told himself, was going to be okay. Better than before.

He joined them at the deck steps and talked for quite some time.

Later, when he thought he could, he took Katherine by the hand and slipped away to the old red barn where they watched Tater and Princess frolicking in the garden. They held each other and laughed about how much trouble those dogs would be in as soon as Granny saw them knocking down her corn.

"So you think we should tell everyone our secret today?" Katherine asked, smiling up at him.

"We can if you want. They'll know soon enough anyway."

"What do you think they'll say?"

"Sheri won't be surprised. She's already told me we make

the perfect couple."

"And your mom, Nettie?"

"Mom's pretty instinctive, I doubt she'll be taken off guard. Either way, I know she'll be happy for us."

"What makes you so certain?"

"Just look at how cute you are—who could resist?"

Katherine's smile got twice as big as before. "But...to be engaged? So soon?"

Joe breathed deeply of her perfume. "Trust me."

She ran her hand up his sleeve and squeezed his large arm muscles. He loved the touch of her fingers against his skin like that. It was the "good kind of electricity," he had told her. He leaned over to steal a kiss...and saw Dr. Jones walking their way. The professor had a section of the *Portland Times* in his hands. He held it up and said sullenly, "See the top story in the press today, Joe?"

Joe studied his expression, then reluctantly took the newspaper and unrolled the pages.

The headline took his breath away.

LOCAL HUNTERS CAPTURE WOUNDED "BIGFOOT" NEAR COLUMBIA RIVER. MASSIVE BEAST FOUND BARELY ALIVE, PROTECTING UNKNOWN REMAINS

His eyes jumped to Katherine. Her face went pale. Then, for a split second, he thought he heard someone in the woods near the farm, whispering, *"Joe."*